HOW I AM A JEW

Adventures into My Jewish-American Identity

Howard W. Polsky

University Press of America,® Inc.
Lanham · New York · Oxford

Copyright © 2002 by
University Press of America,® Inc.
4720 Boston Way
Lanham, Maryland 20706
UPA Acquisitions Department (301) 459-3366

PO Box 317
Oxford
OX2 9RU, UK

Library of Congress Cataloging-in-Publication Data

Polsky, Howard W.
How I am a Jew : adventures into my Jewish-American
identity / Howard W. Polsky.
p.   cm
Includes bibliographical references and index.
1. Jews—United States—Identity. 2. United States—Ethnic
relations. 3. Polsky, Howard W.—Anecdotes. I. Title.

E184.36.E84 P65 2002
305.892'4073—dc21   2002032326 CIP

ISBN 0-7618-2423-5 (paperback : alk. ppr.)

For Roni, Josh and Dan
My Unwitting Collaborators

I want to express my gratitude to Ms. Lisa Cammitt for her careful editing and in-depth critique.

Contents

Preface

This book is a personal journey back to my rich cultural heritage and forward to a new commitment to and pride in my Jewish-American identity.

We live in a seductive mass culture that overwhelms us with the selfish delights of individual narcissism. Above all, we Jews constitute a community, which shares the prophetic vision of social justice, truth to power, care for the poor, disabled, and less advantaged, and universal peace.

I am proud a be a Jewish-American.

CHAPTER ONE
I COPE WITH ANTI-SEMITISM

The last anti-Semite will die when the last Jew does.

W. Adler

I am a Jew because of my upbringing, my dreams and my minority status in a democratic gentile society. I lazily accept my Jewish identity. I have not really thought much about how I am a Jew. I read straight through to the end every article in the New York Times on the holocaust and Israel. But that was then and Israel is out there and I'm here comfortably tenured at the Columbia University School of Social Work. Maybe my stirring is related to the student caucuses that have sprung up in my School ---- Black, Latino, Jewish, Asian, Gay and Lesbian, Feminist, etc., --- and the pride they feel about their heritage and struggles not to be swallowed up by the stereotypes in the American mash potato culture.

I represent the American Jewish "lost generation," a first native born child of Russian immigrant parents. My first language was Yiddish and I was coerced to attend Hebrew school every day after public school. I became an American and learned all about George Washington and the cherry tree he cut down and his refusal to lie to his father. I became an academic example of Budd Shulberg's <u>What Makes Sammy Run?</u> and fitfully celebrated major Jewish holidays.

A new journey begins when you decide to turn off the main highway and take an unfamiliar road. Sometimes it is necessary to go somewhere else even if you are not sure where you are going. New ideas are welcomed. My wife and I were having dinner with a visiting elderly Israeli couple. In the midst of our conversation I mused that Jews growing up in Israel and in the United States must have quite different personalities. I went on to say that I experienced anti-Semitism from the ages of 6 to 72 and that I was always keenly aware of Jews in my company. It was as natural as breathing. I learned later the Jewish saying that "anti-Semitism will die when the last Jew dies." My antennae were always alert to the slightest hint of anti-Semitism.

I wondered about living as a psychological alien in my country. And how does this differ from a Jew growing up in Israel without anti-Semitism? What a powerful natural cultural comparative study! In the course of this journey I want to speak to many Israeli and American Jews of all ages and walks of life to plumb this difference. Israelis make fun of each other's ethnic origins. A Polish Jew is regarded as somewhat stuffy, cautious, overly proper and conformist. A German Jew, a Yeki, is considered arrogant, pedantic and superficially superior. A Persian Jew is stingy, an Iraqi, shrewd, a Moroccan, hot-headed, a Yemenite, graceful and delicate, and so on and so forth. Among American Jewish immigrants the "Litvak," from Lithuania, was considered unsophisticated. These generalized personal characteristics of country of origin fade away with the first and second native born generations. They are not encased in sealed categories like Jewish-gentile relationships in the United States.

Joel, my Israeli friend, a thoughtful and somewhat subdued menche (his son was killed in one of the Israeli wars), adamantly maintained that he considered himself a Jewish Israeli, not an Israeli Jew. After some discussion we learned that his Eastern European Orthodox background is vastly more influential in his life than the Israeli culture that he absorbed while living in Israel for over forty years.

This made me think of myself as an American Jew. Most ethnic minorities refer to their national origin first, Polish-Americans, Italian-Americans, etc.. "Jewish-American" does not sound right. This may be because of religion, anti-Semitism and resistance to assimilation.

It may seem odd that a native-born American Jew at the age of seventy-two has become so concerned about how he is a Jew. I began to feel an inner compulsion for clarity. Running away from a disturbing part of myself is living a lie that cripples relationships and the kind of person I want to be. Goethe said that when he hears the phrase "know thyself," he runs away as fast as he can from himself. I do not want to run away anymore; I want to know the reasons for Joel considering himself a Jewish Israeli and also reclaim the deep cultural roots of my Jewish history.

I want to pass on this struggle to my son Josh. This is a serious unfinished business for me. I was thirty-six years old when Josh was born, securely tenured at the Columbia University School of Social Work, heavily involved in writing and teaching and a Jew in name only. I routinely celebrated Passover and Yom Kippur and was an excellent model for Josh's adolescent escape into a gentile world after his obligatory Bar Mitzvah when we showed him off to all our relatives and friends.

Like Josh, I turned away from Judaism, but the difference is that I turned my back on a rich Jewish education (after a Hebrew school disaster) whereas Josh revolted against my present nominal Jewish identification. Josh cannot be a proud Jew because he was robbed of immersion in our rich cultural heritage. I deprived him of choices of how he wants to be a Jew. I hope this memoir makes up for some of my dereliction.

My Jewish past haunted me when I decided to remember it. The French historian Pierre Nora exactly expressed my feeling: "To be Jewish is to remember being Jewish." Although this journey is in the here and now, I bring to it luggage and "dreams" from the past that are important to open up. In the fourth grade at Lloyd Street public elementary school in Milwaukee, Wisconsin, the teacher mispronounced my last name and kept doing it to the laughter of the class. I was terribly embarrassed. To this day I don't know if this was an attack on my Polish sounding name or that I was Jewish or both. I remember her horrible ugly florid face as if it happened yesterday. At the time I assumed it was an attack on me as a Jew, which is how stereotypes are nourished; I automatically interpreted this ambiguous situation as anti-Semitic. A friend, Joe Cohen, was treated badly recently by customs officials and routinely attributed it to anti-Semitism.

When I was about eleven or twelve years old I hung out with two Jewish buddies. One day after school we were picked on by five or six gentiles who called us "dirty kikes" and dared us to fight. They called us "Christ-killers" and "Roosevelt-lovers" (Roosevelt was widely believed to be the Jews' champion and special friend). My friend, Martin Slutsky, stood up to them and was badly beaten, while Melvin and I cowered in fright as we were punched about. I have lived with the shame of this cowardice all of my life. It will not go away. I linked anti-Semitism with my cowardice that fed a huge inferiority complex. I excused my shameful action because they were bullies and stupid anti-Semites. But I could not really fool or forgive myself. I became a "good boy," an expert at conforming to authority and the status quo and obsessively concerned with what others thought about me. I vainly covered up my shame with athletic and intellectual achievements. That didn't work too well. My cowardice still haunts me and wends a torturous journey through my soul. I had a terrible fear of sticking out. I admired friends and colleagues who took chances, dared to be different, fell on their faces and pick themselves up as if nothing happened. I didn't take chances ---- with ideas, girls, stupid authorities, God, friends, enemies ---- you name it. I became disgusted with all my artful stratagems for avoiding defeat and exposure. It is certainly okay to retreat from a battle against overwhelming odds in order to fight another day. I did not fight the next day because I was a coward the day before. Martin Slutsky fought back and was beaten up. And I was bigger than Martin Slutsky!

I had some restitution thirty years later when I was about forty-two. I was driving a car with my wife at my side and Josh in the back seat. At a four way stop I did not fully stop and scared several burly fellows on motorcycles. I motioned that I was sorry. But this was not good enough for them. They parked their motorcycles in front of my car and approached me on foot with clenched fists and bared tattooed arms. I opened the door of my car and my wife tried to restrain me. I shook her off and got out of the car and walked toward them. They continued yelling and cursing but stopped moving toward me. We glared at each other and they turned around and gave me an obscene finger and got back on their motorcycles. My wife berated me for "going nuts," but after some thirty years since my first cowardly withdrawal, I finally was able to accept some relief from the heavy burden that I had carried so much of my life. I had to confront the hoodlums and I did not care what they did to me. I wanted to fight; to give and take a good licking! I was "nuts." I think that Josh in the back seat had something to do with my "going nuts." I was exhilarated with this breakthrough.   .

My father was a broker in Milwaukee, Wisconsin. He bought in bulk jeans, shirts, ties, gloves, scarves, hats, etc., from New York and sold them to local clothing stores. I made the rounds with him and carried merchandise from the back of the car into the store. One day, I was about twelve years old, one of his customers, a gentile, yelled at him and put him down and threatened never to buy from him again, and I began to cry. My father took me outside and tried to comfort me. I finally calmed down and I never went again with him to stores and we never spoke about this incident. It was the first time I sensed some tears in my father's eyes (the only time I ever saw him cry with tears was the day Roosevelt died). Jews have been taking this kind of crap from gentiles for 2000 years and I believe that Israel will help Jews everywhere challenge this humiliating defenselessness.   .

My "baby brother" was a star swimmer at Washington High School. In his third year, he and the only other Jew on the team were suddenly thrown off the team for coming late to one practice. Naturally we all assumed that it was because of anti-Semitism. And we were right! Several weeks later KKK propaganda and the Protocols of the Elders of Zion were found in the coach's locker, and he was fired.

My "middle brother" was asked by the owner of a shoe repair shop in downtown Milwaukee to hand out flyers advertising his business. At the end of the day the owner decided not to pay my brother anything at all and called him some dirty Jewish names as a bonus.

After I received my Ph.D. and came to New York, I was fortunate to receive a two year post-doctoral foundation grant to study the subculture of a residential institution for delinquent and emotionally disturbed children. Occasionally, I visited the foundation in Manhattan that gave me the grant. Several prestigious sociologists had offices there. One day I was passing an office with its door ajar and heard one person say, "I don't think the Jew-boy will get the grant." I was stunned and then furious and then helpless and then mad. I thought that if I burst into their office I would be accused of secretly over-hearing their conversation. I was scared of making waves. I didn't say anything to them. I am still mad at myself and ashamed.

Two weeks ago I was chatting with several colleagues in the School café. The desultory conversation turned to travel and a colleague, not Jewish, remarked something about "cosmopolitan Jews." I exploded. I wanted to know what he meant by "cosmopolitan Jews?" My colleague defended himself and said he meant that they were not provincial and very worldly. I asked him if he knew about any other cosmopolitan ethnic or religious group. He was non-plussed and recovered and said, "gypsies," and everyone laughed. We then got into a discussion about how "cosmopolitan Jews" often had the connotation of disloyalty and betrayal to one's country. My colleague swore that he was totally ignorant of this connotation which is probably true. Was I compensating for my previous cowardice? Probably. Two years ago (in 1998) my step-son attended a suburban high school, Hastings-on-the

Hudson, because of bad schools in Riverdale in the Bronx where we lived. During the lunch recess and after school a band of senior students hung out near the school and yelled dirty epithets against Jews and Blacks and taunted them to fight. My step-son was expelled from school for getting into a fight with one gang member. The bureaucratic-idiot principle told us that the rule was "no-fighting," and automatic suspension. The father of the leader of the gang was a fairly well known member of a militia organization in upper New York State.

My wife and I were furious. We went directly to the Superintendent of the school district and demanded that my step-son be reinstated. The superintendent told us that he was aware of this gang, but that his hands were tied because every youth must attend school. We threatened to call the Anti-Defamation League and write to the local press. Miraculously within one week the leader of the gang was expelled and the gang disappeared (our son was of course immediately re-instated). The school also followed up on my suggestion that it have assemblies on the nature of prejudice and discrimination and strategies for dealing with it. The lesson that has to be learned over and over again is that doing nothing and standing-by in the face of prejudice is to support and encourage it to continue and expand.   .

Ralph Waldo Emerson said that an institution is the lengthened shadow of its leader. Certainly the President of the United States is the standard bearer of our beliefs and values as American citizens. The Jewish community was stunned by the open, gross and vicious Anti-Semitic smears in the White House Watergate conversations between Nixon and his staff. Not once did any of his staff try to temper Nixon's outlandish statements. I believe that the crime of breaking into the office of the Democratic party and the use of the Internal Revenue Office to blackmail his opponents pales in significance to the despoiling of the Oval Office with the crude anti-Semitic slurs by the leader of the free world. International response to this foul language seemed to be muted because apparently this occurred only in private conversations. But this is precisely how Anti-Semitism continues to flourish as a vast subterranean river of muck in our society. The "Nixons" of the world are forgiven and excused as some minor aberration, although they are the rule rather than the exception, and will continue to be so with our "civilized" understanding and "tempered proportionality. In this way, we all nourish the noxious weeds that everywhere sprout small-minded competitors, exposed liars, sneaky cheaters and secondhand failures that need to boost their fragile egos. Anti-Semites can gain a cheap status by putting down Jews and increase their status and power in corporations, government and academia.

I was thunder-struck recently with the revelations in Mosco Boucalt's film "Terrorists in Retirement." This film provoked a scandal in France sixteen years ago when it was initially banned from French television. I have to explain that I was personally violated as no other political event has done to me in the last fifty years. In my late teens and young manhood, as I will reveal in due time, I was a member of the Young Communist League. We prided ourselves in an unrelenting war against all prejudice (except of course against the capitalist class).

The French film presents a group portrait of several surviving members' recollections of the immigrant, mostly Jewish, arm of the French Resistance to the Nazi occupation. Jews never received recognition accorded to the French resistance. The movie depicts how anti-Semitic Communist leaders for political expediency betrayed the Jews. Beginning in 1943, the Communist Party began deliberately dispatching the Jewish partisans on missions the Communist leaders knew would lead to their arrest and execution. Eventually almost all of the 200 Jewish members were rounded up and executed by the Nazis.

This betrayal by the Communist party, the champion of the working class and all under-privileged minorities, profoundly depressed me. I took it as a personal attack and I was convinced more than ever that the Jew has absolutely no one that can be trusted as an ally against anti-Semites. When "push comes to shove," as the saying goes, all the noble egalitarian socialist theory and rhetoric evaporates into thin air, and once again we are taught the bitter lesson that self-serving anti-Semitism trumps all ideologies and that we can count only on ourselves to survive. A bitter, bitter lesson.

The above betrayal affected me personally much more than the early pact Pope Pius XII made with Hitler. This despicable behavior is an everlasting monument of self-interest over conscience. This anti-Semitic Pope did not bother to protest the deportation of Jews from the Roman ghetto in sight of the Vatican. How could he possibly claim ignorance of what was happening in his backyard? To cap this anti-human cowardly spiritual or vacuity, the anti-Semitic Pius XII is soon to be canonized. The fact is that the Catholic Church was the chief instigator of the Inquisition, the massacre of Jews and their mass deportation from Spain 450 years before the even more zealous Nazi scheme of killing and cremating alive all Jews. One would have to deny all the influence of history not to realize that the Inquisition paved the way for locking Jews up in ghettoes for five hundred years. It is difficult to grant the present Pope more than a fleeting gesture of approval for coming to Jerusalem, praying before the Western Wall and placing a traditional note in a crevice. I wish it would make a difference among Catholics' attitudes toward Jews, but for now I see it only as tokenism, a symbolic act that is too late, too little and ineffectual for making a real difference.

Sixty years have passed since the genocide of Jews by the Nazis. Almost every year new revelations appear to document in horrifying detail the gruesome, barbaric actions and the equal viciousness of a variety of collaborators. But now a backlash is percolating to condemn the witnesses and researchers who are digging up new revelations or spelling out the details of "old" documents. Sadly, the investigators of all this bestiality feel defensive about their revelations just because some people are saying, "enough already." Well, it's not enough and never will be enough to continue to uncover every last thread of the barbarism if it takes another 1,000 years. We should never become so accustomed to these atrocities that we are not overwhelmed by the sheer inhumanity of these murderers.

In April of this year, 2001, a new book, Neighbors: The Destruction of the Jewish Community in Jedwabne, (Princeton University Press, 2001) written by Jan T. Gross, a historian at New York University It reveals that on July19, 1941, nearly the entire Jewish population of the Polish village of Jedwabne were murdered by their neighbors. Some Jews were hunted down and killed with clubs, axes and knives; most were herded into a barn and burned alive. A famous Catholic writer, Zofia Kossk-Szczucka, in a letter to a friend after the war, described a wartime incident on a Warsaw bridge ("New York Times," Saturday, March 17, 2001, p. B9).

"…. A German saw a Pole giving alms to a starving Jewish urchin. He pounced and ordered the Pole to throw the child into the river or else he would be shot along with the young beggar. 'There is nothing you can do to help him. I will kill him anyway; he is not allowed to be here. You can go free if you drown him, or I will kill you too. Drown him or die. I will count …1…2…" The Pole could not take it. He broke down and threw the child over the rail into the river. The German gave him a pat on the shoulder. "Braverl Kerl.'

They went their separate ways. Two days later, the Pole hanged himself."

People in Poland knew that they moved into the houses from which Jews were expelled and herded into the ghetto. Poles turned Jews in, others hid Jews for money. Now the counter-attack begins. "Poles should not feel a collective guilt; the writer has fallen victim to lies; in fact, the murder is a lie concocted by a Jewish conspiracy; Poles were not alone in their complicity. Lithuanians, Estonians, Ukrainian, Russian, and Belarussian neighbors also murdered Jews and profited from their deaths; Jozef Cardinal Glemp, the former Catholic Primate, and President Aleksander Kwasniewski have publicly asked for forgiveness."

Pardon my cynicism, but to all the above "excuses" I give a resounding, "so what!" I don't give a damn for all the perpertators' contrition as far as continuing the documentation of the most heinous mass murder in the history of this globe. I hope the exposure never ends and goes on and on and on! And the rest of you can go on asking for forgiveness until the end of this century.

Another recently dropped "bombshell" is the revelation that IBM, one of our leading corporations, assisted in the destruction of European Jewry indecisive ways (IBM and the Holocaust, The Strategic Alliance between Nazi Germany and America's Most Powerful Corporation, by Edwin Black, N.Y., Crown Publishers, 2000). I don't think it was a "strategic" analysis as much as a "bloody" or "avaricious" or "greedy" alliance. The fact is that IBM did do business with Hitler from 1933 until America's entry into the war and contributed machinery for mechanizing the sizeable job of tracking the murder of Jews. Hopefully his book will stimulate researchers to uncover the perfidious role of other corporations, which, I bet, are furiously working overtime on their paper shredders.

I don't think the fat cat greedy corporations who did extensive business with the Nazis should be condemned less than the concentration camp workers who gassed the Jews. If this bald indictment makes them squirm, good, so much the better.

In the heated awareness in our time of prejudice against minority groups, negative symbolic acts have enormous political consequences. Although Jews and Blacks in recent years have come to respect each other more, the Reverend Jessie Jackson's comment about New York City as "Hymietown" continues to haunt him and Jews despite all the serious regard that he has shown for Jews since making that comment.

The above anti-Semitic incidents do not discount the de-institutionalization of discrimination in the United States and other countries. Much has been written about how universities, corporate businesses, country clubs, banks, governments, etc., would not dare to discriminate openly against Jews. These are important victories. I became a University professor, Martin Slusky, an outstanding surgeon, one of my brothers a drama education consultant and the other brother a successful pharmacist. All of us and our children from graduated college and were successful. Nevertheless, hundreds of thousands of daily encounters with prejudice have taught us that we are different. Nothing is more devastating than to experience anti-Semitism as a child or youth. My scar of exclusion is deep and I don't want to heal it. It took me almost my whole life to realize that I don't want to be with "them," "the anti-Semites," and there is nothing to heal. "They", the perpetrators have deeper scars to heal; they are so deep that they do not realize that they are there.

Two other associations come to mind about the deep, insidious reservoir of anti-Semitism. Clearly, all the anti-Semites cited above were not born anti-Semitic. They absorbed anti-Semitism like sponges in a sea of hate and loathing. During the middle fifties we read in college and graduate school Gunner Myrdal's exhaustive study, The American Dilemma, which developed in depth the thesis that despite all of American society's vaunted allegiance to equality, freedom and justice and the progress of "Negroes", a persistent, pernicious and widespread subculture of discrimination and prejudice against Blacks existed. It is so deep and pervasive that Myrdal could not suggest ways to combat this "virus." My other association is Goldenson's book, One Hundred Thousand Willing Executioners, about the historical deep-seated anti-Semitism among Germans that enabled the Nazis to dare and to succeed in the mass slaughter and cremation of six million Jews. With the possible exception of Denmark, the same virulent anti-Semitism prevailed and prevails throughout Europe.

One of the most shameful and disastrous results of anti-Semitism in the United States is the refusal of the anti-Semitic State Department to permit the migration of hundreds of thousands of Jewish refugees from Europe prior to World War II. Apparently Roosevelt was not fully aware, or was simply indifferent, to the eventual mass murder of many of these refugees. I believe that the vast increase of the power and influence of American Jews since 1945 would make enough "noise" not to allow such flagrant institutional anti-Semitism to occur.

It is noteworthy that in all the intense introspection of our life in America, no one has proposed an in depth study of anti-Semitism on the scale of Myrdal's study. To be sure, we have a meticulous accounting of every anti-Semitic incident and yearly statistical comparisons which is extremely important. But this does not begin to probe the powerful latent reservoir of hatred that is hypothesized here. In my informal interviewing of scores of Jews, I have yet to come up with one person who has not experienced multiple incidents of anti-Semitism, especially during childhood, and these do not figure in the Anti-Defamation League's records. Perhaps as social scientists become more sophisticated about hermeneutic research, which probes deeper levels of the motivation and interpretations of peoples' cognitions and attitudes, we can tackle the roots of present anti-Semitism in American society. One model of the kind of approach advocated here is the studies of the authoritarian personality undertaken by Brunswick and Adorno at the end of World War II.

The most serious aspect of Anti-Semitism is not the open proud bigot who will probably always be with us. The much more dangerous issue is the support that they receive from good people who stand-by with acrobatic rationalizations in order not to 'make waves." The recent debate over John Ashcroft's nomination for United States Attorney is an instructive lesson of how prejudice against minority groups is perpetuated by the passive acceptance of good people who should know better. In the hearings over his nomination, Ashcroft insisted that he was not a racist. Yet he militantly opposed a State Supreme Court African American, Ronnie White, for a Federal Court position because of distorted trumped up charges that he was "soft" on criminals. This was proven to be false. Arlen Spector, a Republican Senator, told Ashcroft that he should apologize to the American people, which of course he did not do. Ashcroft then took refuge in the glib generality that he voted against White because of the totality of his record, whatever that means. .

An additional accusation of prejudice emerged in the hearings around Ashcroft's vigorous opposition to Mr. Hormel, an elderly gay person who was nominated by President Clinton to be ambassador to Luxembourg. Ashcroft accused Hormel of "recruiting" him for the University of Chicago Law School. This turned out to be a lie. The use of the word "recruit" is extremely relevant because of its connotation of gays recruiting men and boys for sexual exploitation. Ashcroft refused to apologize or speak to Hormel despite the latter's attempts to clear this matter up. Then Ashcroft slickly responded to questions submitted to him that he opposed Mr. Hormel's nomination on the grounds that Luxembourg was "the most Roman Catholic in all of Europe." This strongly suggests that Ashcroft's opposition was based, all his denials notwithstanding, on crass anti-gay bigotry. The fact that Ashcroft is not even aware of the depths of his prejudice is most disturbing of all about this sorry incident. It teaches us that prejudice and its denial can be so inbred in us that we are not able to recognize it much less do anything about it. Further documentation of this thesis was revealed when a Georgetown University professor reported that Ashcroft asked him about his sexual preference during a job interview in 1985. Naturally Ashcroft disputes this, but using Ashcroft's favorite response, the totality of his bigotry suggests that Ashcroft lied, or even worse, he doesn't remember his prejudice because it is an integral part of his character. It is truly like the fish in the water unaware that it is swimming in water.

Throughout the hearing by the Senate Judiciary panel, Ashcroft steadfastly maintained that he is not a racist. After Judge White documented Ashcroft's blatant bigotry, White also refused to label Ashcroft a racist. Under cross-examination by Senator Charles Schumer, White again refused to call Ashcroft a racist, but then he was asked whether Ashcroft was using a double standard in evaluating prospects for the Federal Court. White admitted that he thought that Ashcroft was indeed using a double standard. The use of a double standard is the telltale sign of a bigot, be he / she a racist, a bigot or an anti-Semite. The use of a double standard means essentially placing the less favored or regarded person(s) in a special derogatory category and justifying discrimination based on race, religion, sexual preference, etc.

The last act of this disgusting drama took place on February 1, 2001. The bigot triumphed after a full hearing. The triumph was not Ashcroft's nomination as Attorney General, but his supporters who were prepared to forgive and forget and let by-gones be by-gones. I am certain many of the readers will feel Polsky has certainly gone too far in the following analogy, but I believe a powerful causal chain exists between ignorant low-level Nazi thugs and the educated silent perpetrators of anti-Semitic crimes.

Four days before Ashcroft's nomination an article in the International section of The New York Times (page 8), reported highlights of Polish researchers' compilation of the most authoritative history of Auschwitz, the vast killing center for the extermination of the Jews. The report is called "Auschwitz 1940-1945", a five volume work replete with the names of the killers and victims. It tallies property systematically plundered from the prisoners, including gold teeth and hair by the train-load and convoys of empty baby carriages that, one prisoner reported...."were pushed in rows of five, and the procession took more than an hour to pass."

About 8,000 SS men and women ran the camp and largely escaped justice after World War II. In the whole history of Auschwitz there were few instances of SS members refusing to carry out orders and no documented instance of any guard who was punished for refusing to carry out the mass murder. This is truly a remarkable record of conformity because there are very few organizations that do not have to some degree a counter-culture to the official culture of the system. Of course the Nazis were vicious in punishing any one that broke their rules. Nevertheless, the complete conformity to bestiality indicates that all these guards must have completely accepted the anti-Semitism spewed out by the Nazi propaganda machine. They must have been "true believers" to have participated in the mass murder and cremation of men, women and children just because they were Jewish and therefore some kind of sub-human animal.

When Heinrich Himmler, the SS commander visited the camps and the killing fields he congratulated the SS murderers for not allowing any humanitarian impulses to stand in the way of their mass murders. However nauseating anti-Semitic propaganda is, I would not curtail bigots' freedom to spew their filth. Very few "true believer" bigots are going to change their minds. Bigots have become much more careful and subtle about how they peddle their filth and as a Jew I have to be super vigilant to nail anti-Semitism and racism and bigotry whenever they appear. I am sure that many readers believe that I have gone too far in some of my analogies. So be it. Mighty trees from small acorns grow. I have decided at this time in my life to make a really big deal about exposing and fighting bigotry at all levels.

This brings us back to Ashcroft's supporters. The litany of "explanations" for supporting Ashcroft is instructive: he is a former Senatorial colleague, so senatorial courtesy was a factor, the President "deserves latitude in picking his cabinet," etc.. Another tack is addressed to Ashcroft's character: sensitive, honest, religious and does what he says he will do. I think the same could certainly be said about

Pope Pius XII who institutionalized Catholic anti-Semitism with his eloquent silence and noble do-nothing actions of inhumanity in his face by the Nazis. Pius in fact is described as deeply pious and spent many hours of the day in prayer. I don't know if he prayed for the Holocaust victims, but in any case God was not listening. The equation of "religious" with non-racism and anti-anti-Semitism belies 2000 years of Catholic bigotry. Some scholars inevitably excuse Pius because we do not have as yet all the records that can give us a full picture of the complex interplay of political and moral considerations that necessarily inform papal actions. Thus the canonization of PiusXII continues to go forward.

During the hearing on Ashcroft, Judge White recounted his early deprived childhood and how he stood up to racist bullies. Given my own sorry childhood record I am especially envious of this man's courage, his eloquence and judicious temperament. Too bad Judge White will never be canonized, much less appointed the U.S Supreme Court; he certainly deserves to be.

"Nothing happens unless there is much of it," goes the saying. I have a lot of catching up to do to expose anti-Semitism and apologetic supporters. And yes, extremism in the service of anti-Semitism is loyalty to the best virtues of American society. I stand prepared to struggle against cowardly appeasers, be they Jew or Non-Jew.

Considerable confusion has arisen between anti-Semitism and anti-Israeli actions and policy. Recently the Freud Society of Vienna canceled a lecture by Edward Said, the Palestinian American professor, after members saw a photograph of him poised to hurl a stone at an Israeli guardhouse. Mr. Said claimed he was having a stone-throwing contest with his son and called it a "symbolic gesture of joy" at the end of Israel's occupation of Lebanon. He said it was a pebble and the guardhouse was at least a half mile away. Mr. Said is professor of English and comparative literature at Columbia, my University. Jonathan Cole, our provost, defended Said's right to free speech.

Some members of the Freud Society of Vienna acted out of concern for the anxieties of Austria's remaining few Jews in a climate of Pro-Nazi and anti-immigration statements by Jorg Haider, the former leader of the extreme right Freedom Party in Austria's ruling coalition. A spokesperson said that many Jews fear xenophobia and anti-Semitism will grow and they feel that they will be forced to leave the country again. Before World War 11 190,000 Jews lived in Vienna, only 5,000 to 10,000 live there now.

I have terribly mixed feelings about the Said incident. I think it is disingenuous of Said to claim that he was only playing a game with his son. I think that is nonsense at least at a symbolic level. Do we here in the States permit rocks to be thrown at our army or at government officials in the guise of free speech? I doubt it. Yet I am pulled strongly to support his free speech and gestures. But, as I have argued above, the holocaust has changed my thinking drastically. Later I will talk about my encounter with Martin Buber, but I remember Buber writing that during the 30's in Nazi Germany he was obviously certainly aware of anti-Semitism. But then, he pointed out, did not especially make a big deal out of it because he had always been aware of anti-Jewishness in Germany. What he did not know and what all of us Jews everywhere vastly underestimated the German anti-Semitism would lead to genocide. In this context it is understandable that anti-Israeli sentiments would make the Jews everywhere, but especially in places like Austria today, very very nervous.

My major at the University of Wisconsin in the early 50's was in social psychology. One of the most influential psychologists that we studied was Kurt Lewin, a brilliant immigrant scholar from Germany. He wrote several important articles about the marginality of the Jews in American society. His topographical approach concentrated on boundaries between groups and between the individual and the group and how people negotiated crossing those boundaries. Comparing the isolated European conservative ghetto to the emancipated American Jewish community, American Jews more easily passed boundaries and lessened differences (and tensions) with non-Jews.

Kurt Lewin assumed that the restlessness (and tension) of the American Jew was due to an intense desire to belong to the socially higher gentile group now in his / her grasp. The pay-off was more money, more prestige and more power. This often led to less identification with the Jewish community. No doubt Israelis eager to improve their class position are also restless and tense, but American Jews in addition have to cope with anti-Semitism, hence the creation of the "marginal Jew", caught between two cultures.

The challenge today to the above marginality thesis is the increasing doubt among many American Jews of the gentiles' higher social (and cultural and intellectual and moral) status. Why should Jews pass over to "them?" American Jewish institutions --- synagogues, community centers, study groups, schools, camps, colleges and universities, Israel exchange programs --- have an unprecedented opportunity to step into a yawning cultural gap and create a renaissance Jewish culture. Jewish institutions have failed miserably to attract Jews to a new vision of who we are and what we can become. Our self-development as a viable Jewish community is our strongest offense against bigoted enemies that want to destroy us. A Jew proud of his cultural heritage is the best way to eliminate his \ her marginality in American society. The highest ideals of Judaism and America are identical. My proud "return" to Judaism has changed my attitude about marginality. I am not an uncertain Jew. I know where I belong. I'm not marginal, the anti-Semites are, and we will never stop exposing and combating them. As has been often said we have a "majority problem," not a "minority problem."

Conflict within the Jewish community has changed dramatically with the first, second and third native born generations. Previously German Jews put down Russian Jews and the more settled Jews made fun of the "greener," most recent, immigrants. Now the battleground is between the Orthodox and Conservative-Reform wings of Judaism about the degree of change of rituals and procedures, but much more important is the largely silent struggle between 50% of Jewish youth who are assimilating (mainly through inter-marriage) and the others who are not. The Jewish community is at a loss of how to stem this assimilation avalanche, assuming that it should.

The capacity of institutional Jewish leaders to deny their failure in keeping Jewish youth Jewish is extraordinary and perhaps the most important factor of the "vanishing Jew" in America. In the tug of forces between the attraction of non-Jewish life and maintaining Judaism it is clear who is winning. If Jewish youth are fleeing to the gentile world --- freedom, sex, prestige, money, identity, variety, etc. --- because of little attraction to Judaism, then they are double losers. They lose the warmth, humanity and wisdom of Judaism and gentile authenticity because of their birth and guilt. They are the marginal people Kurt Lewin described so well.

Feelings about Jewish marginality are often a step away from self-hatred. Increasing identity with gentiles and avoidance of Jewishness very often leads to adopting negative attitudes about Jews. One day recently in Bloomingdale's cafeteria I met an acquaintance that I had not seen for many years. He was waiting for his wife to finish her shopping. She eventually appeared and my friend took out from his bag the jacket of the book he had been reading and wrapped it around the book. The title in large black letters on the cover was <u>Jew Versus</u>

Jew, by Samuel G. Freedman. I really don't know the reason for removing the cover in Bloomingdale's cafe, but I don't think that it is far-fetched to hypothesize that he did not want others to know that he was reading a book about Jews by a Jew. My assumption of self-hatred could be way off the mark because of my new sensitivity and his reason for removing the jacket in public could be quite innocent. I never asked him about his action.

Jews who cover up their Jewish identity in subtle ways often adopt negative Jewish stereotypes. I don't believe that I am a self-hating Jew or that I harbor Jewish stereotypes, but I definitely do not go out of my way to broadcast that I am a Jew and that I am immensely proud of it. Jewish self-hatred to me denotes that a person has adopted gentiles' definition of Jews as bad in one way or another and that being Jewish will hinder their success or their identity as "Americans." In the twenties and thirties scores of Jews changed their name in part to disguise their ethnicity. Weinstein became Winston and my childhood chum changed his name from Slutsky to Slater.

One way to erase Jewish marginality is to erase the margin. These Jews either do not reveal that they are Jewish or deny that it has any importance in their lives. Robert King Merton, Columbia University's distinguished professor emeritus sociologist, the son of a Jewish tailor in Philadelphia, never hinted that he was Jewish and kept it a dark hidden secret. Walter Lippman, the distinguished journalist and writer bristled at any allegation about his Jewishness. J. D. Salinger was touchy about any mention of his Jewish background. Going back further Marx referred to Jews as "hagglers" and the worst bourgeois representatives of capitalism. Leon Trotsky once said that he was not a Jew but a social democrat.

I am an extremist in the opposite direction. I have become over-sensitive about any hint of anti-Semitism. I think that this stems in part from the Holocaust. The bigots will not disappear but the silent stand-bye and unwitting anti-Semites will not go by unnoticed by me. In a discussion of terrorism in a small group of "intellectuals," the Serbs' attack on Kosovo was grouped together with the Israelis' counter-attacks on the PLO (Palestine Liberation Organization). To some this may be fuzzy anti-Semitism or a legitimate political point-of–view. I assumed it was anti-Semitic and explained to the group my reasons. It is true that one can be anti-Zionist and not be an anti-Semite, but I prefer to err on the side of attacking ambiguous statements rather than assuming their innocence.

I don't know if Senator Joe Lieberman really helped Gore or contributed to his defeat because he is Jewish. But I certainly can raise the question. I don't know whether President Clinton's rejection of the pardon of Jonathan Pollard is tinged with anti-Semitism or not, but I certainly can raise the question. Am I somewhat paranoid about anti-Semitism, seeing it when it is not there and therefore helping to bring it about as a kind of self-fulfilling prophecy? Probably not.

Over-sensitivity can lead to the accusation of bigotry when it is not there. This happened to me. Once a year I went to the University of Minnesota for an intensive five-day retreat One time I attended a story telling presentation and afterward criticized a presentation and thereafter was called anti-Indian. Despite all disavowals I was never invited back to Minnesota after five years teaching at the retreat. I was insensitive and apologized for that. There is a difference between an anti-Semitic remark and labeling someone an anti-Semite. Jesse Jackson once referred to New York as "Hymietown," which is an anti-Semitic slur for which Jackson has apologized. But I would not call him an "anti-Semite." Phillip Roth wrote a book recently about a very liberal professor who inadvertently referred to a "spooky" act by an African American. He was labeled a bigot and anti-Black and was pressured to leave the University.

The best way I have found to deal with anti-Semitism and root out vestiges of Jewish self-hatred is to go out of my way to identify myself as a Jew whenever and wherever I can. When I tell a story that has a Jewish source I always identify it as such. The pride of my Jewish identity is forcefully presented so that the fact that I am Jewish is as unambiguous as the fact that I am a Professor of Social Work. I greatly admire the writer who wrote a letter to "The New York Times" recently protesting President Bush's plan to give government support to religious faith based anti-poverty programs in churches. An example that is cited is a Pentecostal drug rehabilitation program whose method is "intensive Bible study and cold turkey detoxification." The writer identified herself as a Jew and protested the use of his tax money for Christian conversions and targeting the vulnerable homeless and addicted for such ends. "Right on" to this letter-writer. The fact that she identifies herself as a Jew reveals to me someone who has the guts and the pride in her Jewish identity, which adds a special force to her argument.

Like this letter writer, "in your face" is the best way to cope with my Jewish identity and anti-Semitism.

However, the myriad of books, films, photos of Nazis, visits to memorial sites and museums in the United States, Israel and Europe, have deeply affected me. I personally feel obligated in the name of all those who horribly perished to confront even the hint of anti-Semitism anywhere. And I prefer to attack anti-Semites and anti-Semitism when the situation is ambiguous. As I said before, ordinarily this is not me, but I have made myself outrageous and outspoken and on the attack at the least wisp of anti-Semitism. This is how I cope with anti-Semitism ---- not good for my pacemaker, but balm to my soul.

CHAPTER TWO
THE PRACTICAL SPIRITUALITY OF MY ANCESTORS

A Hasid was on his way to visit the Karliner Rabbi. A Rav (nickname for very learned Rabbi) met him, and said: "Cannot you find a Rabbi nearer than Karlin?"

"No, I cannot," answered the Hasid. I read the thoughts of all the Rabbis and I find them to be spurious."

"If you read thoughts," said the Rav, "then tell me what I am thinking now."

"You are thinking of God," answered the Hasid.

"No, your guess is incorrect; I am not thinking of God."

"There you have it," remarked the Hasid. "You yourself stated the reason why I must go to Karlin." (30A)

My warmest Jewish feelings stem from Rabbi Twersky's Hasidic shul where I prayed every Saturday and holidays throughout my childhood. My father was one of his faithful Hassidim. The shul was in the Rabbi's house and as I struggled to learn the Hebrew prayers and rituals I never for even a moment did not feel fully loved, accepted and at home. I spoke Yiddish fluently, the Hebrew and Yiddish melodies entered my soul and I became used to each person praying out loud at his own pace. I can still smell the snuff that members used and visualize their beautiful snuff boxes. In my mind's eye I see the constant flourishing of the talith round the members' shoulders. And when we had a special visiting chazen, like the great Pinchick, the nigunim (melodies) pierced everyone's heart and I sensed for the first time, soaring to heaven. It is impossible for me to enter a Reform temple today with its organ and stage choir without feeling alienated. I feel as if I am in a church rather than a synagogue.

Rabbi Twersky's presence suffused every nook and cranny of the shul's large windowed living room and despite important individual differences and grudges among the congregation, the overwhelming feeling was total belonging. As my father aged, he spent more and more time in shul and totally exchanged his nightly pinochle game at the O.K.U.V. Hall to sit daily at the Rebbe's feet. My father's total identification with Rabbi Twersky gave me some inkling of the Hassidim's total allegiance and faith in their Rabbis. Only many years later after reading Martin Buber's Legends of the Masters about the eighteenth and early nineteenth centuries of Hasidim did I grasp more fully their philosophy and magnetic religious fervor. Rabbi Twersky embodied this legacy and personified a joyous Hassidic spirit and was profoundly accepting of everyone, including the most obnoxious members of his shul. He serenely took delight in every moment. He glowed. When he spoke to you it was like a father, mother, friend, Rabbi and God Himself all wrapped up in one. Only later was I able fully to understand the total identification of the Hasid with their Rebbi. Martin Buber, in his Legends of the Masters, recounts a story about a young student who traveled many miles away from his own village to study several years with a renowned Rabbi. When he returned to his village he was asked what he had learned and he replied: "I learned how the Rabbi ties his shoelaces."(3B) The Rabbi personifies total righteousness and therefore his every act is filled with divine sparks.

Rabbi Twersky was often called upon to mediate conflicts among Jews who could save the money given to lawyers and the courts. He had a special relationship with the President of Marquette University in Milwaukee and sent one of his five sons there, and he eventually became a psychiatrist. Although he was a very strict Orthodox Jew, he reached out successfully to non-observant Jews as well as non-Jews. On Simchat Torah, the joyous holiday that celebrates God's presentation of the Torah to Israel, Jews and non-Jews from all over Milwaukee and the Midwest came to watch him dance. He persuaded me to attend the Yeshiva in Chicago to pursue Jewish studies, but more important, to escape all the secular influences that were beginning to work on me. Ultimately that backfired, because I was not ready to leave my family and it soured my attitude toward the yeshiva.

After all these years the sources of the power of Hasidism have become more clear to me. Yaella Wozner and I wrote a book called, Every Day Miracles, The Healing Wisdom of Hassidic Stories, in which we analyzed over 500 stories that were widely told and retold among Hasidim and are often cited today for their wisdom by Jews of every persuasion as well as by gentiles. The stories reveal the philosophy and values of the Hasidim and the new revolutionary role and function of the Rabbi that began in the early 1700's.

In their fight against the Mitnagdim, whose supreme value was the exhausting study of the Talmud, the Hassidim poured all their energy directly into God and felt His presence in every aspect of their lives. The Hassidic revolution began in earnest with the emergence of the Baal Shem Tov ("Owner of a Good Name," or "Man of Integrity") about the year 1700. For hundreds of years the Rabbi-scholar and wealthy Jews dominated the Jewish shtetl. The ideal model was the Gaon (Genius) of Vilna, who had a brilliant mind and photographic memory who settled all differences in interpretation of the Torah and Talmud. He was the Chief of the Supreme Court and the Attorney General.

The early Hassidim delighted in constantly contrasting themselves with the Mitnagdim. For example, Hassidic Rabbis listen to and help people with their troubles and problems; the Mitnagdim are concerned only with teaching themselves and learning more and more. In one story, the Hassidim, bear nourishing fruit like the date palm; the Mitnagdim are like the cedar --- lofty and unfruitful. (#46C).

Another story refers to two kinds of men, those with black gall and those with light. The dark-tempered read their books and are of a miserly disposition; the light tempered (Hassidim) love company and are generous and give freely of what they possess. The Mitnaged serves God with study and prayer. The Hasid serves God with eating and drinking and earthly delights, raising all this to holiness. (53D) The Hasid finds the holy sparks, which are buried in all things and make all holy things their concern. (72A)

According to the Hassidim, the Hasid has fear of the Lord and the Mitnagid has fear of the "Shulchan Arukh" (Rabbinical legal code). (74E) The Hassidim regarded themselves foremost with concentrating on God directly and His concern with every Hassid whatever his level of learning. Rituals were still meticulously followed, but in the context of never superceding direct communication with God with heartfelt prayers. (Jesus of course did away with most of the rituals, but the direct personal relationship with God has echoes among the Hassidim.) Hassidic Rabbis became extremely introspective and sophisticated psychologically and believed the best way to help others repent is to examine their own impure motives and repentance. In one story the Rabbi refused to offer counsel until he was able first to deal with the sense of pride that he felt when someone came to him for help. It was far better to instruct a follower to read his own soul rather than have the Rabbi read it. (86E)

A Hassid is not a person who preaches the Torah, but rather lives the Torah. (89A) The Baal Shem Tov (The "Besht"), founder of Hassidism, taught that God is within us and about us....the lowliest material things are divine. The divine light descends directly into men's hearts. Before the Besht, Jews found God above us, now every Jew's heart glowed with "the inner light." (89B)

In the Talmud Shabbat is a saying, "If our ancestors were like angels, we are like plain folk, and if they were like plain folk, we are like donkeys." I never quite realized before how much our present life is influenced by our great ancestors. America continues to be great largely because of the exceptional brilliance of the heritage that was created by founding fathers like Adams, Jefferson, Madison, Jay, Franklin, etc.. The American Jewish community was shaped largely by the two million Yiddish-speaking Jews who flocked here from Eastern Europe in the late 1800's and early 1900's. The earlier, much smaller migration of German Jews was swamped by the Russian-Polish Jewish immigrants. The vast majority of the latter were bred in small towns, called shtetls, which for the most part were dominated by Hassidism. The ideals for behavior of the Hassidic culture powerfully influence American Jews. The Hassidic configuration of beliefs and practice has an inner coherence compelling that continues to shape the character of the American Jew. This tradition also overwhelmed the more assimilated German Jewish culture and eventually had a much more important impact on American society.

The assimilated 19th century German Jews are an object lesson for American Jews and for their growing loss of a distinctive cultural identity and a high degree of cultural similarity with non-Jews. A similar cultural drift seems to be occurring among American Jews as they totally and unconsciously accept their integration into a homogeneous American culture, propelled by big business and the commercial advertisement media, which abandon the basic Prophetic and Hasidic principles of caring for the less well off within a community of caring and justice.

As we shall see, significant cultural parallels exist between many of the values underlying the God-centered philosophy of Hassidism and the secular, pragmatic, individualistic and independent ethic of Americans. In the following pages I shall point out the similarities between important features of the two cultures despite the overall distinctive unique structure of the two ways of life. Ethical norms need not be judged solely within the unique context of each culture; comparative appraisals and mutual interactions of specific values can be very instructive and need not be enclosed in separate locked cultural boxes.

In many stories Hassidim are encouraged not to be preoccupied with all the interpretations of the Torah, but to observe the Rabbis' or Zaddikim's (righteous Hassidim) conduct from their arising in the early morning until the time of their lying down to rest at night. The previous chief value of obsessive learning was transmuted into living "right," a populist revolution from below that increased enormously the "divinity" of the hardworking uneducated Jew who can be as good as the most learned scholar. What constituted that "right living" or moral life in practical terms would now be the task of the Rabbis to model for their followers.

To be a leader or model means that the followers are in agreement to conform with the leader's course. When the followers accept the leader's right to prescribe the right course then the leader becomes a legitimate authority. To overcome traditional leaders' authority, new charismatic leaders "claim", and followers often attribute to them, extraordinary personal qualities that give them precedence over Establishment leaders and their code of conduct. In the 17th and 18th centuries Jews in Europe were simultaneously given more economic freedom and severely threatened with anti-Semitism and outright violence, often against entire communities in the form of pogroms. Life was more promising and dangerous, ideal conditions for fostering all kinds of psychological difficulties. Jews were "ripe" for new leadership that could address, in practical ways, their everyday tensions and troubles by incorporating God into their daily life. This was embodied in the charismatic Baal Shem Tov.

The Baal Shem Tov (Master of the Good Name), nicknamed Besh, who was born about 1700, drastically changed the role and function of the Rabbi in the creation of the radical values and philosophy cited above that eventually came to be known as Hassidism. These values were expressed and taught through explicit every day events and stories. The Besht never kept money in his house overnight. After paying off all his debts, he gave the rest of the money to the poor and needy. One day he brought a large amount of money home to pay his debts and give the rest to the poor. His thrifty wife this time kept a little of the money so she would not have to buy on credit. That evening in shul the Besht felt something impeding his prayer. He went home and asked his wife if there was any money left in the house. His wife confessed that she kept some and he took that money and gave it to the poor that evening. (35C)

Obviously all Hassidim or even all Rabbis could not practice this kind of generosity. It was an ideal that nevertheless influenced every day behavior and the responsibility of those who are better off to help those who need support. Those who more nearly followed the Hassidic ideals were called "Zaddikim", the righteous, whose conduct was according to divine moral law. Thus late one night a man came to the home of Rabbi Liber and asked for lodging. Rabbi Liber graciously welcomed the stranger, gave him food and drink and prepared a comfortable bed for him. The stranger asked him the reason he went through so much trouble, whereupon Rabbi Lieber replied: "It is not for your sake but for my own that I am doing this." (27A)

The Hassidim ascribed all their moral laws to God and it was the task of the Rabbis to interpret them in very practical terms to their followers. Thus a merchant once came to Rabbi Meir Shalom to complain about a competitor who opened a shop next door to him. Rabbi Shalom pointed out that he set his heart on his business instead of God, his real support. He reminded him of the commandment to love his neighbor as himself, which here means that he should want for his neighbor what he needs for himself and thereby will find God. And God will provide for all. (62A)The Hassidic Rabbis and the Zaddikim constantly reminded their followers of their responsibility to the needs of the less fortunate and to the community. The Rabbis spoke about three types of people: the person who says that he will do a mitzvah (good deed) soon has a poor character; the average character who says, "I am ready to do a mitzvah now"; and the person who says, I am doing it," who has a praiseworthy character. (3A)

The Baal Shem Tov taught his disciples this morality of righteousness. This deep concern for others and God, in very homely stories and parables in many respects like Jesus, including eventually, the making of miracles. The big difference between the Besht and Jesus is that the Besht portrayed himself as bedeviled with the same sins as everyone including pride, greed, lust, etc.; he portrayed himself as not a divine but very ordinary emissary of God. Before the Baal Shem died his disciples asked him about his successor. He replied that it would be someone who could teach how to overcome pride. One of his disciples, Rabbi Baer, maintained that it cannot be overcome, but struggled with all of one's life and thus he became the Besht's successor. (12C)

The legacy of the Baal Shem Tov is captured in the following story. Moshe Efraim, the Besht's grandson, became a renowned scholar and was tempted to join the Mitnagdim, known for their scholarship. The two went for a walk and met a man from another city. Besht asked him about a great scholar who lived in his city. Then, parenthetically, the Besht turned to his grandson and admitted that he envied the man's scholarship, but that he had no time to study because, "I have to serve my Maker." The message was clear. The Besht felt that it was more important to help others than to spend all of his time in the study of the Torah. From that moment his grandson, Efraim, returned to Hassidim "with all his strength." (19C)

On another occasion the Besht went for a long walk with another young scholar who was not certain about becoming his disciple. On the walk they got lost and the potential disciple seemed to have doubts about the Besht as his teacher. The Besht said to him: "It is written... `that God will fulfill the desire of them that fear him.' God has fulfilled your desire to have a chance to laugh at me.'" This pierced the young man's heart and he joined the master with his whole soul.

Stories like the above endlessly retold gradually built up an image of a Zaddik with super-human spiritual powers. There is no doubt of the Besht's psychological skills in influencing and helping people and creating, wittingly or unwittingly, an image of legendary proportions.

Central to the Hassidim's way of life is their relationship to God. A simple (and innocently paradoxical) self-sealing formula was created which proved that God always had the best interests of Jews at heart even in the most egregious calamitous situations. Thus, when a Jew breaks a leg, he gives thanks to God that both legs were not broken. When both legs are broken, he gives thanks to God that he didn't fracture his head. A Tzaddic's wife held their hungry child who was too weak to cry. The Tzaddic sighed and instantly caught himself. A voice came to him: "You have lost your share in the coming world." The sigh represented a shadow of doubt. The Tzaddic's response to his "sigh" was that now that he could not expect any help, he could serve God in earnest without any expectation whatsoever of help. (20D) And it also left it up to him find food for his child.

A Zaddik is someone who is known only to himself and God. Many stories abound about how Rabbis and Hassidim who have attained some measure of a Zaddik status let that go to their head. This lust for vanity is constantly fought. (11C) A man who pursued honors reported to Rabbi Bunam that he had a dream in which his father told him he would be destined to be a great leader. This man appeared again several months later to report that he had the same dream. Rabbi Bunam told him the next time that his father appeared to tell him that he should also appear to the people that he is supposed to lead. (15B)

Rabbi Bunam, a celebrated follower of the Besht, had the uncanny ability to talk to throngs of followers and despite their many differences, gave to each "his own perfection." (1A). When the Besht spoke to his followers they quarreled about whom the Besht was speaking to. One time they all began to speak at once and then suddenly "fell silent." (1C) The Besht stressed serving people. He once said that when he has reached a high rung of knowledge, he has learned nothing if he has not " taken a step in the service of God ...", which to him is the equivalent of serving people. (23B)

Many stories elaborate in different ways the highest Hassidic virtue that defines the Zaddik, which is finding oneself by giving to others. One gives not only to help others, but because the giving is self-satisfying. A Zaddik gives zedakah, does good deeds, because it is the human and Godly way to live. I think that this concept is extraordinarily difficult for us to understand because our lives are so individualistically self-centered and competitive that our need, and hence chief virtue, is to look out for number one first, foremost and exclusively. Everyone else is far secondary. And as we shall see, this did not mean that a small group of people gave and a large group took. Quite the contrary; individual independence and self-sufficiency were highly prized.

The Rabbi of Kotzk once commented about a famous Rabbi who bought himself a fur coat: "One man buys kindling for a fire, another a fur coat. The latter keeps only himself warm, whereas the man who buys wood gives warmth to others." (71D) One beautiful story about Rabbi Riziner tells of a fellow Rabbi who complained that when he studied the Torah he felt the holy light encompass him, but when he stopped studying he felt himself chilled and surrounded by darkness. Rabbi Riziner suggested that when he finished studying that he do a Mitzvah, a good deed, and the light will not be lost. Then he added : "The light, which you feel round about you during the studies, is borrowed from the souls of the Sages. A light of your own is from your own Mitzvahs."

The use of metaphors and easily recognized events were frequently employed by Hassidim to drive their points across. A storekeeper once complained to the Premislaner Rabbi that a rival opened a store next door and was taking some of his business. The Rabbi asked him if he ever saw a horse drink water and stamp his feet at the same time. The storekeeper said that he had noticed this. The reason the Rabbi told him is that he sees a reflection in the water of a horse and tries to chase an imaginary foe away. But God's abundance flows like a river and it is He who sustains everyone according to His will. (92A)

At the same time that the Hassidim valued zedakah, doing good deeds, they also emphasized independence. They believed that accomplishments only through one's own effort is worthy. A poor Rabbi, Yehiel Meir, gleefully once reported to the Kotsk Rabbi that he had won money in a lottery. The Kotsk Rabbi responded that that was not through his efforts so Rabbi Meir went home and gave the money to the poor. (10D) Rabbi Hirsch Rimanover once said that some Zaddikim serve God on the main highway, that is the traditional course, other adopt new ways, but those who choose to walk on their own path are the first to reach their destination. (74A) The art (and science) of Hassidic counseling consisted in matching cures according to the needs of each Hasid. Treatment varied from reading ethical books or psalms to doing good deeds and communal work. (80E) The Rabbis warned that when a person becomes dissatisfied with his business or profession "it is a sure sign that he is not conducting it honestly." (90D) Underlying all of the Rabbis' counseling and help is the idea of empowering the Hassid to help himself and to rely on his own skills. The Rabbi of Roptchitz, Rabbi Naftali, got up early in the morning and prayed that all those in need of help may find it in their homes and not have to go to Roptchitz and be deluded into thinking that the Rabbi has helped him.

The Hassidim often used irony, sarcasm and sardonic humor to get their points across. Rabbi Isaac Zidichover was fond of saying that when someone visits the first time, he gives him his blessing; when he visits a second time, he penetrates his soul; if he returns for a third visit, he carries him on his shoulder. (82A) Once Rabbi Yehudi was walking cross-country and came to an overturned wagon. The driver asked him to help raise it. The Rabbi tried but the wagon would not budge. "I can't," he finally said. The wagon driver corrected him: "You can, you don't want to." In this way Yehudi learned how to serve God better. (6A)

The emphasis of Hassidim helping themselves rather than Rabbis or God helping them is described in a story about the Rabbi of Koznitz. A villager and his wife came to him for help with prayers for having a son. The Rabbi asked for 52 gulden which is the numerical sum of <u>ben</u>, son. The villager had only ten gulden and the Rabbi refused to help him. A month later the villager returned with a sack full of coins and spread them out on the table. The sum came to twenty gulden and the Rabbi still refused to help him. The villager became very angry and told his wife to leave with him immediately and that God would help them without the Rabbi's prayer. The Rabbi then told him that he had already been granted his help (by accepting responsibility) and he was right.

Over the years the Hassidic Rabbis developed a counseling theory and method that I call "practical spirituality." The Hassidim believed that God's spirit or divine sparks are manifested in the most mundane and ordinary events and objects on earth. Hence the way to reach God and all the comforts and enlightenment of spirituality were through every moment and thing. In many ways this practical spirituality has many characteristics in common with Zen Buddhism. Thus a Hassid would respond to the question of what is most important by saying "this moment." If asked how he prays, he would respond, "with a bench and the floor." Asked if he needs anything, the Hassid would say, "I have what I need." The busy man would find solace during the hectic day by total absorption in prayer, which probably is just as effective as meditation. A student traveled a long distance to study with Rabbi Dov Baer of Mezeretz. When he returned after several years and was queried by the villagers about what he had learned, he responded: "I learned his way of tying his shoelaces." (3B)

One of the best stories in Buber's <u>Legends of the Masters</u> that describes the holiness of everyday life is about a disciple of Rabbi Shmelke who sought his help about how to prepare his soul for the service of God. He told his disciple to go to an inn where he would find Rabbi Abraham Haryyim, who at that time was innkeeper. The disciple went to the inn and was surprised to see the innkeeper, after morning prayers, devote all his time to his business. The student finally asked Rabbi Abraham what he did all day and he responded that he cleaned the dishes thoroughly so that not a trace of food was left on them and scrubbed the pots and pans until they were spotless. The student worked in the inn for six months. The disciple then returned to Rabbi Baer and reported what he had seen and heard and done. Rabbi Baer told him that now he knew how to prepare his soul for service to God.(43A)

The phrase, "practical spirituality," is an oxymoron. The term refers to upsetting conventional modes of thinking which delighted Hassidim. For example the Kossover Rabbi once said: "If you give a donation to a poor man, and the latter returns it, asking for a still larger gift, your acquiescence to his request will bring you a boundless reward, since it is contrary to the nature of man." (9C) The Rabbi of Kotzk said: "Everything in the world can be imitated except truth. For truth that is imitated is no longer truth." (2D) This statement forces you to think in terms of opposites and is very powerful if you assume that one person's truth is his or her truth and is never quite the same for other people who must find their own truth. It is similar, but certainly not the same, to Rabbi Pinhas declaration that a "man's soul teaches him." When a disciple asked him why the soul is not constantly teaching us and why we don't obey the soul, Rabbi Pinhas explained: "The soul teaches incessantly, but it never repeats." (18D) I feel this conundrum is important, but I still have not figured it out completely to my satisfaction.

The reason why "things are often not what they seem," is that the Hassidim plumbed the motivation of people, the feelings and thinking that drove their actions and often included covering up true intentions. The Rabbi of Zana once asked a Hassid what he would do if he found a purse full of money. The Hassid indignantly replied that he would return it immediately. The Rabbi asked the same question to another Hassid who replied that he was not such a fool as to return a purse full money. A third Hassid answered the same question by saying that he was not sure what he would do, but he would fight his evil inclination as hard as he could and return the money. The Rabbi responded to him: "These are good words. You are a true sage!"

The complexity, depth and brilliance of the Besht's motivational psychology is revealed in a story he told about rich and poor brothers. The rich brother "had no scruples" about doing wrong. The poor brother began to misconduct himself but he remained poor. He complained to his elder rich brother who said to him: "… your transgressions have not made you wealthy because you did them solely to become rich and not from the conviction that it matters not whether you did good or evil." Then the Besht concluded, as he always did, with the lesson: "How much more applicable is this to doing good with the proper intention." (78A)

One time the grandson of the Besht was told that he delivered his teachings very well. The grandson replied: "Rather than speak so well, I should be stricken down." (47D). The paradox that reveals the truth can be found in an admission told by Rabbi Elimelech Lizensker. He told his followers that he was sure that he would have his share in the world to come. When he was asked the reason, he replied that when he would be asked by the Heavenly Tribunal whether he had studied as duty-bound , he would answer "no;." he also answered "no" to praying as duty-bound and "no" to doing good as duty bound. He then explained to his shocked followers: .... "judgment will be made in my favor because I have spoken the truth." (2B)

The powerful focus on "intention" and its analytical separation from behavior opened up a wide arena of insights for the Hassidim. In Lublin lived a great sinner. The Lubliner Rabbi saw him frequently and conversed with him as if he were a man of integrity. This upset the villagers so the Lubliner explained. "... I know he is a great sinner... but he loves gaiety and hates dejection, has no regrets and no repentance ... and lives in happiness as in a tower. ... the radiance of his happiness overwhelms my heart. (12B) "The Rabbi of Mesritch admired strong thieves who know how to open locks without keys. He explained: "God loves the thief who breaks locks open; I mean the man who breaks his heart for God." (18C) From gamblers the Rabbis deduced that they were able to stay up all night which would be valuable to them when they turned to study. (16C) From a hopeful thief they learned never to give up in the pursuit of Mitzvahs (good deeds) and serving God. From scoffers they learned to be as bold in serving God as they are bold in ridiculing others.(83D) From Satan and Haman they learned to be diligent in serving God (85F and 85G). From a Smith who got up early to work Rabbi Yaskov Yitzhak was inspired to begin his work earlier to serve God.(69B).

Hassidim learned from everyday situations and objects valuable lessons about how best to live. Rabbi Hanokh moved to a house in Warsaw that was next to a house from which he heard the sound of music and dancing. He asked a friend about what was going on and was told that it was a house for wedding celebrations. Rabbi Hanokh sighed; "Now I know why our sages compare this world to a house of weddings." (7C) When the Koretzer Rabbi saw the rain he remembered a passage from Deuteronomy 32:3: "Moses said:. 'My doctrine shall drop as the rain.'" This in turn led him to associate with the rain falling among many different plants with each one growing according to its own nature and students responding differently to the same instruction. (8C)

The son of the Rabbi of Lentshno saw Rabbi Yitzhak praying quietly and simply and was amazed at his lack of ecstasy. His father explained that great swimmers do not thrash about, but let the tide carry them (10B). Today we say "go with the flow." A grandson of Rabbi Pinhas of Kinsk entered Rabbi Yerahmiels room and was surprised to find him lying down and playing with his watch. The Rabbi explained: "You look surprised at what I am doing. I am learning how to leave the world." I don't think it is possible to understand this strange reply to our ears without grasping the Hassidic belief that a watch is every whit sacred and divine as a prayer. (12D) A Hassid excitedly told Rabbi Bunam that he had become an expressman. Known far and wide as a great wit, Rabbi Bunam replied: " Your head will now be occupied with the horse; hence it appears that you have made of your mind a stable." (29C)

Once the Baal Shem Tov came to the entrance of a shul and refused to enter. He sardonically replied that it is crowded with teachings and prayers from wall to wall and there was no room for him. Then he added the punch line. "The words from the lips of those who are teaching and praying do not come from the hearts and are not lifted to heaven. They cannot rise but fill the shul from wall to wall and from floor to ceiling." (32) The Besht compares a crowd of people to a crowd of prayers in a shul. The prayers are stuck together and not heaven bound because they were said mechanically and are not heart-felt. This brings up again that it is not prayer as such, but the feeling and motivation behind the prayer that are important.

The Hassidim were ingenious in finding, in every object, a hidden practical lesson of how to live. One Rebbe asks another: " Do you know why the railway engine has the strength to draw all the carriages behind it?" Answer: "Because he restrains his steam within himself. (41B). A congregation in a small town assembled to welcome a master Rav. One show-off tried to impress the Rav with his learning. The Rav turned his back on him and kept staring out of a window. The show-off demanded to know what he was looking at. The Rav replied: "I am amazed to see how such a small lump of earth grew into a tall mountain." (48A) Rabbi Hayyim of Krosno once was totally absorbed in watching a rope dancer. His disciple was surprised at his behavior and the Rabbi replied: " The rope dancer is not thinking about the 100 gulden he is earning, but what he is doing: if he thought about the gulden he would fall." (50A) The analogy with how to pray to God would be obvious to a Hassid. The Koretzer Rabbi said once to a disciple: "Long ago I conquered my anger and put it in my pocket. When I need it, I take it out." (54E) This remarkable story underlines the tremendous psychological sophistication of the Hassidim 200 years before Freud and his principle of " psychological determinism." Anger is a powerful feeling that does not evaporate after it is triggered, so why not put it to good practical use? A somewhat similar story is told about Rabbi Leib Dimimies of Lantzut, who was a wealthy merchant and very learned in the Torah. He lost his fortune, but seemed to pay no heed to his loss and continued his studies. He was asked about this lack of concern and anxiety. He replied: "The Lord gave me a brain which thinks rapidly. The worrying which another would do in a year, I have done in a moment." (74A)

Rabbi Moshe was fond of telling the following story to himself as well as to others. A high ranking officer ordered an expensive suit from a well-known proud tailor. The suit did not fit at all and the tailor was dismissed in disgrace. He sought the help of the Rabbi of Kobryn who told him to go back to the officer and offer to remake it. Then to rip the suit to pieces and do it all over again. Humbly the tailor remade the suit, which turned out to be perfect.(61B) This story, like many of the preceding ones, again highlights the importance of feelings and motivation underlying behavior. Together the stories weave a tapestry of the positive and negative motivation that propels actions. The Hassidim were 300 years ahead of the current preoccupation of psychology with the motivation of behavior.

Like other populist religions, Hassidic Rabbis, in their zeal to speak directly and simply and be helpful to their followers often lapsed into a pop psychology that was as simple as it sounded. Sometimes the obvious can be profound, but more often it can be banal. To be sure, what is obvious or profound is in the ear of the listener. For example, Rabbi Yehiel Mikhal told his Hassidim that a carriage traveling up a mountain can tire the horses. The foolish traveler will let the carriage roll down the mountain; the wise traveler will place a stone behind the wheel so the horses can rest and is like one who has to interrupt his service and is able to pause and then proceed to the top of the mountain of the Lord. (16B) Rabbi Meir learned from his teacher that the commandment, "thou shalt not steal," refers not only to not steal from others, but from "oneself." (29E) That is certainly sensible, but to my ears, not profound. The Rabbi of Sadagora once told his Hassidim that everything can teach us: "from a train we learn that because of one second, one can miss everything; from the telegraph that every word is counted and charged; and from the telephone, what we say here is heard there." (67E) And from the game of checkers, Rabbi Nahum, the son of the Rabbi of Rizhyn, derived the following lessons: one must not make two moves at once; one may only move forward and not backward; and the third is that when one has reached the last row, one may move to where he likes." All these quips seem to me to be dressed up as profound wisdom that are uttered by wise sages.

The practical spirituality of the early Hasidim enabled them to avoid bestowing messiah status on anyone (although the Baal Shem Tov came close, unwillingly, to this bestowal) and also to avoid falling into spiritual mysticism or the spell of Cabala. But there certainly was some ambivalence about miracles and the messiah. Mostly, however, they made good fun of the miraculous. Rabbi Zalman used to say: "In the house of my teacher…. Miracles lay under the benches, only no one had the time to pick them up." (49D) "Those in heaven wanted to reveal to Rabbi Sheloma of Karlin the language of the birds, the trees and the serving angels, but he refused until he found out of what importance each of these languages was for the service of God. (54D) Rabbi Bunam said: "Before the Messiah will come, there will be Rabbis without Torah, Hasidim without Hasidism, rich men without riches, summers without heat, winters without cold, and grain stalks without grain." (75G) One implication of this story is that the world will never be this topsy-turvy so you can forget about the Messiah coming here.

The Hasidim were too practical to be carried away by mystical beliefs. Rabbi Mendel once boasted to his teacher, Rabbi Elimelekh, that in the evening he saw the angel who rolls out the light and in the morning the angel who rolls away the darkness. "Yes," said Rabbi Elimelekh, "in my youth I saw that too. Later on you don't see those things any more." (38C) The Rabbi of Kobryn said: "We paid no attention to the miracles our teachers worked, and when sometimes a miracle did not come, he gained in our eyes." (68E) The Hasidic way of making fun of the idea of miracles. In place of miracles the Hasidim created a spiritual life that is akin to Zen. The young people attracted to Buddhism are ignorant of the powerful spiritual tradition engendered by the early Hasidim. One story tells about a Hasid who lost all of his money, but continued to pray and study. He said that he learned that he who wants to be rich, let him go north; he who wants to

be wise, let him go south. He was then asked about the man who
wanted to both rich and wise. He responded that he who thinks nothing
at all of himself, and makes himself anything, grows spiritual, and
spirits do not occupy space; he can be north and south at the same time.
I think this a powerful lesson because it teaches us that each one of us
is much more than whether one invests himself in study or making
money. We can transcend our achievements or the lack of them and
when we shed these encumbrances we can be everywhere. (30D) Very
powerful!

      Although the Hasidim belittled miracles, they had a profound
understanding of the importance of trance and mind altering
experiences. The most mundane objects and experiences can trigger an
altered state of mind. A grandson of Rabbi Yerahmiel once came to the
master's room and found him lying down and playing with his watch.
He said to his grandson: "You are surprised at what I am doing? But do
you really know what I am doing? I am learning how to leave this
world." (12D) The Hasidim were utterly entranced by the skills of tight
rope walkers and likened them to the faith that they had in God. (50A)
The Hasidim believed that their faith used them as vehicles to express
God's truth. The Baal Shem said; "When I weld my spirit to God, I let
my mouth say what it will for then all my words are bound to their root
in Heaven." According to Rabbi Ber of Meseritz, when he is
discoursing on a subject of the Torah, he neither feels or hears the
words he is speaking. As soon as he hears himself talking, he stops.
(90C) Rabbi David Moshe once held an extremely large Torah in his
hand and one of his Hasidim wanted to relieve him. He responded:
"Once you hold it, it isn't heavy any more. (37E)

      The Hasidim were utterly opposed to asceticism. On the
contrary, they believed that God created a world that should be
thoroughly enjoyed with all the senses. One interesting legend reports
that when the Baal Shem was young, he used to take six loaves of bread
and a pitcher of water at the close of the sabbath and went into
seclusion for an entire week. At the end of the week the Baal Shem was
surprised to discover that when he lifted his sack to return home, he
found all the loaves still in it. The story concludes: "Fasting such as
this, is allowed." (45C) Like all values and philosophies that the
Hasidim opposed, they made fun of or at least wryly commented on the
miraculous. Rabbi Zalman once said about his master that every day at
dawn his master went to the pond and stayed there for a while: "He was

learning the song with which the frogs praise God. It take a very long time to learn that song. (47C)

The Hasidim had a unique concept of the messiah. In the Talmud Sota is the provocative assertion that, "when the Messiah comes, impudence (chutzpah) will grow." The coming of the Messiah is linked with radical change and the courage of revolutionaries. In one of the most moving stories by Martin Buber, "The Judgment of the Messiah," a young scholar broke an agreement with an intended father-in-law to marry his daughter because instead of marriage, he wanted to travel to a far away town to study with a great teacher. The young scholar subsequently died and when he appeared in heaven before the Messiah, he declared that he had to go to the master Rabbi. The Messiah responded: "The father-in-law is right because he followed the authority of the Rabbi, and the Rabbi is right because he took the law as his authority." And then he added: "But I have come for those who are not justified." (3C) In other words, authority can be challenged and is not always right!

In summary: Six major values are taught over and over again in stories, sermons, songs, proverbs and sayings:

1. God is in every thing and every act and every thought every moment of our lives; heartfelt prayer is the way to reach Him.

2. God will not enable you to get what you want; you and you alone can get what you want only through your own efforts. Believe in God unconditionally, whatever the consequences may be.

3. To give to the less fortunate is the highest ideal in life.

4. All of us, including Rabbis and Zaddikim, are tempted to sin and must struggle all of our lives against the temptation to do so.

5. The motivation steering one's actions are of prime importance in getting what you want and living a righteous life.

6. Although the Hassidim challenged the predominance of study and learning, they nevertheless remained a cardinal virtue. "A learned bastard is superior to an ignorant high priest." (Talmud Horayot) "Let a father wed his daughter to a scholar, even if he spends all his money on her dowry." (Tanna Deve Eliah)

Of the above ideals, one stands out as the distinctive characteristic of our Hasidic ancestors and before them to the great Prophets of the Old Testament. Rabbi Moshe Leib once asked: "To what end can the denial of God be tolerated?" The answer is that deeds of charity triumph over God Himself: "if someone comes to you and asks your help, you shall not turn him off with pious words, saying:

'Have faith and take your troubles to God!' You shall act as if there were no God, as if there were only one person in all the world who could help; this man --- only yourself." (68C) No story in the hundreds of stories we have about the early Hasidim matches its chutzpah in the service of the poor and the needy over all pious abstractions including God.

Often the values and philosophy of a group contain contradictory norms. For example, although the Hassidim prized self-sufficiency, they also had a profound faith that God looked out for their best interests, however the obvious reality was just the opposite. The great Bratslaver Rabbi once said: "The knowledge that whatsoever occurs to you is for your good, raises you to the heights of living in Paradise." (74G) The obvious danger in this kind of "God-philosophy" is that it can also engender passive resignation to evil in seeing in it an ultimate good. The Holocaust challenged severely this naïve and overly optimistic attitude.

Today we all believe in cultural relativity. This means that ideas and practices that we now oppose have to be seen in the unique context and time-period of the total culture. Despite all of the rationalizations of the woman as the queen of the house and the Sabbath, the Hassidim practiced the belief in a secondary status of the woman. The Rabbi's authority was rarely seriously challenged. All in all, however the six orientations described above had and continue to have a profound influence among Jewish people and are important values of our cultural heritage.

The special thrust of the Hassidim is making God as much a part of their lives as their paias and tallis and the sun and the moon and washing dishes. But what a price is paid for this piety! Hasidism became a cult because it brooks no dissent from its rituals and values. Those who dissent are simply ex-communicated. Like every cult, Hasidim is an all or nothing affair. Their great virtue was embodying God with joy and faith in all their routines and in the case of their Tsadikim, their "Saints," in all their relationships. But like every religion, it became institutionalized, clannish, intolerant of other points of view and sealed itself into a totally segregated community that is culturally and intellectually incestuous and turned into a modern antique like a preserved armchair of the 18th century.

In Rabbi Twersky's shul many of the members were not really Hasidim in practice or belief. The magnetic charisma of Rabbi Twersky drew them into his shul and they were accepted without any pressure to reform. As my father aged, and especially after his heart attack, he gradually became a totally observant Jew and president of the shul. But there was always some gap between him and the "true Hasidim." As I look back now I feel the shul was my father's second home and Rabbi Twersky became the father that he left when he immigrated to the United States at the age of fifteen. It is clear to me now that an unbridgeable gap exists between today's Hasidim and Jews who refuse to adopt totally their way of life. And this only increases their cultist society.

Even in Rabbi Twersky's warm "womb," however, I was far from totally religious. When an important baseball game was played on Saturday morning, I found ways to play hooky. After my Bar Mitzvah I was seized with the holy spirit and spent a very lost unhappy year in a yeshiva in Chicago. Upon my return to Milwaukee I continued my Hebrew studies with increasingly diminished fervor. Because of my unusual height, I became a pretty good high school basketball player.

In high school my "secular" studies gradually took over, and I realize in retrospect that this was a key aspect of my assimilation to American culture. It was extremely important for immigrant parents for their children to succeed in public school. For thousands of years learning, first and foremost the Bible and all of its commentaries, was the cardinal value in Jewish life; Jewish immigrants became obsessed with transferring this deep and abiding value to their children succeeding in schools, colleges and universities. In this way, a cardinal Jewish virtue succeeded in subverting youngsters' attachment to Judaism. Later I will explore in depth Ahad Ha'am's formulation of the supreme irony of Jews' outward success and spiritual (cultural) poverty.

Success in American schools and colleges prefigured a massive identification with American values on many different levels. But this process proceeded below our consciousness. Ahad Ha'am, the pen name of Asher Ginzberg, a leading cultural Zionist, explained this phenomenon very clearly: "What is the true national education? That which makes children absorb the national spirit unconsciously." So what happens when two "national" spirits compete with each other? Very simply I moved away from Judaism and adopted American values and philosophy of achievement and success. My new heroes were Washington, Jefferson, Lincoln and Roosevelt. I learned the "Star Spangled Banner" national anthem and pledged allegiance to the flag every school day and celebrated Thanksgiving with all the trimmings.

Every year Christmas flooded America and was a major force in maintaining my outsider's status in American culture and society.

I grew up in a kind of Jewish shtetl in a working class neighborhood on the lower North side of Milwaukee. I belonged to a Jewish gang that fought against Irish, Polish and German kids. We had our own bakeries, kosher butcher shops, delis and grocery stores. We had a funeral home, mikvahs, hot Russian steam baths and religious stores. On Jewish holidays we traveled up and down "synagogue road" from one shul to another looking for Jewish girls to taunt and tease. All adults went to shul on the holidays and everyone past the age of thirteen fasted on Yom Kippur. The more religious built a makeshift sucha (hut) that was attached to their homes. During the eight days of Succoth we would visit the sucha for delicious Magen David red wine and pound cake.

I grew up in a Jewish home. We had a mezuzah on the door entrance, a huge brass menorah in the living room, several pictures of Rabbis praying with their tallish and a beautiful embroidered linen tablecloth for the Sabbath. Friday night was always special. My mother welcomed the Sabbath with a cloth over her head and a prayer over lit candles. My father said the blessing over wine and bread. Invariably we had challa, half sour-pickles, chicken soup with mondlach and kreplach, chicken, and compote for desert.

These are the practices which formed my way of seeing the world for the most impressionable years of my life through adolescence. I carried this culture as I would shirts and pants. It located me in a special network of friends and relatives with goyim on the outside of the circle and stamped me with religious beliefs that I uncritically accepted as I did the sun, the moon and the stars.

My family, neighborhood, shul, cheder (Hebrew school) and all the holidays were all of one piece. In the back alleys of my neighborhood we stole plums and apples daily. We belonged to the Jewish center where we learned basketball and other sports and competed against each other. Summers we went to Camp Sydney Cohen and sat around the huge bonfire and sang songs and cried and swore we would be in touch with each other in the city and be back in the same bunk next summer. In high school three of us from the same class played hooky together, landed in a jail for a couple of hours in a Milwaukee suburb and were immediately found out. We caused a sensation in North Division High School. My father had to come to school to talk to the principle and it was one of the few times my father beat me with a strap.

During adolescence, sexual feelings consumed our lives. Sex was never discussed, not even mentioned at home or public school. So the gutter took over. I had a brief puppy love encounter with a religious girl, which her parents thoroughly disapproved of. Jewish boys divided all Jewish girls into three categories: JAPS, Jewish American princesses, "nice" non-sexual girls and "loose girls" who boys were allowed to "feel up" at parties in the bed-room and to "score" was to grope bare tits. The latter girls were relatively few and very well known. For the "real stuff," we turned to "Chikusa's" (derogatory name for gentile "loose" girls). One of my best friends, Marvin, was lucky to have his house free of parents during the day and he discovered an incredibly overweight ugly girl to whom he treated his best friends. Our other sexual outlet was Plymouth, a small town about twenty miles northwest of Milwaukee. It boasted a brothel and bar, a huge garish music box that played very loudly, and a stout madam and a couple of prostitutes that dealt with all eight of us in less than an hour. I couldn't get an erection and the prostitute thought I should see a doctor for some help.

This gentile-Jewish sexual division of labor was institutionalized by young Jewish men of my generation. It contributed to the destructive outlook that nice Jewish women did not really enjoy sex and added to the traditional religious bias that Jewish women produced babies and with shiksas sex was fun and, religiously, even permitted. Is it no wonder that this development was pushed by Freud to the point that young boys, beginning about the age of four, were desirous of possessing their mothers and "killing" their fathers. Is this the real source of the Oedipus complex that Freud disguised with Sophocles' famous tragedy? Once this cat was out of the bag subsequent generations of American Jewish writers had a subject that is still very much alive. Mothers poured out their pent up feelings on to their male children, especially the first born, who at least for a few years could be their exclusive true lovers and Freud universalized this relationship to all of mankind.

My mother was a pushover for us. We turned to her secretly for things that we knew we could never get from my father. She somehow scraped together some money for me to take dancing lessons which I thought would raise my stock among girls. My father lorded over her and could devastate her by threatening not to eat food that she had prepared. She was able to escape by acting in Yiddish plays and singing at informal parties. When my father died at the age of forty-nine, she took the meager savings that we were able to accumulate and fled to South Beach in Miami where she changed her name from Sarah to Sonia and had a ball dancing evenings, working out on the beach and seducing many suitors. I loved her chutzpah and iconoclasm. My brothers and I were convinced that for years she was making out with a friendly burly gentile Acme delivery man with whom she had fun during the days when my father was not around. She was a brave vital woman way ahead of her time. I am so proud of her zest for life despite my father's stodginess and strict authoritarian controls. My father once told me that "even when he was wrong he was right," which puzzled me for years. Later I was to learn that this is true of many power-hungry leaders who were not as honest as my father.

The feminist revolution has changed the subservient status of women. And is it no wonder that leading phalanx in the movement are Jewish women? I felt it when I moved to New York City at the age of thirty. Independent Jewish women here were neither JAPS nor nice girls, but rather enjoyed sex and were not obsessed with having children right away. I think that this development ended the Oedipus Complex, but a serious cultural lag prevails among psychiatrists and American Jewish male novelists who try to convince us that the over-protective enmeshing mother still is alive and well. This is an excellent example of the self-fulfilling prophecy vigorously peddled by self-interest. Here I hold with Lincoln's assertion that you can't fool all of the people all of the time. Some beliefs unfortunately have a slow lingering death.

During adolescence, I dealt with sex by not dealing with it. I substituted God as a very personal guide and savior. I think adolescents who are religious tend to see God as actively intervening in their lives to overcome problems and help to get them what they want. It took some time for me to learn that that is precisely what God does not do. God does not deal with quid pro quos. It took a long time for me to learn that God wants me to find God within myself. I now just don't believe in miracles and that is the reason I have never stepped inside a gambling casino. I remember a Hasidic story in which a student ran breathlessly to his Rebbe to let him know that he had won a lottery. The Rebbe told him in effect that that was no big deal and didn't change his opinion about the student. The student gave all the lottery money to some poor people.

Over the years reading and re-reading the early Hasidic stories has given me insights into myself and others, patience with my various projects and serenity of mind and body. I do not believe in God as fervently as the Hasidim, but I did learn from them not to take myself too seriously and that waiting for something to happen is every bit as important as making it happen.

The greatest contribution that Hasidism has given to the Jewish culture and the world is the concept of Tzadik. The typical translation is "a righteous person," someone who acts in accord with moral and divine law. It also has connotations of someone who acts from an outraged sense of justice and is free from guilt. But in addition to blamelessness, righteousness has come to connote sanctimony as in the term "self-righteous." The concept is often ridiculed today because it is unrealistic for anyone to be "so good," and besides, since we are all to some extent Freudians today, such goodness is suspected of covering up not-so-nice qualities as insecurity, desire to be liked, narcissism, etc. For example, Rabbi Aryeh Levine, as recorded in A Tzaddik in our Time, by Simcha Raz, is considered one of the great Jewish "saints" of this century. To do good so dominated his life that he considered it a favor when people allowed him to help them. This kind of behavior today is regarded as bordering on one of W.C. Fields' suckers or what is called in Israel a "fryer."

This ideal role model emerged within a tight Jewish community called a "shtetl," where everyone knew each other and each other's business. Everyone belonged, the idiot and the rich man, the scholar and the ignoramus. An ideal does not mean that it is practiced 100%, but is a goal to strive for. The ideal of giving first to someone else and then providing secondly for oneself exists in many mothers, certainly if they are Jewish. The contrasting image of Thomas Hobbes who wrote at the dawn of Hasidism is diametrically opposite. For him life is nasty, brutish and short and people are basically wolves toward one another and people are to be used for individual advantage. If I had to choose between these two philosophies, I would opt for the Hasidim.

The Tzadik gradually was transformed into the concept of the mensch, a decent honest person who can be fully trusted. A mensch does not take advantage of others and can always be counted on to be fair and free of self-aggrandizement, that is to relate to others to enhance one's power, wealth, status or reputation. Mensch was emptied out of the Tzadik idea of giving totally to someone else. The Mensch, still a difficult ideal to reach, is much more realistic.

A gentile I played tennis with was somewhere between a Tsadik and Mensch. Tennis is a fiercely competitive sport, but he always made judgment calls that favored me. It was quite extraordinary. I greatly admired him and he had a profound impact on my life on and off the court. In fact, this behavior so shook me up that I tried to re-balance my life to temper my competitiveness with a more honest regard for other people. A French film, "The Taste of Others" portrays the central character as a mensch and he has a profound impact on all the other characters that cannot believe that he really is what he appears to be. Maybe, just maybe, if we can ever overcome the profound alienation in our society, the concepts of Tzadik and mensch will become more widespread and in vogue.

CHAPTER THREE
MY DISPUTATIOUS PEOPLE

When the quarrel between the Hasidim of Kotsk and those of Radoshitz was in full swing, Rabbi Yisakhar Baer of Radoshitz once said to a Hasid from Kotsk: "Why do we quarrel all the time when the difference between us is so simple? What your teacher believes in is: 'If you can't get over it, you must get under it,' but what I believe in is: 'If you can't get over it, you must get over it any way.'" Rebbi Yitzhak Meir of Gar, the disciple and friend of the Rabbi of Kotsk, formulated the difference in another: "The world thinks," said he, "that there was hatred and quarreling between Kotsk and Radoshitz. That is a grave mistake. There was only one difference of opinion: in Kotsk they aim to bring the heart of the Jews closer to their Father in Heaven; in Radoshitz they aimed to bring our Father in Heaven closer to the heart of the Jews. (29D)

The above story is fascinating not only because of the Rabbis' disagreements on how they differed from one another, but how silly the argument was altogether. They simply had to disagree even if the disagreement was ridiculous. They would disagree about anything, including on how they disagree. It is like an obsession over which they have no control whatsoever. Obsessions frequently take over our lives when the means to a goal becomes the end.

A Hasidic story tells about a King who had observed that his musician was growing weary and stale. The astute King invited fresh guests daily to listen to him and he responded by displaying his skill with a new zest. The lesson here is that God enjoys new interpretations of the Torah and its commentaries offered by sages. Therefore He sends new disciples in order to waken a new zest in them and sharpen their intellect. In this chapter I shall explore the deep roots of disputation and its cardinal importance in our cultural heritage.

Although I did not attend shul regularly and was now too old for Hebrew school, my father insisted that I continue my Hebrew studies. I mightily resisted but thank God my father prevailed and I took weekly private lessons with Rabbi David Shapiro for two years.

Rabbi Shapiro was quite a different Tzadik than Rabbi Twersky. He was the extreme opposite. He was a shy retiring person who never raised his voice, never put himself forward, and seemed free of emotion. In our lessons he let me take the initiative and ask questions that enabled me to probe deeply the Prophets, especially Isaiah, Jeremiah and Amos.

Rabbi Shapiro was considered to be a gaon, a genius. His tradition flowed from the Mithnagdim, who valued learning and study as the supreme virtues of Jewish life. He had a photographic memory and could recall instantly any passage in the Bible, knew much of it by heart and was thoroughly versed in the Talmud and its commentaries. His recall was phenomenal. He could play all the major violin concertos without looking at a score; he introduced me to Schubert's divine Death and the Maiden that to this day I feel is the most exquisitely romantic music ever composed. Like Whitehead, one of his favorite philosophers, he believed that by letting things and life unfold gradually, organically, you can eventually get what you mostly prize. He told me the story about the Hasidic Rabbi who explained this view with the story about a very large fish that was cut open and many small fishes were discovered in his belly with their heads facing the tail of the fish. Very few people could appreciate the non-aggressive non-flashy Rabbi and he barely eked out a living with his small congregation.

Except for one professor, Hans Gerth that I had later at the University of Wisconsin Rabbi Shapiro was the only renaissance scholar that I knew personally. He had extraordinarily wide interests and a deep knowledge of subjects in many areas. We spoke about his knowledge of the Bible's commentaries and his grasp of classical music, but this was only the beginning of this savant's mastery. He read Greek and was conversant with Socrates, Aristotle and the brilliant philosophers in Plato's Academy.

He had read Montaigne, of course, and was comfortable with Rousseau, Mills, Hegel, Marx, Marcuse and the Freudian canon. His study was lined with all these books and often he would cite passages from them or give me a book with specific chapters or pages to read which were associated with the Biblical text we were reading. He went to the opera whenever he could accumulate enough money to do so. His wife was a notch below ordinary and very plain looking indeed. But she was devoted to him and if she could not be a peer or companion she could take care of his earthly needs. He had two daughters; but it is my belief that the students substituted for the lack of male children of his own. It was of great importance for him to eventually

pass on the legacy of learning and faith to the next generation. In that
sense I was one of his "designated hitters."

Rabbi Shapiro came across often as detached and
unresponsive to others. He seemed abstract, in another world. In
retrospect I now believe that he was depressed and perhaps even
suicidal. He followed in the footsteps of the great <u>Mitnagdim</u>, Talmudic
scholars, and far surpassed them in his mastery of subjects outside the
Biblical and Talmudic canon. Clearly he belonged at Oxford or
Cambridge or the University of Chicago where he could easily match
their most distinguished scholars. And here he was giving private
lessons to an ambivalent young snot that could barely appreciate his
monumental intellectual achievements. But I could "begin" to do so
and his influence on my life and what I would aspire to be was
incalculable.

Rabbi Shapiro was a master teacher. In two years we covered
in Hebrew Isaiah, Jeremiah and Amos. I never saw him come so alive
as when we were reading and discussing these visionaries. Unlike my
Hebrew and public school teachers, Rabbi Shapiro stressed probing the
meaning of the passages rather than rote repetition. He emphasized
translating the big themes into my own words and than fearlessly
critiquing their validity. The Bible was not revealed wisdom, but a
manifesto open to all kinds of interpretation. He taught me how to think
by challenging ideas, not simply memorizing them. How I wish that
these sessions could have been recorded --- what wonderful testimony
they would be to this seer's extraordinary passion for learning and for
social justice.

Isaiah was Rabbi Shapiro's lodestar, but as he made clear to
me Isaiah was an inspiring model, but not a guide, for a utopian world
of people's peaceful relationships and international conduct. The
foundation of a sane world was of course in the belief of a just and
merciful God. Anything was possible with an unshakable faith in the
Lord and following His commandments and precepts. Obeying God
would create a world of peace, love, and harmony.

Over 2000 years has passed since Isaiah proclaimed a vision
of God creating a world where swords would be beaten into plowshares
and spears into pruning hook "nation shall not lift up sword against
nation \ Neither shall they learn war any more." (Isaiah, 2.4) Martin
Luther King stirred the souls of Americans and the world by reiterating

this great vision of what mankind could become. Moreover, "The wolf and the lamb shall feed together \ And the lion shall eat straw like the ox .... They shall not hurt or destroy." (Isaiah, 65.25) In retrospect I now believe that Isaiah could have been a vegetarian.

The grandeur of Isaiah's vision was also simplistic. Isaiah had a marvelous grasp of the rise and fall of nations in the Middle East. Actually, he had a theory of history in which nations prospered when they obeyed God and were laid waste when they did not do so. By obeying God's commandments Israel shall blossom and bud \ "And the face of the world shall be filled with fruitage." (Isaiah, 27.6)They that lost in Assyria and dispersed in the land of Egypt... "shall worship the Lord in the holy mountain at Jerusalem." (Isaiah, 27.13) Furthermore, the deaf shall hear, the blind shall see, the humble shall find joy in the Lord... "And the neediest among men shall exult in the Holy One of Israel." (Isaiah, 29.19). Obeying God fundamentally alters the world so that the sun's course can be reversed and, "take a cake of figs and lay it for a plaster upon the boil and he shall recover." (Isaiah, 38.21)

The promise of salvation is breathtaking. All this is what psychologists today would dryly say is the "carrot" for being good. But 90% of Isaiah dwells on the evil and wicked ways and "the stick," the terrible consequences for disobeying God. The kings and princes, the elders and the prophets and priests and man people have abandoned the fatherless, no longer plead for the widow and stand by while people oppress one another. They have eaten up the vineyard and the spoil of the poor is in their houses. The child behaves insolently against the aged and the base against the honorable.

Most of Isaiah is taken up with God's retribution for Israel's wicked ways. When the anger of the Lord is kindled awful things happen: the lofty are laid low, the hills tremble, carcasses abound on the streets, there is total destruction of cities, the world is turned upside down, tables will be filled with filthy vomit, people eat their dung and drink their water (urine), oppressors will feed on their own flesh and become drunk on their own blood, and a variety of earthquakes, floods and fires will be visited upon Israel.

How can all this be turned around? This becomes a little ambiguous. On the one hand the Lord is Judge, Lawgiver, King, and, "He will save us." (Isaiah, 33.22) On the other hand, Isaiah claims that the Lord will send a savior, and a defender, who will deliver Israel. (Isaiah, 19.20) Most of the time it is God Himself who is rewarding the good and punishing the evil and only glancingly Isaiah refers to deputy saviors like Immanuel (God is with us) (Isaiah, 7.14). It is quite clear that Isaiah is extremely wary of saviors and their potential corruptibility. So he has God working directly to rehabilitate Israel.

Rabbi Shapiro, but includes also thoughts and ideas that have evolved over the years as I returned repeatedly to Isaiah's immortal words ignited much of the discussion above. My most vivid recollections, however, are when we dwelled on the subjects of authority, power and corruptibility. This, in addition to Isaiah's magnificent vision of a utopian world of peace and brotherhood, is his most important lasting legacy. Isaiah was fearless in his condemnation of a whole slew of corrupt authorities including Kings, princes, elders, prophets, priests, the haughty daughters of Zion, etc.. He minces no words: "And the loftiness of man shall be bowed down, \ And the haughtiness of men shall be brought low; \ And the Lord alone shall be exalted in that day." (Isaiah, 2.17) Princes are fools and easily deceived. Since no one can be trusted God has to do the job himself.

Isaiah is a historical account of the rise and fall of nations as they believe in or fall away from the Lord. The irony is that the most fervent believers often become the most haughty and vicious in the name of the Lord. Isaiah is the Lord's watch-dog. He was one of the first investigative journalists to search out the historical and political sources of all the misery, cruelty and indifference to suffering and offer a solution. Since mankind today has pretty much co-opted God, the corruptibility of power continues to haunt us. If not the Lord, who will govern the authority of the powerful? Clearly, what has proven to be the best alternative is democratic institutions including most of all a Constitution and two and four year elections in which the rascals can be thrown out of power.

But who will control the powerful behind the scenes that dictate the choices people have? Rabbi Shapiro took out his copy of the Communist Manifesto and asked me to read it. In subsequent discussions we dissected the problems of the "masses" gaining this authority, and the untrammeled power of the dictators over the dictatorship of the proletariat, to speak and govern on behalf of the masses without democracy.

All this was very heady stuff for a very impressionable seventeen year old. I don't remember if he used the phrase "truth to power," but that certainly was the thrust of the meaning of Isaiah. But he told me something else which at first I did not grasp but over the years became increasing clear to me. Isaiah, as well the other prophets,

were outsiders. They did not belong. They were isolated and had only
the Lord on their side. Later I came to understand that the Jewish
people as a whole are outsiders which is a source of great strength and
vulnerability. We are not only isolated from the mainstreams of
societies, but for hundreds of years, were quarantined as outcasts that
simply did not belong because we would taint others' purity.

It also took me a long time to realize that Rabbi Shapiro's
beloved Prophets as outsiders was how he also felt about himself. The
Prophets had the Lord to comfort him; Rabbi Shapiro had God and the
Prophets, and, a seventeen year old disciple.

With Jeremiah it became clear that the Lord had now become
a puppeteer with a whole string of nations that He moved around
depending on their wickedness and repentance. The Lord now
determined directly the fate of all nations, not only his chosen people.
And all these nations prospered or fell depending on how they treated
the Hebrews and the latter's obedience, waywardness, and repentance.
His prophet, Jeremiah, became an early warning system that foretold
the dismal future of the fickle Hebrews.

Jeremiah apparently was a knowledgeable, shrewd politician.
He counseled the Hebrews to go into captivity in Babylon where they
would be reasonably treated until they could return sometime later to
their own land. If they did not go they would be wiped out by the
Chaldeans. Thus captivity was a relatively good thing. But later
Jeremiah wrote about how the "broad walls of Babylon shall be utterly
overthrown." (Jeremiah, 52.58) No person or nation could escape for
long the Lord's wrath. The Prophets depict a perpetual war between
wicked people and nations constantly testing Him, their eventual
downfall and inevitable redemption. A couple of new "wrinkles"
appear in Jeremiah, including a lot of false prophets and that before
Jeremiah came forth from the womb, the Lord sanctified him a prophet
unto the nations. Both Isaiah and Jeremiah foreshadowed Jesus, but
neither had the chutzpah to take them to the next "logical" step and
make themselves actual Sons of the Lord. They of course spoke in His
name and had special access to Him but they stopped short of
immaculate conception. The best metaphor they could come up with is
the modest analogy that the Lord is like a potter and if the pot is faulty
it can be broken up and replaced with a new pot.

God influenced people by working through the prophets who
would challenge kings when they overstepped their boundaries by
disobeying God. In a sense this was a rough approximation of the

executive, king, judiciary, the prophet, and a "constitution," the Ten Commandments, and a host of rituals. But God had a different mechanism for succession than elections, namely the creation of hereditary kings that stemmed from highly successful and obedient leaders. Hence in Jeremiah, the Lord raised.... "unto David a righteous shoot, \ And he shall reign as king and prosper....."(Isaiah, 23.5) This "shoot" {new growth} will save Judah and Israel shall dwell safely. Clearly in Jeremiah's time people believed in the genetic transfer of power from one generation of leaders to the next and that God blessed the whole process. It is quite amazing that this divine right of kings to rule by virtue of God's support and blessing has lasted for thousands of years until the advent of the democratic revolutions of the seventeenth and eighteen centuries when God lost this divine prerogative.

It may seem strange to the reader that an orthodox Rabbi and scholar of such prodigious talent would also be so critical and innovative in analyzing the Biblical text. Rabbi Shapiro of course was familiar with the burgeoning field of deconstructionism and fascinated me with his critique from the vantage point of historical developments since the time when the texts were first written. Rabbi Shapiro suggested lines of inquiry documented above, but I certainly cannot vouch for what he said to me and what I have confabulated since then. No matter. What is important is the fabulous legacy of the many-sided critiques and disputations that he bequeathed to me, giving me so many years of pleasure and enlightenment. God bless him.

Like in Isaiah, Jeremiah is filled with rich and glorious imagery that heighten his story of betrayals and redemption: mountains tremble, hills move to and fro, playing the harlot with many lovers, take away the foreskins of your heart, chariots like the whirlwind, horses swifter than eagles. Here's how Jeremiah describes Israel's adultery: "They have become as well-fed horses, lusty stallions, \ Everyone neigheth after his neighbor's wife." Those accustomed to evil are compared to a leopard changing his stripes. The wicked shall be slain and be like dung upon the face of the ground.

This hyperbolic language certainly portrays the depth of the Prophet's revulsion and dire warnings, but one cannot help feeling also that these poetic flights also bespeak of an artist carried away by his own rhetoric. Shakespeare might very well have been influenced by these glorious metaphors in his dramas, which in some ways reflect the same conflicts, except which the source of wickedness lies in human nature rather than disobedience to God. The most striking image in all of Jeremiah prompts me to think of the alienation, deceit and indifference portrayed by Kafka, particularly, in <u>The Trial</u>: "As a cage is full of birds \ So are their houses full of deceit; .... They are waxen rich.... Become sleek; .... Overpass in deeds of wickedness... plead not the cause of the fatherless.... The right of the needy do they not judge." (Jeremiah, 5, 27-28.) Mankind trapped in a cage of deceit and indifference best describes all of Kafka's work.

In a fascinating passage the Lord tells Jeremiah to write all the words He has spoken to him. The reason is that He thereby can demonstrate His power in the validity of His prediction that He will end Israel's captivity and return His people to their native land. Doesn't that prove beyond doubt God's awesome power and His faith in Jeremiah to tell it to the people? In effect Jeremiah tells the people that out of the time of trouble, Jacob shall be saved. (Isaiah, 30.2-7) Perhaps this is the first documented example of the "self-fulfilling prophecy?" In the days of the Prophets "every man that is mad, ... maketh himself a prophet." Jeremiah had a lot of competition. A true prophet like Jeremiah therefore had to constantly raise the bar. This was accomplished by passing a series of tests that demonstrates that the Lord indeed is interceding on behalf of a true prophet. For example, Jeremiah was placed in a pit with no water but mire. {Jeremiah, 38.6} Zedekiah, the King, saved him and he in turn saved him and his people by telling him when to submit to his enemies and when to challenge them. Jeremiah, a consummate politician, had a keen political sense of the strengths and weaknesses of the various nations at war with each other until a conqueror like Nebuchadnezzer conquered everyone and imposed a Babylonian kingdom on the whole region. Minor kings who did not know when to submit would have their eyes put out after they personally witnessed all their princes and noblemen slaughtered. Clearly a true prophet must have the Lord's ear to escape all the scheming and plots that dominated relationships. Ultimately God brought Israel back to His pasture and punished the kings of Babylon and Assyria. Amen.

Rabbi Shapiro taught me to "fight" (his word) to get the main ideas and significance of a text, always referring to and backing-up assertions from the text. He mastered this kind of analysis by hundreds of hours of studying the disputes among Rabbis and scholars on the commentaries of the Bible. This often led to scholars becoming obsessed with fighting with the text and each other for the correct interpretation. It was like massive legal briefs interpreting laws and using the interpretations for further disputes in an endless circle of controversy.

Although Rabbi Shapiro was a master at this, especially because of his photographic memory, he was able to escape intellectually this hermetically sealed world of religious texts. One of Rabbi Shapiro's most anomalous traits was his adherence to the Orthodox religious tradition and the utter delight he took in the Prophets' challenge to corrupt Kings and authorities. Although he would never evince openly his disdain for the mediocre Rabbis in Milwaukee, I could sense at times his impatience with their preoccupation with blind obedience to rituals. I did not grasp at first the importance of challenging authorities. I had to learn this lesson over and over again. Rabbi Shapiro certainly planted the seeds for this belief and I will always be grateful to him.

Another lasting lesson was how to think. Rabbi Shapiro taught me how to get the gist of an argument and back it up with evidence, data. I learned how to criticize faulty arguments fairly. The most important legacy that Rabbi Shapiro imparted to me is the love of teaching and learning as a conversation. The sheer pleasure of learning in itself was the opening of two minds to one another and however limited I was in my analytical skills, Rabbi Shapiro fully respected me and paid close attention to whatever I said, which sometimes were pretty stupid things. All the bad teachers that I have had since Rabbi Shapiro could never erase his enduring legacy.

Over the years I have become increasingly convinced that disputation, argument, debate, are central characteristics of our Jewish heritage. Jews must disagree with one another and they do so on everything. Many jokes make fun of this trait. A Jew was once marooned on an island and a passing ship discovered him ten years later. The Jew proudly showed them the two synagogues that he had built. "Why two?" he was asked. The Jew replied pointing to one synagogue: "this one I like and that one over there I don't like."

Nothing is free of disputation among Jews. A recent book, The Holocaust Industry, written by an American Jew, Norman Finklestein, whose parents were holocaust survivors, claims that the holocaust has long since ceased to be a source of moral and historical enlightenment and has become a straight-out extortion racket. Of course his opponents were quick to reject Finklestein's allegations as reckless and insubstantial. Even those who say a little of the truth lies with each side will never resolve this dispute. I once heard Elie Wiesel debate Goldenhagen, the author of <u>Hitler's 100,000 Willing Executioners,</u> about the holocaust. Wiesel maintained that the Holocaust is too horrific and bestial for us to ever understand. Goldenhagen took precisely the opposite position, saying that the roots of the holocaust can be understood, and they lay in the anti-Semitism of gentiles since Jesus Christ, and most specifically and virulently, among the Germans for over 500 years.

One of the most stirring debates in recent years concerns Jerusalem as the undivided capital of the Jewish State. Elie Wiesel wrote an eloquent editorial for the "New York Times," claiming that Jerusalem is the undivided capital of Jews all over the world since King David. The implication was that the Arabs had no claim to any part of Jerusalem. A number of letters quickly appeared in response that in effect attacked Wiesel for his "chauvinism" in totally ignoring Arab claims on some parts of Jerusalem. A very controversial article claimed that Israelis are extremely short sighted in not recognizing that from the Arab point of view, the Israelis are a colonial power with the typical prejudices of superiority attributed to any occupying country. This in turn produced a host of responses attacking this position.

The skill and courage to dispute authority are the two great lessons that the Prophets bequeathed to the Jews and the world. Actually, Adam and Eve at the very beginning of creation disobeyed the Lord. Many believe that it was downhill after that. I believe the just opposite.

A new kind of authority has risen under democracy. People have unprecedented freedom to choose how to live and what to believe in. The question now is, do people choose what they want, or do they want what they are supposed to want? Here is where disputation is critical to avoid falling into the trap of the anonymous "them" authority. One has to dispute unthinking choices of how to live.

But the greatest modern enemy is unqualified belief in any authority. At the end of his book, "On Being Red," Howard Fast proclaims the great tragedy and lesson that he learned as a member of the Communist party. Despite all of the talk of democratic decentralization, the Communists unquestioningly believed that their leaders knew what they were doing. What made them so smart? In most ways they are no better or worse than we are. The main difference is that many leaders can give the impression that they know where they are going, but for the most part are as uknowing as most of us. The

belief in an authority that can protect us and bring us happiness is a
persistent pernicious myth. Authorities fill a critical gap in our lack of
self-confidence. The search for someone who can tell us how to live
disables us from the need to depend on ourselves and makes us seek
constantly someone to lead us out of the wilderness of our alleged
limitations and inadequacies. The way out of this dead end of looking
for authorities to tell us how to live and meet pressing needs, is to
challenge and dispute every authority that impinges upon us. What is
worse than being helped by an authority is to uncritically submit to it.
But submission is difficult to maintain in the face of disputation and
here we find a key contribution of Judaism to civilization.   Every
despot is keenly aware of this principle and quickly moves to restrict
and abolish dissent. The way out of submission is to abandon the idea
that your life should be determined by others' authority, and this is best
accomplished by unremitting disputation with every one who claims to
be an authority. Of course, some people are more skilled and
knowledgeable than you are. So what. A profound difference exists
between learning from others and elevating them therefore to have
authority over you. A helper can assist without glorifying a helper into
a magician.

        We Jews are blessed for a heritage that values critical thinking
at an early age. However dated much of the content of the Talmud is, it
is a profound laboratory for critical thinking. It is assumed that every
position taken by any scholar can be disputed. Nothing is taken for
granted as the truth. Rather the truth lies in the disputation of a never
ending series of points-of- view. One result of this critical thinking is
not to find the answer, but to find the best critical way to defend your
point-of -view. My ideas stem from criticizing and evaluating others'
ideas. This is the true meaning of having thoughts of your own.
Ultimately this right and freedom to be critical of everything includes
God. There is no higher power than the unique individual self.

        The Prophets exposed the kings, leaders and false prophets of
their time to settle on the Lord as the only inviolate authority. But that
authority was too abstract and "fickle," so Jesus Christ was invented to
give the Lord a more palpable presence. But this too had its limitations
when one considers all the variations in the belief in Christ and of
course the Jews who do not believe in Him at all.

        Rather than questioning the existence of God, except in recent
times, the Jews fought over interpreting His Holy Scriptures. The
Talmud stands as the monument of all times in its seemingly endless

unresolved rational disputations and interpretations of the Torah.
Jewish religious scholars still spend endless hours deciphering
opposing positions. Truly the disputations here became the quest, not
the goal of some truth. All the great controversies among Jews since the
Talmud have proceeded in the same disputatious tradition. This left no
room for a Messiah.

The one big disadvantage of critical thinking is that it leads to
an emphasis upon rejecting others' opinions without building viable
alternatives for fear that they too would be critically rejected. One way
around this pitfall is the idea that when two ideas oppose one another,
they also contain elements of each other's point of view, which then,
dialectically can be synthesized much like the celebrated metaphor of
heated water turning dialectically into a qualitatively new state, steam.
But this dialectical thinking was also challenged by Adorno's concept
of the "negative dialectic," which refers to conflicting ideas simply
holding their own until one or the other or both simply fade away
without their synthesis. This is humorously illustrated in the Jewish
story about the Rabbi's wife overhearing her husband telling separately
the wife and husband that came for counseling that each one was right.
The Rabbi's wife asked her husband how each one could be right. He
replied, "You're right too."

Jewish history is replete with examples of the negative
dialectic. The Bund, a Jewish Socialist Party founded in Russia in
1897, bitterly opposed Zionism as a bourgeois utopia and eventually
faded away. Jesus and Judaism never "synthesized," unless you
consider the pitiful "Jews for Jesus" as some sort of synthesis. The
Jewish Trotskyites and Stalinists never synthesized. Likud and Labor
are not about to synthesize. The Orthodox, Conservative, Reform and
Reconstruction religious movements are experiencing considerable
difficulties synthesizing

I believe that the best way to understand Jewish history is to
see it as a series of epochal disputes, disobedience, dissents and
challenges over the last 5,000 years. Below is a sample of the
highlights of these disputes. Cutting across all these disputes are
opposing positions about the degree of change or conservation of our
rich cultural heritage.

THE BIBLICAL PERIOD. Eve challenges Adam and together
they challenge God. Abraham challenges his father's worship of Gods
and idols; Cain kills Abel; Jacob and Esau fight over Isaac's blessing;
Joseph's brothers try to dispose him; Moses challenges Pharaoh and in

turn is challenged and challenges the Israelites in the desert; Nathan denounces King David for killing Uriah and taking his wife; Delilah double-crosses Samson; the Prophets challenge false prophets and Kings; Job timidly confronts God about his punishment; Jonah flees God and is swallowed up by a whale; Elijah confronts Ahab and Jezebel; Esther and Mordechai defeat Haman; and so on and so forth.

THE SECOND COMMON WEALTH, THE ROMANS AND THE MEDIEVAL PERIOD. The Maccabees execute eight hundred Pharisees; Hillel, a liberal interpreter of the laws, challenges Shammai's more strict and conservative interpretation of the law; Paul rejects the Torah's laws and ethics as the basis of obeying God and substitutes faith in God for following the rituals in the Torah; The Pharisees, believers in the oral law, challenge the Sadducees who favored Temple rituals and sacrifices and a strict literal interpretation of the Torah; the Essenes, a third sect during this period, was an ascetic, celibate and disciplined monastic commune who minutely practiced a variety of cleansing and purifying rituals; the Zealots challenge Rome and are defeated; Masada defies Rome; Rabbi Akiva and the Bar-Kokhba rebellion; the Jewish-Christian disputations about Jesus as the Messiah in Barcelona in 1263; and so on and so forth.

THE MODERN PERIOD. Baruch Spinoza, 1632-1677, is excommunicated from the Jewish community because of his pantheistic views that God is the universe and everything in it is a manifestation of Him; Ashkenazim and Sephardim; Hasidim and Minagdim; Moses Mendelssohn, 1729-1786, initiates the Haskala or Enlightenment movement, "Germanizing the Jews;" Rabbi Samuel Hirsch, 1808-1888) introduces neo-Orthodoxy into Judaism by fostering a secular University education alongside Orthodoxy; Jews prominent among the Trotskyites and Stalinists fight it out; Herzl "floats" Uganda as a Jewish homeland and is soundly beaten; the Bund, a Jewish Socialist Party is founded in Russia in 1897 and opposes Zionism's bourgeois utopia; Jabotinsky, 1880-1940, opposes both Weizmann and Ben Gurion and advocates violence to get the British out of Palestine; the Haganah and Irgun fight over the use of violence against the British; Labor and the Likud become leading oppositional parties; the Refuseniks emerge in the 1960's in Russia and eventually over a million Russian Jews emigrate to Israel and the United States; true to the glorious heritage of disputation the Knesset, the Israeli Parliament, harbors twelve different parties and factions with constant wrangling of coalitions to get a majority of votes to govern; in the United States a plethora of conflicting articles and books appear about the vanishing, assimilating, inter-marrying American Jews and what to do about it.

The cursory historical view above of the role of disputation in our heritage attests to our vigor in ceaselessly challenging authority and the status quo. It shows a profound and abiding belief in rational discourse, however bitter the debates and antagonisms. But this great strength of belief in reason failed us in the rise of Nazism, because it was difficult to anticipate and imagine that one of the most enlightened modern nations in the world could totally abandon reason and institute a regime based on the bestial violence of the jungle. Thousands of years of rational debates disarmed us from shifting to an opposition of violence early on and then it was too late.

Genocide was not foreign to us before the Holocaust. Abraham bargains with God to save Sodom and Gomorrah and is unsuccessful; Jonah is taught God's mercy in saving Nineveh. Because of the Amalekites' cruelty to the defenseless Israelites while they were still wandering in the desert, God instructed the Hebrews to wipe them out. Many years later the prophet Samuel orders Saul to wipe them out. Saul does not execute their King Agog and is replaced with David. Still several hundreds of years later Haman, believed to be a descendent of Agog, tries to wipe out the Jews.

The Nazis use of violence to wipe the Jews out is not unique. What is unique is abandoning the ancient retribution custom of wiping out those who would wipe us out. Of course many of the Nazi leaders were executed, and as for the rest, all we are left with is our Eleventh Commandment ---- "never to forget, never to forgive" ---- and to be eternally vigilant.

Especially since Freud, conflict, and disputation have been judged to be therapeutic. In fact people who always seem to get along with each other and never disagree or fight are suspect of repressing and harboring hostility and gobs of unexpressed anger. The result is the displacement of the anger onto innocent people or onto oneself. The biggest fallacy in not disputing is the mistaken need always to be liked and that opposition will result in others not liking you. That may be so, but that after all is their problem, not one's own. Several disputes a week are healthy for keeping one honest and for peace of mind.

And not every dispute has to be settled or compromised. For example, my wife is a Sabra (native-born Israeli) and a former captain in the Israeli army and professor at Tel Aviv and Hebrew universities.

Now she is a professor in Social Work at Adelphi University. Over the last dozen years we have had a continuing dispute about permitting the Neo-Nazis in Cicero, Illinois to march and have the freedom to spew their garbage. I take the American Civil Liberties Union position that the freedom to assemble and speak is inviolable even for the Nazis. My wife believes, like many Israelis, that they should be locked up. I can understand her position, even more so in light of my discussion of the Amalekites above. Our disputes are very heated and we have a kind of truce to live with our differences. Perhaps here is where cultural relativity has a role to play. If I had been born and raised in Israel and if I lived there and continue to feel the effects of the Holocaust there much more than I do here, I may very well take her position.

I am proud of our disputatious Jewish heritage. Ben Gurion once said that the true test of democracy is the freedom to dissent and criticize. This freedom of speech is the foundation of a humanitarian society and we Jews will protect this right with all our resources.

CHAPTER FOUR
AT THE CROSSROADS OF MY TWO UTOPIAS

Mr. Marcus was our advisor to the AZA, American Zionist Association youth group I belonged to which met at the Milwaukee Jewish Center. I still remember a refrain of our song that we sang at every meeting: "Up you men and sing to AZA / Time will pass and we'll be on our way." Mr. Marcus was a very special person in my life, mostly, I think, because I was always attentive to what he told us and because I was far more knowledgeable about our Jewish cultural heritage and knew much more Hebrew than the other kids in the group.

In fact, that is what I most remember about Mr. Marcus. His favorite phrase was, "our Jewish heritage," and he always kept saying it whenever he could so the kids began calling him "the Mr. Jewish Cultural Heritage Man." I think that he enjoyed the nickname because he always smiled when anyone referred to "our Jewish cultural heritage," hesitated, and then looked for a reaction from him. In our weekly meetings Mr. Marcus always took about fifteen or twenty minutes to tell us something about Palestine, or some Jewish hero. He referred most often to Ahad Ha-am ("One of the People") and the need for a Jewish spiritual revival and the importance of our own Jewish homeland. I remember he once brought a large map of Palestine and spoke enthusiastically about Tel Aviv as the first modern, all-Jewish city. Mr. Marcus visited Palestine every year and brought back craft objects from the Bezalel School of Arts and Crafts in Jerusalem. I still remember him telling us that Bezalel was named after the chief architect of the Tabernacle and that he is mentioned in the Bible. "That's what I mean by 'our Jewish cultural heritage,'" he would proudly say as he showed us what he had brought back.

Mr. Marcus always wore brown suits with shirt and tie. He had jet-black hair, kind brown eyes, was about six feet tall and somewhat stooped. He was quietly muscular and never showed off his great agile strength. Every morning he "opened" the Jewish Center at 6:30 a.m. and practiced shooting baskets from every angle on the gym floor for about an hour. He asked me to join him, and taught me some invaluable lessons not only about shooting baskets, but life itself. He taught me to be much more conscious about how I shot the ball and to imagine the curve of the ball in the air just before I shot so that I could be clearer about adjustments that had to be made. I learned to "fly" through the air with the ball.

Later in college I was introduced to Eugen Herrigel's <u>Art of Archery</u>, which is about the six years that the author spent in Japan learning how to shoot an arrow so that he fused the bow, arrow and target and self and became one with the shot of the arrow. I shot basketballs and occasionally competed with Mr. Marcus one-on-one in a game of "horse" every day (except Saturdays) for a whole year. These mornings were clearly the happiest times of my teen years. One result was that I became a member of the varsity basketball team my first year in high school and eventually made the basketball all-star team of the entire city.

Mr. Marcus was not married, at least that is what we assumed because he always showed up alone at Bar Mitzvahs and never referred to his family. I was very surprised to hear whispers that he was a homosexual, which was scary to many kids. Some kids began to tell stories about him touching them and implying some inappropriate behavior, but I always defended him and said that was a lot of bull. I remember getting mad at my parents who kind of rolled their eyes upward at the mention of Mr. Marcus as if there was something not quite right about him. And once, I overheard some adults refer to him as a "feigele," which is Yiddish for "bird," but is also used derogatively to describe a homosexual.

But all this slander did not seem to affect Mr. Marcus. He seemed to be aware of anything "Jewish" that was going on anywhere and usually was present not only at Bar Mitzvahs, but special events like when Richard Tucker came to Milwaukee with other great cantors to give concerts. When a <u>shiliach</u>, a Zionist delegate from Palestine, came to Milwaukee seeking donations, he was Chairman of the Zionist Commission that collected money from the <u>pishkas</u>, blue and white collection boxes of the National Jewish Fund that planted trees in Palestine. He started a great Jewish book study circle that met regularly at the Center. He introduced Chanukah awareness and celebrations alongside Christmas into the schools. As I look back, Mr. Marcus was truly a "universal Jew." He showed up at Rabbi Twersky's shul to watch the Rabbi dance on Simchat Torah and the next week he was at Emanuel-El, the Eastside reform temple, to hear the charismatic Stephen Wise passionate speeches on Zionism and social reform.

The outstanding Zionist event that took place at this time in the mid-forties in Milwaukee was a panel discussion which actually turned out to be a debate among the Habonim (the "Builders"), the Socialist labor Zionist youth organization, and the more leftist Communist-Socialist Ha-Shomer Ha-Tzair (literally, "The Young Guard") and, Mr. Marcus, who said right off that he disagreed with both groups and was speaking just for himself. The largest group in attendance were the Labor Zionists, the largest Zionist organization in Milwaukee, in part because of Golda Meir. She grew up in Milwaukee and was a teacher there. The Jews in Milwaukee considered her "our Golda," and the Habonim had a huge picture of her in their club room. (Incidentally, Golda Meir's family name was "Mabowitz," and Mr. Marcus' family originally had had the same name; he was apparently related to Golda as a second or third cousin, or perhaps a nephew.) Ha-Shomer followers were a smaller group but more vociferous. Milwaukee once had a Socialist mayor and still had many Socialists and more extreme radicals, the Communists. I don't think Mr. Marcus had any followers except for me, but he was very well known throughout Milwaukee as a passionate Zionist and was invited as a speaker on the panel.

The differences between the two groups were foreign to me and I had difficulty sorting things out. I knew that in Russia the Labor Party began a big battle which was waged between Jewish Marxists who had rejected Zionism as a reactionary bourgeois movement, and Zionist Socialists who saw the solution of the "Jewish Question" in a utopian classless society in their own homeland in Palestine. Moses Hess was the great Jewish Socialist leader to take on the Jewish Marxists. The Socialist Labor Zionists predictably split into left and right wings and sometimes united and at other times opposed one another.

In Milwaukee the Hashomer Hatzair group was an extreme radical group that was intent on creating an American kibbutz in Palestine. Some of my friends joined this group and prepared for Palestine in a camp, hachshara, in New Jersey where they learned agricultural skills, Hebrew and Zionist-Socialist ideology. Eventually a large contingent from Milwaukee helped create Kibbutz Sasa in the Gallilee and stayed there for many years, though most of them eventually returned to the United States. Whenever I go to Israel I try to visit Sasa and spend some time with old friends.

Hashomer was far too extreme for the Habonim. The latter were not prepared for living on a kibbutz where the men and women took showers together and had quite loose sexual mores. All the children were raised together in youth houses and a strict communal routine of everyone in the dining room and regular rotation of jobs and leadership existed. Apparently, the Hashomer tried to put into practice on the kibbutz the Marxist slogan "from each according to his ability, to each according to his need." Hashomer in Milwaukee was considered "Trotskyite," because they sided with Trotsky against Stalin and believed that Marxists should wage a war for world socialism rather than building socialism in one country at a time, emphasizing of course, socialism first in Russia.

Habonim was equally dedicated to Zionism, but much more neutral about socialism, and had a much larger variety of diverse political ideologies. Many of the Habonim were also making aliyah, but were not planning to live in a kibbutz.

I was on the periphery of both groups, had friends in both groups, and eventually opposed both groups. I was against the Habonim because they were too bourgeois and I opposed Hashomer because at that time I sided with what later turned out to be Stalinism, which greatly dismayed me in later years.

In the panel discussion between Hashomer, Habonim and Mr. Marcus, there was a lot of discussion about the "true Zionists." Habonim was adamant that Palestine was the only place Jews could live fully as Jews and that a national homeland was the answer to anti-Semitism. Creating a Jewish State was the mission of this generation. Hashomer emphasized Palestine as a socialist homeland where the great principles of the Prophets could be achieved in innovative communist institutions like the kibbutz, and eventually, a socialist state.

I was surprised to hear Mr. Marcus say that he agreed and disagreed with both Habonim and Hashomer. Mr. Marcus identified himself as a follower of Ahad-Ha-Am, "One of the People," [a pseudonym for Asher Ginzberg] a foremost thinker and essayist in Hebrew literature. Citing Ahad-Ha-Am, Mr. Marcus made an impassioned speech that Israel must first become a cultural and spiritual center before it could develop into a viable Jewish state. Both Habonim and Hashomer united in putting down Mr. Marcus because they claimed he drew necessary energy away from the concrete political creation of a national homeland for the Jews and that the whole idea of a "spiritual center" was much too vague to organize

People. Besides, the Jews would get into a bitter internecine battle on the nature and content of such a spiritual revival. Mr. Marcus was ignored for most of the panel discussion. I felt sorry for him and after the discussion I rushed up to the stage and told him that he did a very good job in presenting his position. He smiled and thanked me and then stretched out both arms and hunched his shoulders in a typical Jewish gesture and said, "but who listens?" (This is based on the joke all Jews are familiar with about a new psychiatrist asking a veteran psychiatrist how he could sit all day and listen to patients' woes. The veteran psychiatrist stretched out his arms and replied, "who listens?"

I sincerely said that I was very interested in learning more about Ahad-Ha-Am and I could see that this perked him up. The very next day Mr. Marcus gave me two essays by Ahad-Ha-Am to read: "Priest and Prophet" and "Slavery and Freedom." He laughed when he gave me the essays to read and remarked that Ahad-Ha-Am was his prophet and that he was the priest. I knew that Mr. Marcus would follow this up with a very serious discussion of the essays so I spent a lot of time studying them, read them several times, and made an outline of what I thought were his central ideas. Here is where Rabbi David Shapiro's instruction on how to get the gist of an article proved very helpful. I did not want to discuss the essays in vague generalities as a topic, but preferred to get to the guts or the themes of Ahad-Ha-Am's national Jewish spiritual center and how this is to be accomplished. I knew that much of this was way over my head, but I also felt very responsible about meeting Mr. Marcus' high standards.

I was so desirous of getting Mr. Marcus' approval that I "cheated." I went to the biggest library in Milwaukee downtown and took out two books of essays by Ahad-Aham. I also did this because I found out that he was very easy to read and did not resort to abstract generalizations that were over my head. I was going to prove to Mr. Marcus that I was a pretty smart student. I re-read the two essays that Mr. Marcus gave to me, but I had a lot of difficulty understanding the main thesis of a national spiritual center.

Mr. Marcus was a great teacher. When we met to discuss the essays, the first thing that he said to me was to tell him in my own words what I got out of them. I told him that the Prophet and Priest essay was the easiest to understand. The prophet is a man with a great new vision and is very extreme in sticking to it whatever the opposition says. I said that he was like a prophet in the panel discussion because he stuck to his point-of-view even though everyone seemed to be against him. I noted that Mr. Marcus was pleased by this comment. The prophet speaks the truth which I really did not understand, maybe because I didn't know what the truth was at this abstract level. The priest was easy to understand. He was the operations person who tries to put the vision into practice. He is the operations person who makes all kinds of compromises and is very political in assessing what can possibly be accomplished. Aaron was the priest to Moses' prophet, Harry Truman was the priest to Roosevelt the prophet. I broke Mr. Marcus up in my comment that "The Lone Ranger" (a popular radio series), was the prophet to his Indian sidekick, Tonto. Mr. Marcus laughed so hard that tears began streaming down his face and he tapped me on the shoulder and said, "that's a really good one." In rare instances, a person can be prophet and priest like leaders as diverse as Thomas Jefferson and Napoleon.

The other article on slavery and freedom was very clear and straightforward. Ahad-Ha-Am maintained that the spread of democracy, freedom of speech, right to assembly and so forth had enabled Jews to succeed beyond their wildest dreams. But in their pursuit to become American, French, English, German, etc., had abandoned and impoverished their own cultural heritage - "external freedom, internal slavery." Mr. Marcus congratulated me for getting to the heart of the essays. We had several hours of discussion and we talked about a lot of things but after so many years, the best that I can do is to summarize the highlights. Amazingly, I found in my files my original notes and summary of our discussions. I was even more impressed of how Ahad-Ha-Am (he died in 1927) speaks to us today about one of our most burning issues, the revitalization of our cultural heritage. Mr. Marcus agreed that the idea of "truth" in the essays was very fuzzy. The best definition of truth Mr. Marcus told me is that it is above all "righteous," which means that a person's actions should be guided by a sense of justice and morality. Justice is more important than mercy, although the latter is also very important. The Talmud is a monument to reasoned (obsessively so) discussion of fairness and justice. "Subjective altruism" is very unreliable when it is not accompanied with justice.

I was to learn later in graduate school, America's most talented thinker, Talcott Parsons, distinguishes between "universalism" and "particularism," which is very close to what Ah-Had Ha-Am had formulated in distinguishing between mercy and justice.

Particularism is favoring anyone on the basis of a special connection like a relative, friend or even a friend of a friend; universalism is treating everyone, friend and foe alike, on the basis of the objective (justifiable) merits of the situation. Thus the prophet Nathan upbraided King David for his despicable behavior in sending Uriah into battle to be killed so that he could marry his wife Bathsheba. While I am writing this the former President Bill Clinton was sharply attacked by foes and friends alike for giving pardons to criminals on the basis of friends' and donor connections rather than on the objective merits of their cases. Of course, Jerome Pollard, accused of spying for Israel, did not receive a pardon despite the intervention of several Israeli Prime Ministers. Another ambiguous case of anti-Semitism.

To me Ahad-Ha-Am was an example of an outstanding thinker who used our culture to develop his philosophy and theories. Mr. Marcus explained to me that this was the basis for his belief in the creation of a bi-national state in Palestine, which now of course, is out of the question. Mr. Marcus stressed that Ahad-Ha-am was a Zionist and a fervid believer in the necessity of creating a Jewish homeland and state, but he also warned with all of his skill and passion that an exclusively political-Zionist approach could further degrade our Jewish cultural heritage.

In retrospect the modernity and relevance to today's issues of Ahad-Ha-Am's thinking casts him in the role of at least a minor prophet. He foreshadowed a host of recent studies, foremost by Erich Fromm and Phillip Slater, of the extreme individualism rampant today in which each person is out for himself and "the devil take the hindmost." The disconnect between people and any sense of a meaningful community were sharply criticized from a Jewish cultural heritage point-of-view.

The latter diagnosis and warning may be his most enduring legacy. A relatively recent sociological study, Habits of the Heart, describes in detail the break down of community in the United States. Amitai Etzioni, an Israeli and American scholar in the United States, recently published a profound study of the connection between a viable community and responsible individuality. His book, The New Golden Rule, will be discussed in a later chapter.

Mr. Marcus had a profound impact on my thinking and life. His approach to Zionism steered me away from Habonim and Ha-Shomer. His devotion to all aspects of the Jewish community I was not able to put into practice, but admired all my life and now realize, was lurking in my soul waiting to be sprung. Mr. Marcus attended all my high school basketball games and when I went away to college, he gave me a copy in Hebrew of Ahad-Ham's essays which I still treasure in my library.

When I was away in college at the University of Wisconsin in Madison, I read in the Wisconsin Jewish Chronicle that Mr. Marcus had died. I hurried home for his funeral. Goodman's Funeral Chapel was overflowing with people and I was surprised to see that Rabbis from all of the synagogues were present. Orthodox, Conservative, Reform, leaders from the Labor Zionists, the conservative World Zionist Organization, Hashomer and Habonim, the entire Jewish Community Center staff, many Jewish storekeepers, and so on and so forth. Many wonderful tributes were given, but the one I most remember is the brief eulogy by Rabbi Pastor of the new Reform Temple Hashalom. I recently thought about it when I heard President Kennedy's inaugural address with the famous line, "ask not what your country can do for you, ask what you can do for your country." Rabbi Pastor said something similar: "Mr. Marcus was a Tzadik who gave and gave to our Jewish community and asked for nothing in return."

Two months after his death several huge cartons arrived at my parents' home. They were filled with hundreds of books in English, Yiddish and Hebrew, and yes, Mr. Marcus had bequeathed them to me. I still have many of them in my library.

Ahad-Ha-Am's ideal utopia has not been realized. So what? This is the reason for prophets --- to envisage an ideal future to live by. We are not ready yet to achieve it.

After I graduated high school in January 1946, I enlisted in the United States Army with my friend Marty Slutsky. The GI Bill of Rights was still in effect which gave two months, for every month in the army, free college tuition and books. I was at loose ends and did not know what I wanted to do so the opportunity appealed to me. Martin Slutsky and I were separated immediately, and after three months of basic training, I was sent to Fort Sam Houston in San Antonio Texas. But, after several months of milling around, I developed a polonoidal cyst which was operated on three times before the doctors got out all its roots.

I was in the hospital for two months. My roommate was Richard Attenboro, who was in for some back trouble. He was a tall, thin, bespectacled, quiet, extremely well mannered fellow who stuck out as a kind of nerd among the more rough and tumble guys. He went into the army to get the GI Bill of Rights, could not wait to get out and was using his backache to get out of the army.

Richard's mother was English and taught English literature and poetry at the highly rated Beloit College in Wisconsin. She instilled in Richard a love for English poetry, which entranced him. He became my first peer mentor. Richard explained to me that the best way to really appreciate poetry is to learn by heart those poems that catch my fancy and to say them to myself silently or out loud to deepen my appreciation for them so that the poems will continue to give me endless delight and wisdom. "A poem," he often repeated, "is a trusted friend that will never let you down."

For two months I was reciting poems to Richard and myself and learned perhaps a hundred poems by heart. The poetry ranged from the Twenty-third Psalm to Michael Drayton ("Since There's No Hope") and Robert Herrick ("Delight in Disorder") to Marlowe and Shakespeare (a dozen of his "best" sonnets), Blake, Byron, Henley ("Invictus"), Kipling ("If") and Yeats. But above all, Richard felt most passionate about Wordsworth and could recite pages and pages of "Ode Intimations of Immortality from Recollections of Early Childhood".

To this day I can recite many of the poems by heart. I love especially Caliban's rhapsody with nature from The Tempest:

> Where the bee sucks
> Where the bee sucks, there suck I:
> In a cowslip's bell I lie
> There I crouch when owls do cry.
> On the bat's back I do fly.
> After summer merrily,
> Merrily, merrily I shall live now
> Under the blossom that hangs on the bough.

By reciting his poems over and over again, I developed a deep appreciation of Shakespeare. For example in "Hark, Hark, the Lark," from "Cymbeline," is the passage …. "And winking Mary-buds begin / To ope their golden eyes; With everything that pretty is…" Sheer magic.

One day Richard noticed that I had extremely flat feet and suggested I could probably get discharged if they were hurting. I got the message and the doctor that looked at them knew that I was faking, but he didn't care and I was honorably discharged with 36 months of free college tuition and books ahead of me. Of course, Richard and I said we would keep in touch, and every couple of years we do meet for lunch or dinner and talk about our discoveries of new poems and "the good old times." Richard teaches English literature at Yale University and has received acclaim for his book on Wordsworth.

I think of Richard from time to time and continue to be enthralled by his passion for poetry. Richard shared his great passion with others and it seems to me not only was he blessed with a great gift, but also wanted very much to bless others with it. "To bless and be blessed," Yeats says somewhere is the essence of our humanity.

Since the government was paying, I decided to go to the top rated University of Chicago and received a B.A. two years after successfully passing entrance exams. UC was a hotbed of radical student groups and several boys I knew in Milwaukee invited me to come to a Marxist study center. Within a month I was sharing a basement apartment with three students (one of them a girl) of the Young Communist League. At UC, Chancellor Robert Hutchins was a great believer in reading the classics and for two years I read Aristotle and Plato, Hobbes, Rousseau, Mills, Marx, Freud and many others. It was very heady stuff, especially since the campus was like the classroom where students continued debating the "big philosophical issues."

I liked my roommates a lot, especially Gloria, who was a free spirit and generously had sex with each of us guys. The rule was that when a door of one of the bedrooms was closed, it was off limits to the rest of us. I was quickly brainwashed by Marxist ideology, especially the idea that in a classless society everyone would love their work and be responsible to each other and that, with the elimination of exploitation, each person would expand forever his creative powers. We studied dialectical materialism, knew about surplus value, and could distinguish between scientific and utopian socialism. We were "experts" on alienation: between man and work, man and man, the individual and society, and in the family. We believed a communist revolution would end it all, initially of course with the dictatorship of the proletariat. The capitalist and their toadies were powerful dictators and could only be fought, fire with fire.

Marx was the real messiah. All past history was "pre-history," a history of self and self / other alienation. Socialism will bring forth human history, real freedom, justice, brotherliness, reason, and a new utopian world that is the next inevitable stage all previous history was moving toward. The free development of each person is the condition of the free development of all, not only those who own everything and exploit everyone for their profit. Work could be enjoyed and creative for everyone because it would correspond to each person's different interests and potentialities. Here again I was back into a new version of utopia that was different from Isaiah's God-centered paradise and Ahad-Ha-Am's creative Jewish cultural heritage community.

We deeply believed that humankind's emancipation required not only democracy, but a social and economic transformation of society for a truly representative government. The above concepts fueled our passion to convert students to our cause and collaborate with other student groups to fight against repression for a more progressive America.

We were terribly naïve. We vastly overestimated the political will of the working class. During the Henry Wallace campaign for presidency we went into working class areas to pass out leaflets and talk to people. No sooner had we appeared than we were attacked by Chicago's Mayor Daley's thugs with bats and clubs and fled for our lives. I slipped and fell and had a deep gash in my leg and a very healthy respect for Mayor Daley's Democratic machine.

Although we spent all of our free time on political work, we remained devoted to our studies, and each one of us graduated with honors and went on to become extraordinarily successful bourgeois lawyers, doctors, and University professors. I don't know of any one who became a businessman or a factory worker.

As I look back on this exciting, and intellectually fulfilling, deep camaraderie with its shared mission and optimism about creating a new socialist society that would be based in part on the dazzling success (we thought) of the Soviet Union (including its impressive defeat of the Nazis), we became inoculated to any criticism. We were democratic because of Lenin's concept of democratic centrism. The Soviet Union was a dictatorship because it was surrounded from the outset by predatory capitalist nations, so we took no notice of the gulag camps or rationalized their existence.

But we were intellectuals and gradually our rationalizations began to explode in our faces. The untouchable supremacy of the economic forces was exaggerated; the working class was idealized to the point of fantasy; Marx vastly underestimated the proletarian leaders' lust for power; man would not be transformed by the process of removing economic shackles. He underestimated the moral dimension of achieving a new Socialist man; he underestimated and did not foresee at all the rise of Fascism; he had an oversimplified rationalist picture of man; he also underestimated peoples' deep tendency for dependency, which paved the way for the success of dictatorships. Finally, no one would dare to challenge the methodological bastion of dialectical materialism, which was finally taken up by Adorno with his concept of the "negative dialectic" that all contradictions do not eventually culminate in a new synthesis.

All of the above gradually emerged after I left the University of Chicago and during my graduate days at the University of Wisconsin. Kruschev's expose of Stalin finished our association with the Soviet Union and the Communist Party. In retrospect, I believe two major factors kept many of us in the movement longer than we should have been. One was certainly the utopian mission of really free creative people in a communal society, and the other factor was our deep personal affection and trust for each other. We have kept in touch with each other for fifty years since we left the University of Chicago.

Mr. Marcus joined my parents at my graduation at the University of Chicago and he was instrumental in persuading them that it made a lot of sense for me to spend the remaining year and a half of the free GI college tuition at Hebrew University in Jerusalem. Rabbi Twersky gave his blessing and Rabbi Shapiro was also helpful.

I went to Israel on a Greek vessel, took it pretty well, and made some excellent friends. One folk singer, a former postman and Communist Party member, was looking forward to starting his life over. He was headed for a kibbutz and, after learning Hebrew, became a pop singer and guitarist. For Americans, Israel represented a new life, especially for those who witnessed the collapse of the progressive movement. The trip was great in part because both old and new lefties every night joined in singing all "our" songs from Birobijan to Woody Guthrie's "This Land Is My Land," and Pete Seeger's "Wine Sweeter than Life."

Tel Aviv was already a crowded, bustling city with enormous energy and horses and wagons, broken down cars and camels. Every other corner it seemed had outdoor stands with fabulous overflowing humus and falafel sandwiches which were cheap and filling. I arrived in the hot summer and I thought the women in short light summer dresses or shirts or blouses, with bare legs and flat sandals, were the most beautiful in the world. Everybody was very, very busy, but at night people recovered on the seashore, swam in the warm water, drank filtered black Turkish coffee, and ate cookies and cake. The dense fog of gas fumes that later were to engulf Tel Aviv had not arrived and the nights were cool, the stars were bright and plentiful, the sea was calm and the moon was a yellow cheese. I loved Tel Aviv and my Hebrew was good enough to catch a lot of the conversations.

I soon headed for Jerusalem by bus. Going up to Jerusalem after innumerable visits over the last fifty years is still a mystical experience. Anybody who knows anything about Jewish history certainly is familiar with the passions going to Jerusalem arouses and how, through all the wars, captivities and expulsions, it remains the heart of our Jewish identity. It is not, of course, a physical reality of residence for the millions of Jews all over the world, but many of those millions will say at the end of the Passover meal --- "next year in Jerusalem."

Last year (2000) my wife and I were in Spain and we went to Cordova, one of the oldest Jewish ghettoes in Europe. We visited a 12th century synagogue where Maimonides prayed. It is tiny, but stately and royal in its structure and furnishings. On the wall above the entrance is carved the following in Hebrew "This is a temporary refuge before we return to Jerusalem." This was a powerful bridge from me to Jewish people and a Jewish place 800 years ago, but it was as palpable to me as when I went up to Jerusalem. The Arabs occupied the old city, but we could see its walls and from the roof of Terra Sancta, where Hebrew University was temporarily located, we waved to the Arabs with their cafir head-dresses in the old city.

I found a room with a family in the German colony. The neighborhood was populated with many Germans who had come to Israel during the 1930's and German was spoken as much as Hebrew. The neighborhood was dotted with Jerusalem white brick houses with large balconies that flooded the house with brilliant sunshine and intoxicating fresh air. The nights were magnificent and were like a canvas filled with stars everywhere. I lived near the University with two other students in a comfortable, airy, clean apartment with a large veranda. The husband was an editor of a local Hebrew newspaper, and his solicitous wife frequently invited us for tea, coffee, cake, and to occasional lunches.

My housemates were Asaf and Sarah and the three of us became inseparable. Asaf was a tough five feet, six inch wiry Sabra (born in Israel) who was from Degania Aleph ("A"), the first kibbutz settled in Palestine in 1910. There, the first born child was Moshe Dayan, the famous one-eyed Israeli General and Defense Minister.

His kibbutz had sent Asaf to the University to become a teacher, but he vacillated between studying education and physics. He was also an outstanding violinist. Sarah once wryly commented that "people were talking" about us being together all the time and even holding hands when we walked together to and from the University (which we immediately stopped doing). Sarah was a thin redhead and was very fair with an attractive non-sexy body (but this did not stop me from making a pass at her which she declined). Asaf was a very straightforward, seriously dedicated kibbutznik and Sarah was a light-headed, cynical student who was not sure what she wanted to study. They were "secular" Israelis who never went to the synagogue or ever referred to God. Both of them spent a lot of time trying to convince me to settle in Israel because of the necessity for us to have our homeland and because anti-Semitism in their view, would eventually drive most Jews to Israel. This was an argument I was to hear constantly from all sorts of people during my 1949-50 year in Israel.

One of the most memorable events of my Israeli stay was my visit to Degania Aleph for Passover. I was simply overwhelmed on the first night of Passover when I entered the huge communal dining room and was immersed in a sea of white shirts and blouses. Kibbutz members were bareheaded waiters scurrying around with huge platters piled with roasted chicken, potato kugels and vegetables, and later, with cornucopias of fresh fruit. But the most astonishing scene of all was an Israeli string quartet playing classical music (later joined by Asaf) in the center of the dining room. The kibbutz had its own original version of the Hagadah, the story of the Jews going forth from Egypt, with much more description of the most recent exploits of the Palmach (Israeli commandos), Haganah, and the Army. (The kibbutzim supplied many of the front-line soldiers and officers in the Israeli-Arab wars.) At the end of the seder everyone joined in folk dancing which ended with the hora. That night I thought of Mr. Marcus and Ahad-Haam and I wondered if this was the kind of innovative cultural heritage that he dreamed about.

I took courses at Hebrew University with two outstanding scholars, S.N. Eisenstadt and Martin Buber. Eisenstadt was a brilliant rising sociologist whose mentor was Talcott Parsons, America's leading theoretician. Martin Buber is the world-renowned philosopher and scholar whose Legends of Hasidim (see Chapter Two), and his book, I and Thou, an influential study of the human encounter, are well known among Jews and Christians. I cannot think of two scholars more different than these two professors. Both lectured in English. Eisenstadt spoke non-stop without notes about the history and sources of the current Functional School of sociology. We read Kingsley Davis' textbook on functionalism, which I still have in my library. The main idea of this School is that institutions fulfill important needs of society, but also produce latent dysfunctional consequences in the process. For example the capitalist economic system is efficient and productive, but also produces widespread poverty. Democracy can also result in the most wealthy people having the most influence in the government. Eisenstadt was a master expositor of the great theorists that included Comte, Marx, Simmel, Spengler, Durkheim, Weber, Mannheim, Parsons, and Freud.

Eisenstadt's biggest influence on me was to give me a powerful alternative to Marxism. Sociologists at this time were most interested in the problem of order, that is, how societies are stabilized, not "revolutionized," so to speak. The "solution" was precisely in the opposite direction of Marx. Marx considered "culture," society's system of beliefs, values and philosophy, as extremely important, but nevertheless secondary to the economic structure, particularly social classes. Parsons and others believed that first of all society was much more orderly and stable than Marx envisaged, and secondly, this order was precisely maintained by the belief in a common culture of values and beliefs that cut across and included all the classes.

I was not fully aware at the time of Eisenstadt's influence on me, but in retrospect my decision to become a sociology (and social work) university professor was planted in his class. I think he scarcely knew me for there were over thirty students in the class and I don't think I spoke to him, not even in class, because I was intimidated by some of the older students who seemed to have had other courses with him. And yet he had this profound impact on me! I'm sure Rabbi Twersky, and Rabbi Shapiro, and Mr. Marcus also influenced my decision to become a University professor, but not nearly as much Eisenstadt. How come?

Perhaps this is an example of the wondrous hidden ways Hasidim believe God works His will upon us. I have a much simpler and more mundane hypothesis. I believe that all of us are agents for changing each other, often without either party realizing what is occurring. Eisenstadt's magnificent scholarship and his clear expositions inspired me to follow him and perhaps be like him, at least in some respects. For example, he told us that one article that Kurt Lewin wrote, "Knowledge, Conduct and the Acceptance of New Values," summarizes and encapsulates theoretically his considerable body of work. And he was absolutely right.

A half dozen years later in my preparatory doctoral examination we were given a choice to select one of several social psychologists for analysis and discussion. Yes, Kurt Lewin was one of the possible psychologists to write about and I, of course, selected him. The professor who read my exam thought that my essay was good enough to be published. Lewin's main thesis is that durable change entails an articulated synthesis of a shift of behavior, values, and cognition. Who knows? Maybe God does work in wondrous ways.

My experience with Martin Buber was not so fortuitous. Actually the course was a seminar of about twelve students. Buber's style was to ask questions and answer very few of them. Students asked questions and sometimes he responded and sometimes he did not. I think that he was hard of hearing. Buber did about 90% of the talking in the seminar. He retired the following year. He was allegedly discussing Marx and Freud, but "I and Thou" of course frequently crept in. I think that much of Buber's thinking was influenced by Marxist concept of alienation, but more of that later.

In a nutshell, the I-Thou relationship is one in which the individual responds to another person with his whole being, cognitively, emotionally and spiritually. I-Thou includes a similar relationship with God. The I-It relationship is a much more limited, much less emotional encounter; like for example someone giving directions how to get to Timbuktu. I-It relationships are of course necessary, the problem arises when I-Thou relationships are conducted like I-It relationships (and vice verse, I might add). I-It is a functional relationship in which the other person is used to further one's purposes. It is of historic interest to note that Freud's <u>Ego and Id</u> was published the same year as <u>I and Thou</u> (there is no "sex" in <u>I and Thou</u>, and strangely, well after Marx, there is no discussion of the work place).

Buber's writing is difficult to penetrate. This always raises the question of whether an obscure book is also profound. C. Wright Mills in his book, The Sociological Imagination, ripped apart the writings of Talcott Parsons, America's preeminent sociology theorist, and tried to show that underneath a lot of the so-called profundity was an obscure jargon that was actually saying some pretty simple things (most of which Mills happened to disagree with). I think it is important for a scholar not to be intimidated by a prestigious thinker and deconstruct his writings and make your own critical judgments, "wherever the chips may fall." Reputation should not be allowed to triumph over your independent critique.

At this point I feel that I am "on the narrow ridge," a metaphor frequently used by Buber to describe his ambivalence or mixed feelings about one or another issue. For example, when he speaks of mysticism he is sometimes walking on the narrow edge between two abysses, on both sides, a risky ridge. Maurice Friedman is to Buber what Paul was to Jesus. He has written and edited over a dozen books on Buber and several hundred articles and was in close dialogical contact with Buber for over 30 years. According to Friedman, Buber (1878-1965) was one of the truly universal figures of the twentieth century, a great philosopher, a consummate writer, a world famous scholar, translator of the Bible into German, and a literary re-creator of Hasidism, (which he single-handedly made part of the heritage of the Western world). In short, he was a genius with an amazing command of language and disciplined knowledge, possessing an inexhaustible store of creativity that produced a treasury of books, essays, poems, stories, a novel, and a play. After all of this prodigious output some "amen" is of course in order. Walter Kaufmann, who translated I and Thou into English is another Buber Hasid (passionate follower). His translation has some fifty editions, which certainly makes Buber's book one of the most contemporary unread books in the United States. I say this outrageous statement advisedly, because with a stout heart and a major exertion of will power, I have strived mightily to decipher its passages without any success. Moreover, I asked an unrepresentative select circle of friends and acquaintances whether they had I and Thou on their bookshelf. Of the 15% who had it, not one had read the slender book. After all it was not War and Peace.

Any hesitation to criticize a world renowned thinker of the 20th century is certainly understandable. I am intimidated. I do want to hasten to say that Buber's collection and translation of Hasidic stories in his Legends of the Masters is brilliant and a lasting monument to world literature. The stories capture the enormous vitality and spirituality of enterprising and persecuted Jews in the shtetls all over Eastern Europe and Russia for over 200 years, from 1700 into the 1900's. Dr. Yaella Wozner and I wrote a book, Every Day Miracles, The Healing Wisdom of Hasidic Stories, which uses largely Buber's and Newman's translations of Hasidic stories.

The stories help me personally deal with many problems. For example, when I am angry with someone who has screwed up on one thing or another, I instantly recall the story, "Doubling a Loss," in which the Lubliner Rabbi was about to scold his wife for not preparing a meal in time because he had an important appointment to keep, but then he caught himself and said: "I wished to gain time to please the Lord, shall I displease Him by becoming angry and thereby double my loss?" (4E) Beautiful (despite the understandable, culturally speaking, put down, and patriarchal domination of his wife). When I get caught up in some tension or am stressed out I think about the wonderful story, "The Busy Man's Prayer"(15C), in which the Baal Shem Tov asks us to imagine a man who is hounded by business all day and then he remembers it is time for the Afternoon Prayer, heaves a sigh, and runs into a by-street to pray. Or, when I push myself foolishly to my outer limits, I remember the wise story, "What You Pursue,"(4D) by Rabbi Pinhas: "What you pursue, you don't get. But what you allow to grow slowly in its own way, comes to you. Cut open a big fish, and in its belly you will find the little fish with its head pointed to the tail of the big fish"(4D).

When my Columbia University School of Social Work was searching for a new Dean, I believed that we should select someone from our own faculty so I told the told the story, which has many versions, about "The Treasure at Home"(24B). The version by Rabbi Bunam tells the story about Rabbi Eisik, the son of Rabbi Yekel, who dreamed three times of a treasure hidden under a bridge that leads to the King's palace in the city of Prague. After a long journey he came to the bridge which was guarded by a soldier. The soldier asked Rabbi Eisik what he was doing in Prague, and Rabbi Eisik told him about his dream. The soldier laughed and told Rabbi Eisik that he had a dream about a Rabbi Eisik who would come to the bridge in Prague to look for a treasure, when in fact, a treasure was hidden under the stove in a house of Eisik, the son of Yekel. Rabbi Eisik hurried home, found the treasure under the stove, and built a House of Prayer.

The heart of Buber's work is encapsulated in the concept of I and Thou. I have tried to pull out from his work and its many exegeses its core meaning. I have used a circuitous strategy of surrounding the concept with a variety of expositions I have found in the hope of finding its central them. Please bear with me.

I-Thou is true knowledge because it preserves the uniqueness and integrity of the other. A man inhabits his love and love is between I and Thou. In each Thou we address the Eternal Thou. God wants us to believe that we are interwoven with one another. We meet God in our human relationships. Self-realization emerges in the I-Thou relationship and when two are truly together, it is in the name of God. It is not the absoluteness of God, but our relationship which makes up His profound mystery. The closer the I and Thou, the more we speak from our hearts. Whenever one speaks in the third person, it is a sign of an I-It relationship. Because each I-Thou relationship is unique, there are no rules or generalities because that would ignore its specificity and particularity (like all rules or non-rules, there are exceptions as indeed there are too Buber's generalities).

The It is the eternal chrysalis, the Thou is the eternal butterfly." Take your pick or make up your own interpretation of this oft repeated aphorism. It, for example, is when you are getting to know someone or are first encountering another and Thou is a fuller realization of the other. The lightening flash of an encounter breaks through the darkness of human estrangement. The heart of the encounter or dialogue is the immediate intuitive presence of the other, the only mode of contact with reality in which value and purpose are manifest.

Buber maintains that he is not a teacher, but carries on a conversation. He shuns any systematizing. Each person can work the redemption of the world, but no one can effect it. Truth becomes evident from my own existence, which seems to indicate Buber's penchant for subjectivism.

Buber formulates two contrasting ways for influencing others. In the first, one imposes one's opinion and attitude in such a way that the other's psychic reaction is his own. In the second way, one discovers and nourishes in the soul of the other what one recognizes in oneself as right. In some ways these two are similar, but apparently in the second, the focus is more on the other in finding points of contact.

In general in therapy or in helping another, one begins on oneself rather than on both parties in a relationship, changing together. Above all, helping starts with understanding the whole other.

Buber's work is fragmentary, and not too connected, which I think this is purposeful. One important difference between Buber and Marx is that the latter focused almost exclusively on alienation, which is similar in many ways to the I-It relationship. Buber talks about I-It, but spends much more effort in probing the I-Thou relationship (often to be sure, in contrast to the I-It relationship). Incidentally, Buber rarely writes about the ordinary meaning of love and practically nothing about women. Legends of the Masters is an important ethnographic study of a ghetto society and culture that has for the most part vanished. We shall always be indebted to Buber for this work.

The first, and most important, comment to make about I and Thou is that today, more than ever, it resonates and its vibrations continue to amplify in a society where 50% of marriages end in divorce, desperate single mothers deposit their babies in trash cans and on the doorsteps of hospitals, and children shoot teachers and other students. Our society is drenched in consumerism and elegant restaurants while forty million people, mostly children, do not have health insurance coverage. Surely, we have reached the summit of alienation, or in Buber's terms, an I-It society of human relationships in which people use people as objects to be manipulated and exploited. Of course not too long ago one people, the Nazis, arrogated to itself the right to completely annihilate another people, the Jews.

Buber promises an antidote to all this barbarism with an entirely different type of relationship, I and Thou. The word "Thou," adds to the concept a Biblical connotation, perhaps a Garden of Eden or the period of King David's tenure in Jerusalem and the Psalms, or perhaps King Solomon and the Song of Songs or maybe Shangri-La, a remote imaginary place where human relationships approach loving saintliness.

Marx wrote a lot about alienation. It is a mode of experience in which the person perceives himself as an alien. His own act as an alien power stands against him, instead of being directed by him. An extreme example of alienation is the bureaucrat who relates himself to the world as an object carrying out his duties. This is also an example par excellence of the I-It relationship.

Furthermore, these roles negate relating to life as a loving person which is then reciprocated by the other also in an I-It way. This one-on-one alienation and alienation from work, expands so that one feels helpless in influencing the social forces that shape life. We relate to each other like machines or computers. In this impersonal world it is vital to appear friendly and responsive so that people turn themselves into marketable packages. Peoples' relationships are cast in a cost-profit nexus and cool deliberations are made about where to invest time and energy. Advertising reigns supreme because it is designed to produce desire for the sake of expanding profits. In place of mutuality, we now relate on the cat and mouse game of exposing each other as shysters.

Buber of course recognized much of the above through what he called "living experience." He makes a valiant call for genuine I-Thou mutuality in which people strive to know the unique 'you' in others and in yourself. The fundamental methods for accomplishing an I-Thou relationship are through dialogue, mutual access and trust, and through one's intuitions and revelations.

In the next chapter, based on a personal experience of great love for another person, I will critique Buber's concept of the I-Thou relationship not only as hopelessly idealistic, but actually harmful. The absorption of two peoples' uniqueness of each other is not only impossible, but if it were to any degree possible, stands in the way of a loving relationship. The I-It and I-Thou dyad completely ignores the positive value of the I-It relationship. I will argue later that a true love relationship is an exquisite balance and an interminable process of making choices of the other and oneself. But more of this later.

My main criticism of Buber has to do with the glib abstract generalities that at first blush seem profound, but upon closer inspection turn out to be empty bombast. I want to start with a simple example for you to get the feel for what I am referring to and then use more substantive illustrations. One commentator remarked about the insight of Maurice Friedman, who once said that if he had to choose one sentence to summarize the whole message of Buber's life and his thought it would be the words Buber spoke at the end of his acceptance speech on the occasion of being awarded the Peace Prize of the German Book Trade in 1953: "Let us dare, despite all, in trust." Now at first blush this seems to be a hopeful, encouraging, even inspiring message. But let's take another look at it. One could ask: "Trust whom? Trust when? Trust How? Trust where? What is the downside? How can Jews trust after the holocaust and should they? Should we trust Halder in Austria who wants to get rid of all the Jews? This is a recipe for insanity. As for me, if I had to summarize my views today, I would emphasize the slogan over which so much of our blood was spilt: "Never Forget, Never forgive."

I pick at random a complete marked off fragment of five lines that are not related to fragments before and after it: (I and Thou, p. 61)

---What, then does one experience of the You?
---Nothing at all. For one does not experience it.
---What, then, does one know of the You?
---Only everything. For one no longer knows
   particulars.

It pains me to say this, but this is gobbledy-gook. It is unintelligible. My translation: I do not experience you, but I know everything about you, but nothing in particular. Words like, "experience,You, nothing, know, everything, particulars," are shorn of all references and context and stand suspended in air to fill in with whatever comes to the mind of the reader. And the whole book is like this. What I find infinitely sad is that an army of prominent scholars declare all of this as the ultimate wisdom of the 20th century. "The Emperor's New Clothes" are still quite fashionable.

Someone did a content analysis of a conversation between Carl Rogers, a brilliant American psychologist, and Martin Buber and found out that Buber did more than two-thirds of the talking. At the University of Wisconsin in the early fifties I took a seminar with Rogers and asked him what he thought about Buber. "Good man, but not a very good listener," Rogers said and he smiled.

My studies at Hebrew University (I also took several Hebrew language courses) were absorbing. Asaf invited me several times to Degania Aleph, and with Sara (a triad is inherently unstable) we met every day, ate suppers together and did a lot of kidding and joshing of each other. During the holiday breaks we went back-packing together and visited kibbutz Sasa in the upper Galille near the mystical city of Sefad. I had fascinating talks with friends from Milwaukee and I was very impressed with their dedication and idealism.

I became knotted up with the idea of actually joining a kibbutz. I knew that I did not know much about what kibbutz was really like, but my contacts with the halutzim filled me with awe and admiration. Surely at this time the kibbutz was the best practical example of a utopia in action. My interest in Marxism began to fade as I became more familiar with the reality of a commune such as the kibbutz. I was invited to stay at Sasa and also to return for an extended stay at Degania Aleph with Asaf.

Sometimes when you are at a crossroads and can't make up your mind it may be best to suspend a decision altogether and "get some distance," before cutting this unique Gordian knot. Sara had a job for the summer vacation, Asaf returned to his kibbutz, and a friend of a friend from the States looked me up just when I was deciding what to do. Alan and I hit it off and decided to go back-packing in the Gallilee. We both had read Herman Hesse and fancied ourselves wandering free spirits seeking adventures and letting happen whatever happens. I promised Sara and Asaf that I would look them up before I returned to the States. We were sad when we embraced each other and our eyes were moist and at the departure. I really felt how much I loved my two friends. I stay in touch with Asaf, but we lost track of Sara. I did not know, of course, at this departure that I was now primed for the greatest adventure of my life.

CHAPTER FIVE
IN LOVE ON A KIBBUTZ

"Are you happy," I yelled in Hebrew across a luscious green and yellow meadow on a soft rolling hill in the upper Gallilee and a more musical yell came back in Hebrew: "Happy?, 'content' is better." The reply came from a beautiful, thin and tall sheep shepherdess with blond hair sticking out from under the blue hat kibutzniks wore at the time. As Alan and I approached her, I could not help associating the staff she was holding with the many pictures of Jesus Christ carrying his shepherd's staff.

I remember whispering to Alan, "this is unreal, reminds me of Heidi." As we came close we were able to make full eye contact and we filled each other up with looks that were locked together and that neither one of us ever wanted to be interrupted. Ariela recovered first and smiled also at Alan and then came back to me. I smiled and said, "A mind at peace with all below," and she replied, "A heart that is filled with innocence." "My God," I said to myself, she remembers the concluding lines of Byron's "She walks in beauty like the night / Of cloudless climes and starry skies," which became our "poem" as some couples have a favorite song all of their lives.

"Hi," I finally said, "I'm Tzvi (Hebrew for my middle name, William,) and this is Alan. We're on our way to Sasa where there are some kibutzniks I know from Milwaukee, my home town in the States." We firmly shook hands and, if my memory does not betray me, Ariela held fast to our grasp several moments longer than usual as if to say already, "let's never let go of each other." Obviously that thought could have been my fantasy.

"Oh, that's where Goldie [Golda Meir, prominent Israeli government official and eventually Prime Minister] comes from. My name is Ariela Robinson, but people call me 'Ari,' and I'm from England." I know," I said, "that accent betrays you," and we chuckled. "I'm from Chicago," interposed Alan, not a little annoyed by all the attention I was getting. We chatted for a while and I discovered, after several hours, that Ari was in Israel about three years. Her mother was Israeli, and her father was English.

Both lived in England and are very pro-Zionist. Ari spoke fluent Hebrew because her mother in England spoke only in Hebrew to her.

We sat, walked a bit, and then sat and chatted all afternoon. Ari graduated from an English University with a degree in literature and made an abrupt decision to go to Israel, joined a hachshara, a left wing socialist Hashomer Hazair kibbutz training farm for youths, and after three months came to Israel and kibbutz Lahavot Habashan (Flames of Bashan in Northern Gallilee. She spoke excitedly about her recent acceptance as a full-fledged member of the kibbutz, how she loved it and the heterogeneous members who were mostly from Poland, but also included English, South African, German, Canadian and American immigrants. She repeated several times that afternoon the phrase, "to build and be built," the rallying cry of the kibutzniks at that time (and to some extent still is).

Finally, she turned completely around to face me and with great seriousness for the first time said "Surely you will come to visit us and stay a couple of days at my kibbutz. I just got through doing a stint building our artificial fish pond and that is what they will probably assign to you. "I much prefer outside work," I smiled, and Ari clapped her hands and jumped up and said in English and Hebrew, "excellent! Then, let's go. I have to set you up in the kibbutz." I was surprised and delighted to be so easily accepted as a volunteer.

It may be of some interest to the reader to explain how I could remember so many details of an incident that occurred over fifty years ago. What comes to mind retrospectively are the opening lines of Shakespeare's Sonnet #30, which was made additionally famous by Proust's classic novel, Remembrance of Things Past: "When to the sessions of sweet silent thought / I summon up remembrance of things past." Don't all of us collect pictures of special meaning and hold them forever in our mind's eye and heart? For example I can vividly recall my Bar Mitzvah and singing from the Torah scroll, feeling scared, and then growing confident that I really knew my stuff. I easily conjure up the birth of my son, Josh, thirty six years ago as he emerged from my wife's womb and the pat on the back and the wonderful cry of life that issued from his itsy-bitsy mouth. The picture of Ari on the grassy hill with blue cap and staff in hand are forever engraved on my heart. This picture "begs" to be filled in with the many particulars of that gorgeous sunny day and I could easily go on for many more pages. I remember, for example, that her white shirt had several unbuttoned buttons and that one side clearly exposed the side of one of her more than modest breasts. I had a diagnostic test of one sure-fire sign of a sexy woman and that was the half-buttoned shirt.

James Barrie once said, "God gave us memory so that we might have roses in December." I would amend that to "roses all of our lives."

It did not take me too long to realize how valued Ari was to the kibbutz. It seems she knew everyone and she began introducing us around as if we were childhood friends. Before the evening was over, she had secured a small room with two cots from someone who had gone to the States, possibly forever. We were set up to start work the following day at 6:00 a.m. to digging a fish pond. After work, about 3:30, we went directly to the very large communal dining room. People were full of grime and sweat. On the oblong tables were huge tin pitchers of hot tea, thick black bread and about a half dozen different jams. We sat with some middle-aged Poles and Americans.

As soon as they heard that I was from the States they wanted to know what I thought about the Rosenbergs and if I thought they would be executed for spying for the Soviet Union during World War II. I naively thought because of the world-wide protest, especially in France, that they might not be executed. The kibutzniks believed that I was wrong and that the real issue underlying the execution was anti-Semitism. They wanted to know how it was possible that in a city like New York, which had millions of Jews, not one member of the jury was Jewish. When I pointed out that the Judge, Kaufman was a Jew, they dismissed this with the notion that Kaufman was a lackey, as an American said, "an Uncle Tom," and that Truman put enormous pressure on him to sentence the Rosenbergs to death. I remember also that they wanted to know why no scientists were called to testify and they knew that the eminent French scientists, the Curies, had said that the Russians had the bomb without any help from the Rosenbergs. The kibutzniks believed that there was no way that a drawing by David Greenglass, the only "real" evidence in the case, had anything to do with the development of the bomb. They knew that the whole case rested on David Greenglass, a very unsavory character, copying a drawing of the mechanism that triggered the bomb. The also knew that the House Un-American Activities Committee was still at work, attacking mostly prominent Jews in the film industry.

I was initially surprised at how informed and how passionate many kibutzniks were about the Rosenbergs. Of course, Lahavot was a

Hashomer kibbutz with many of its members left wing socialists, who at the time were still enormously proud of the Soviet Union's victory over the Nazis. But they were Socialist Zionists. The Rosenberg's case was proof positive that despite very important democratic and constitutional safeguards, two Jews could be deliberately framed and put to death. They firmly believed that the Jews in the United States were not safe in the face of widespread anti-Semitism. Of course, I did not agree with their extreme assessment, but no one really listened to me. They had lived with the Nazi terror in Europe and they believed I should clear out of the United States and get to Israel as soon as possible.

Ari quietly took in all of these discussions and later told me that she agreed fully with the kibutzniks. During the next several months she made many pleas for me to settle in Israel and she used many of the arguments of the kibbutzniks.

Perhaps the disputatious quality of our people that I spoke of before can claim an excellent candidate. Halavot was not only extremely Marxist, but also fanatically ideological, precisely how they referred to all of their capitalist and liberal enemies. By "ideological," I mean a point of view that sees and interprets all events and people's positions according to a pre-digested "theory" which they adhered to and stuck to whatever contrary evidence was presented. One day, Shlomo, an arch unreconstructed Marxist and several kibutzniks were having a big argument about Marx' anti-Semitism. Shlomo was a fighter in the real as well as rhetorical senses. He was in the famed Abraham Lincoln Brigade that fought in the 30's against Franco. The day after the war for independence broke out, he was on a boat on his way to Israel. He was a dedicated Hashomer follower from childhood and as he became older, had the unenvious task of squaring his Zionism with Marxism (the Trotskyite variety).

The argument centered on Marx's anti-Semitism. Heinrich Marx, Karl's father, converted to Christianity so as to be permitted to practice law. In 1824 he converted his children, including his son Karl, so that they too could avoid being victimized by anti-Semitism. Not all converts turned against the Jews. Heinrich Heine and Benjamin Disraeli, two famous well-known figures, remained sympathetic to Jews and Disraeli was actively involved in English Jewry's struggle for equal rights. Karl Marx, the grandson, hated the Jews, and according to some, was an anti-Semite. It is reported that Adolph Hitler gained some "insights" into Jews by reading Marx' <u>On the Jewish Question</u>.

The charge of Marx's anti-Semitism is based primarily on this essay, which is so hateful of Jews that it does sound Nazilike: "What is the secular cult of the Jews? Haggling. What is his secular god? Money.'' Well, then! Emancipation from 'haggling' and 'money,' from practical Judaism would be the self-emancipation of our time .... Money is the jealous God of Israel, besides which no other God may stand." One of the kibutzniks read this aloud in a "chug," a study circle on Marxism. Shlomo's position was quite straightforward Marxistic. Marx was not against Jews, he was against the embodiment of Jews as capitalists, against the merchants and moneylenders. Shlomo repeated this point many times during the evening, but I could see many in the "chug," would not go along with him, including Ari. I stuck in my two cents worth with my assertion that Marx was anti-Zionist because he believed that it is perfectly fine for Jews to be scattered among all the nations. In this sense Marx was a "cosmopolitan," who believed the "Jewish Question" would be solved only with the demise of capitalism. I could see that Shlomo was unhappy with my position and he acted "tentatively" toward me after that until I left the kibbutz.

Ideologically, my kibbutz experience had a profound impact on me. I began to see the dangers of belonging to a group, who in Hoffer's felicitous term, were "true believers." While my affiliation with the Communists served my idealistic beliefs and gave me enormous comradeship and a 'second home," it was also, to my horror, a brain washing machine. Going to Israel enabled me to begin to see myself as outsiders saw our University of Chicago commune in the states: "brainwashed true believers who believed what the party line wanted them to believe." So it was in Israel that the seeds of my abandonment of the Communist utopia began to sprout. The paradox of course is that all the rationalizations I spouted in the States echoed in the kibbutz among the most extreme Marxists so that I began to realize Marxism was no longer a matter of superior dialectical knowledge and prediction of a new world coming, but rather a self-sealed system of thought that successfully parleyed all criticism into substantiation of its doctrine. In later years the Freudians matched this self-delusion of superiority. Of course all this is academic now because Kruschev's exposure of Stalin revealed in one blow the terrible delusion to which the Marxists had subjected themselves. In Stalin's Marxist Garden of Eden anti-Semitism flourished.

I have spent some time on my Marxist disillusionment because I really want to put this aside to get to the most amazing experience of my life. Ari and I fell in love at first sight. I remember we were once talking to Moshe, a grisly, gnarled, totally dedicated veteran who loved to talk about "soft stuff" such as mutuality and affection and comradeship and about the vicissitudes of love. He told us that ...."Love certainly must have attraction, physical, mental emotional, but the beauty of the other person catches us before we love him or her." Ari interrupted him and asked: "But what if each one is caught by the other at first sight?" "Aha," sighed Moshe, "each one attracted by the other at first? This is called the 'Garden of Eden.'" The next day during dinner Moshe came to our table and gave us each an apple and kissed Ari and shook my hand. This is the kind of incident that I, and I think Ari too, will treasure all of our lives.

Alan left after working one day in the field, I think mostly because he knew that he was only in the way of Ari and me. Ari, of course, offered to introduce him to some girls, but Alan was anxious to see as much of Israel as possible since he was leaving Israel in about two weeks. We promised to keep in touch. The day Alan left, Ari moved into our room and we were literally together all the time except when at work. Our love had so much to explore that I had no room or energy left for any interest in the rest of the kibbutz environment. We were sufficient unto ourselves and we became a kind of "kibbutz within the kibbutz." If there is no remedy to love except to love more than our love grew and grew and broke out of all boundaries over and over again.

It is impossible to be balanced and reasonable when in love. Ari was now in between lovers and although I had made some great friendships with Sarah and Asaf, I too was lonely for love. I remember the first night together when Ari and I found a secluded bench among some trees and it must have been for two, three hours, I'm guessing, (for who knows anything about how time passes when one is in love?) we scarcely said a word to each other and began kissing and kissing and kissing. We explored with our lips every inch of each other's face and the inside of each other's mouths. I think it was that evening that I discovered that love really has no language. Declarations of love become irrelevant. When we talked about our first night together later, we both confessed that we had never been so oblivious to the rest of the world. Our love became a tyranny we gladly submitted to. I think Emily Dickinson is absolutely right when she said, "love is immortality." Loving and being in love were fused. And I think it is true that to be in love is to see insistently and freshly all the beauty and ecstasy of everything in the world. There is no need to look for lovely things, because everything and every person has become beautiful and wondrous. That night is locked forever in our hearts.

I think Ari and I became the envy of the entire kibbutz when they saw us together "all of the time." After Ari moved into my room we fell into a routine of making love in the morning, going together to the dining room, going separately to work and immediately meeting after work in the dining room and then off to our room to make love before falling asleep. Then back to the dining room, go for a walk and return to our room by nine for several hours more of love. When two people are in love as Ari and I were, they rarely discuss what to do, or make decisions or explore alternatives; quite the contrary, everything is clear about where to go and what to do. Everything takes care of itself and we don't have to ask anybody for anything.

As I look back at these first few weeks of idyllic simplicity I am amazed about how little we shared about our lives. We simply could not get enough of each other physically. Moshe once said to us that on the kibbutzim the orgasm has replaced the Torah as the focus of longing and fulfillment. How true, how true!

Many people believe or at least practice sex as the last great amateur art. I remember Theodor Reik, a well-known psychoanalyst, said in one of his many books that there is a need of variety in sex, but not in love. Now that is a brilliant observation. Ari was a bit shy in a group, but was a tigress in bed. In her three years on the kibbutz she had over a dozen serial sexual liaisons of varying lengths of time, mostly with men of all ages from outside the kibbutz. She told me it felt too incestuous to go to bed with men from the same kibbutz. As soon as we came to our room, Ari undressed and for most of the time was utterly naked. She told me that she had learned a lot from her various liaisons and loved to practice immediately what she had learned in one relationship in the very next one. Chaucer said of a teacher that first he wrought then he taught. This was Ari. I did not know how little I knew about sex before Ari.

I never tired looking at Ari. Truly, a thing of beauty is a joy forever. I not only got to know every inch of her magnificent body, but also was able to see all of her beautiful flowing movements and gestures that, in my limited use of language, I can only call "poetry in action." I told her once that she defied gravity and seemed to float in the air rather than walk on the ground like the rest of us poor mortals.

The very first night we began rituals that we followed most of the time. We would shower together and after soaping up, mutually explored all our orifices. I was a quick study and learned almost immediately to get to places I had never reached before. Then we meticulously wiped each other reaching into many of the same orifices. Ari had collected a cornucopia of oils, perfumes, scents, perfumes, etc., with which we sparingly smeared and dabbed each other. Then we hugged each other and French kissed and caressed each other's private parts and then we jumped into bed and warmed up under the blankets. We wrapped our legs around each other.

By this time we were fully aroused and then I discovered that the very last thing Ari was interested in was the missionary position with either me or her on top. Her initial move favored the sixty-nine position. She would usually have several orgasms every evening while I tried to contain premature ejaculations. One idiosyncrasy was that she always asked me to watch her when she sucked my cock and would look up from time to time to see if indeed I was watching her. She of course excelled in her movements to the point where I could rarely hold back an orgasm.

The climax of the evening when I finally entered Ari was the magical mutuality of sex when Ari would move her body to synchronize with my thrusts and after several evenings we were able often to have simultaneous orgasms. I think the sexual attraction lasted for the summer because the different surprises sprung on me and after awhile I began to introduce some innovations of my own. As I said, in some things I am a very quick study.

On Friday afternoons and Saturday we went back packing and Ari was a genius in setting up all sorts of rides to a variety of places. First of all we visited Degania Aleph and had a wonderful day with Asaf. We visited Kibbutz Sasa in the Upper Galilee and met with a dozen of the friends, really more acquaintances, that I had from Milwaukee. Wherever we went and whoever we talked to inside or outside Lahavot, the conversation turned to convincing me to make aliyah. It was inevitable that this eventually would became a point of dissension between me and Ari, who could not imagine living anywhere else. My fondest memories of our days off were Ari and I taking a basket of food and hiking in the countryside. We always read poetry to each other and I remember how Wordsworth's lyrical descriptions of meadows, fields and groves and winds and brooks and sleeping flowers, spread out before us as they were for him in England. We reveled in the simplicity and the passion of the innocent brightness of a new-born day. We read all the English romantic poets and the brave love poems of Emily Dickinson and the sad and beautiful poems of Sara Teasdale. Our love for poetry enabled us to reach out together to a passion outside of ourselves and we became enveloped more in each other through the magic of lifting the veil of the hidden beauty of the world before our very eyes.

As the summer wore on scarcely a day would pass that Ari did not raise the issue of our future, especially that the summer was now beginning to draw to a close. In many ways I was ready to join a kibbutz. I grew up in a Hasidic shul, I spent a year away from home in a yeshiva when I was fourteen years old and I lived for two years in sort of a commune at the University of Chicago and then I was in the army. My year at Hebrew University and especially, Eisendtadt, had convinced me that above everything else, I wanted to write, do research, and become a University professor. Only one time in my whole career did I waver from this aspiration. Ari seriously challenged me to submerge myself in our love and life together in the kibbutz.

Two weeks into our relationship we fell into the habit of going to bed earlier and earlier, made love, and began talking in bed about us; what we wanted out of life and where Lahavot figures in all of this. It may be pretentious to call this "philosophy," but we were sharing our most important values and sorting out priorities.

One evening, to my surprise, Ari spoke non-stop for about an hour with great passion about her future. Perhaps in the beginning the firmest love is in the fewest word, but this is certainly not true after the beginning. I will try to summarize as best as I can what transpired some fifty years ago as faithfully as I can. Lying next to me, Ari said that her second most important love is Lahavot. Here is where she found herself and she loves most of the people and the whole way of life and really does want to build and be built by the Kibbutz and the State of Israel. She enjoys giving not only because she enjoys giving, but because she feels that she is creating with her comrades a socialist way of life in the kibbutz that can be a model for all of Israel. When she visits her folks in England and sees her aimless, lost, and egotistical friends, she cannot wait to get back to her "home" in Israel. Ari was realistic enough to acknowledge that Lahavot also had its egoists and braggarts and free-loaders, etc., but they were more than offset by the very wise Moshe

and the incredibly dedicated Shlomo and many others who found their
individual ways for giving, but also getting back.

At one point I asked Ari what she wanted personally for
herself. I remember she sat up and looked at me with wide open eyes
and an unbearable intensity and said pointing a finger at me, "most
important of all I want you," and she laughed and jumped on me and
we had sex. That concluded our discussion for that evening, but I too
can be persistent, and the very next evening I asked her again what she
wanted for herself. I remember her saying, "I have very simple desires.
I want you and I want to get married and have a half-dozen kids, and go
to the University to get a masters degree in education and teach English
and literature in a regional kibbutz high school. And also write poetry."
This was said in one breath and Ari sighed with great relief and looked
for my reaction. I kissed her and said that all that sounds quite
manageable, and then I paused and opened up what was to be the
biggest rift between us.

I told Ari that two big things stand in the way for me.
Although I loved the kibbutz and its way of life, I really was not as
ready as she was to commit myself to it. Now I mentioned a lot of
things that I had seen or perhaps even misinterpreted or distorted, but
underlying all these conscious reasons was a profound resistance to
submerge myself in a commune ---- of any kind. I mentioned to Ari
that I sensed deep resentment by some young kibbutzniks who wanted
to study at the University but were denied the opportunity to do so, and
some of the younger members were chafing at the domination of the
veterans and the leaders, who had difficulty rotating out of their high
status positions. A lot of discussion had begun about hired labor. When
I was in Israel in the early fifties the kibbutzim, only a little more than
5% of the population, had an elite status, some of which came from the
Palmach, the commandos of the Israel Army, who eventually became
the highest officers not only in the army, but in the government as well.

There was a lot of discussion about the immigrants beginning
to come in from the Arab countries, and the role of the kibbutzim in
their migration. The debates could get quite vitriolic, but I did find
them, for the most part exhilarating and of course Ari and I developed
our own ideas and positions and more often than not, were in
agreement on the big issues. I was not quite sure how all of the above
affected me, but reflecting on the issue now there were factors
influencing me. The big difference between myself and Ari was likely
the fact that she was married to Lahavot and I was particularly hesitant,

very, very, very unsure about tying the knot with the Kibbutz. I had two issues inextricably intertwined and I could not unravel one without unraveling the other. Ari would not leave the Kibbutz even if I did. She said this with tears in her eyes and I believed her. I could only keep Ari by remaining in the kibbutz.

I think this is the first time in my life that I had to really decide what I wanted and I knew that my decision would fundamentally determine the rest of my life. All my life up to this point, I went along with others and never had to decide anything significant for myself. I was playing with life. The playtime was now ending and I could no longer drift along and let events decide for me rather than me making a decision of what I wanted and living with the consequences of that decision. And this was truly a momentous decision that I, and only I, would have to make.

I saw no compromises. The alternatives could not in any way exist together. I had to decide to stay or leave Lahavot. When I have big decisions to make, I withdraw completely into my self; I became somewhat depressed and I "tune out" from the world. Ari saw my pain, but she herself was on tender hooks, looking for any clues about what was going through my mind.

During this very difficult time I found myself oddly debating Buber and what he had written and talked about in his "I and Thou," and "I and It" distinction. My basic decision was about remaining on the kibbutz and with the greatest love that I could not even have imagined. And now I knew why I had disagreed with Buber and I was convinced more than ever that I was right that the fundamental decision in life is the struggle between "I and I", and "I and Thou," not with "I and It." I know this sounds unreasonably cerebral and chutzpadich, but this is me at this time, although I was much less conscious of this struggle than I am now writing about it after fifty years. The best way to describe my inner struggle is to compare my University of Chicago "commune" and the kibbutz. In the UC commune however much committed we were to each other and Marxist ideals, we were at the same time completely entrenched in the University. We attended classes, did our homework, got high grades and made plans for graduate education. Among the fifty or so of us students, three decided to go into the steel mills and organize workers for the coming revolution. Two of these three left the mills within six months and went onto graduate study. One, and only one, returned to Milwaukee to join the working class and indeed became a radical union leader. Throughout our stay at UC it never occurred to us that we would not complete our studies and of course we knew and believed all the rationalizations that the radical movement needed intellectuals, theorists, ideological "warriors," etc.. The point I am trying to make is the tension between "I and I" and "I and Thou," simply dissolved in favor first and foremost of "I and I" taking complete precedence. Only one of us, one of fifty, was willing to subordinate I and I for the I and Thou movement.

This is an example of the vaunted individualism of the American culture, "looking out for number one," the competitive spirit that made America so great. There is no tension between what I want and the needs of the community, because my culture has taught me to fight like mad for my portion of the pie. I remember my first male teacher in the sixth grade at Lloyd Street Elementary School in Milwaukee, put up the following rousing lines on the blackboard and had us memorize them:

> If you want to be rich you son of a bitch
> I'll tell you what to do,
> Never sit down with a tear or a frown
> And paddle your own canoe!

Now for the first time in my life the kibbutz was asking for a commitment that seriously challenged my entire upbringing in the "I and I" culture and way of life. Clearly I was totally unprepared to make this decision and fell back on the ethos of the "me-first" culture that I was socialized into. No contest.

In a parallel way, many members of the kibbutz were beginning to ask serious questions about I and I and the kibbutz from the "other side." Increasingly, younger members especially, the kibbutzniks were taking a new look at what was called "mutuality," or "reciprocity." In bald terms the issue became how much do I "give up" of me, of "I and I to remain in what was becoming an overwhelming I and Thou commitment to the kibbutz? Many were beginning to have aspirations that did not fit neatly into the needs or resources of the kibbutz. In other words, their "I and Thou" upbringing was now beginning to be challenged by an "I and I" attitude that set them on a collision course. Of course, at this time, I did not know that this fundamental conflict would obsess kibbutzniks for the nest fifty years, and that they would change their philosophy and way of life to leave much more room for "I and I" deviations and alternative institutional structures for socializing their youngsters to become more individualistic like the rest of Israel and the rest of the Western culture for that matter. Families on the kibbutz began increasingly to set themselves off from many aspects of communal living and even began eating more and more by themselves, away from the communal dining room.

It may be pretensious, and it is certainly not accurate, to allege that I had such a clear definition of the conflict of the personal and the community, of the "I and I" and the "I and Thou." Nor did I know that this issue would fester in my soul all of my life. I became a very successful and esteemed University professor and became more and more concerned about me, and often did not realize that I was denying myself the comradeship and joy of giving and taking relationships. Maybe it is impossible to have a relationship with a community of people anywhere near the intensity of the relationship between me and Ari. That is unreasonable to expect.

The intense conflict I experienced about joining Lahavot made me very cynical when hearing over and over again all the glib, wonderful sounding bromides of community and care for others that is constantly circulated in our American culture as just so much rhetoric:

"No man is an island, entire of itself, every man is a piece of the continent. Ask not for whom the bells toll, it tolls for thee," John Donne, "Devotions" (1624, p. 17) Ever since Hemingway's book, "For Whom the Bell Tolls," has been made into a film with Gary Cooper, Ingrid Bergman, and Akim Tamiroff, it has been a favorite of all classes and cultures.

How many times have you heard this literary one?: "I am a part of all that I met." Lord Tennyson, "Ulysses" (1842).

Bertrand Russell, the great English philosopher, somewhat dourly said: "If you wish to be happy yourself, you must resign to seeing others also happy." ("The Science to Save Us from Science," "The New York Times Magazine, March 19, 1950).

How about the ancient Greeks? "What is not good for the swarm is not good for the bee." Marcus Aurelius, "Meditations."

Or this Cameroonian proverb: "Rain does not fall on one roof alone."

How about the New Testament? "Have we not all one father? Hath not one God created us?" Malachi 2:10.

And Eugene V. Debs heart-felt ringing cry: "While there is a lower class I am in it, while there is a criminal element I am of it, while there is a soul in prison, I am not free." (Speech, Cleveland, Ohio, September 9, 1917.)

Perhaps the following is the most cynical comment ever made about our society: "A low capacity for getting along with those near us often goes hand in hand with a high receptivity to the idea of the brotherhood of man." Eric Hoffer, The Ordeal of Change, 1964, p.11.

No American President has ever forgotten to allude to our common destiny. John F. Kennedy is known by every school child to have said: "Ask not what the country can do for you, but what you can do for your country." And every Jewish child who had a bar-mitzvah or bat-mitzvah knows that Hillel said: "If I am not for myself, who will be for me and if I am for myself alone, what am I? And if not now, when?"

And then of course Martin Buber challenged the I-It orientation with I and Thou.

Is it any surprise then that the most stingy President in years for helping the poor and the needy and the widow and the lame, while increasing the wealth of the rich at the expense of denying 40 million people, mostly children, basic health insurance coverage, should proclaim as the motto of his presidency, "a compassionate conservative?"

The greatest academic industry today is the constant flood by Marxists and non-Marxists alike of tracts of alienation, isolation, the deterioration of communities and the destruction of neighborhoods. In literature, novels, art, poetry, and movies, the most popular subject by far is the various forms of alienation. A funny thing happened on the way to the steel mill, Marxism has become so popular in Universities that the Marxists are challenging the non-Marxists for the leadership of national associations like the Political Science Association.

My short few months on a kibbutz has given me an invaluable education of what it truly means to confront the real, and not rhetorical challenge of self and community. One other thought. I think young people are especially vulnerable and open to uniting with their peers for noble ideals. For most of them, this attitude and commitment will change when they have jobs and family responsibilities. I made lots of mistakes politically, but I do not apologize one whit for my political idealism at UC and my kibbutz experience. I feel great regret that young people today so quickly become alienated by our intensive cultural commercial barrage.

Some of our best literature portrays the adolescent or young man or woman caught up in the corruption and alienation of the adult world and losing their innocence, that is, their concern and compassion for other people. From Hamlet to Holden Caulfield in the <u>Catcher in the Rye</u> and Golden's <u>Lord of the Flies</u>, and innumerable plays, books and movies, children and youth put before us a mirror of our selfish, manipulative and corrupt society.

While I was "torturing" my decision about Lahavot, I was torn apart for my love of Ari and my fear of losing her. Here again, rationalizations "save the day." I said to myself that Ari and I had engulfed each other too quickly and it did not make sense for either of us at this point in our lives to make such a momentous decision about living together and perhaps getting married. Ari knew me well enough by now to sense that I was beginning to withdraw from her and it pained me to see the pain that I was causing her.

Summer was drawing to a close and I could not give up thinking about where I would go next to continue my studies. Ari and I found a way of dealing with our pain by telling each other over and over again that we would be in constant touch and that she would visit me and I would spend summers at Lahavot and we could meet for holidays in England. We put up a brave front but it was not very helpful. Moshe tried to be helpful and I remember distinctly his telling us that "the world is round and the place which may seem like the end may also be only the beginning." This is one time Ari and I thought Moshe was not very helpful. Incidentally, before I left he gave me a book of proverbs and sayings in Hebrew which I often look at and treasure to this day, fifty years later.

Ari insisted on driving me to the airport and arranged well in advance that she would have a car available to take me. We stopped many times on the way to hug and kiss and cry and become terribly choked up. I was driving and had to stop several times to wipe away my tears so that I could see the road.

When we got to the airport, I was determined to find a red rose, which I did and quickly pinned a note to it. It said: "... but thou didst only breathe on it \ and gave it back to me \ and it grow and smells \ not so much of it, but thee." Ari of course recognized immediately the lines from Ben Jonson's "Song to Celia," that begins with, "Drink to me only with thine eyes." Ari smiled, smelled the rose and graciously returned it to me. Then we hugged and hugged and cried and cried.

On the plane I smelled the rose all the way to New York. That did not help. I still have a big ache in my heart that will never go away.

CHAPTER SIX
MY JEWISH AND NON-JEWISH SCHOLARSHIP

Rabbi Joseph L. Baron of the East Side Reform Temple in Milwaukee, Wisconsin was the first (and only) gentleman Jewish scholar I ever met. He combined gentleness with a high standard of propriety. He was about five feet, two inches tall, always impeccably and appropriately dressed with a white buttoned down shirt and dark tie, and a conservative brown tweed Brooks Brothers suit. He had an amiable, welcoming perpetual smile and was the warmest most supportive adult that I had known up to that point in my life; "he was always human when he talked."

I was the first principal of the first Hebrew school in the Reform Temple that had classes during week-days after public school. This represented a sea change attitude for the large wealthy German-Jewish Reform temple, which apparently had decided finally to support enthusiastically, a homeland for Jews in Palestine and introduce Hebrew and more Jewish cultural content into its programs. From the moment Rabbi Baron interviewed me for principal, he was interested in my studies for a master's degree in social work and a doctorate in sociology (social psychology). He knew and admired Rabbi David Shapiro and suggested that I research the Milwaukee Jewish Community. He had a scholarship fund to help young researchers who were interested in Jewish community affairs. I received $1,000 for my study on Jewish youth and $2,000 for my doctoral dissertation of the Milwaukee Jewish Orthodox Community.

Rabbi Baron was a champion of Jewish diversity and had no problem whatsoever about his Reform temple sponsoring a study about Jewish Orthodoxy. Rabbi Baron proudly gave me, as a gift, a book that he edited, <u>A Treasury of Jewish Quotations</u>. I saw a brand new colorful paperback recently in Barnes and Noble and I think it would make him very happy to know the book is still in print fifty years after it was first published. I have very mixed feelings about books with lists, although I did like Moshe's book of proverbs and sayings that he gave me, especially when the entries are carefully and judiciously selected. Rabbi Baron's 600 page book has everything in it, including the

kitchen sink. It now reminds me of a passage by Kierkegaard about
Leporello, who, like the learned men of his time, kept lists. Then
Kierkegaard slyly concludes that while Don Juan seduces girls and
enjoys himself, Leporello notes down the time, the place, and a
description of the girl.

.   Rabbi Baron's book had a profound impact on me, not
because of the proverbs, but in spite of them. In a two-page preface,
Rabbi Baron explains his philosophy of the selection of the sayings. He
said that he uses "Jewish authorship" in a broad sense and that his book
includes sayings of converted and excommunicated Jews like Spinoza,
Disraeli and Marx because they were born of Jewish parentage.   Dr.
Baron's "big tent" included the authors of the New Testament,
practically all of whom were Jews. I was thunderstruck. Since I was
brought up an Orthodox Jew, I simply assumed that the "goyim,"
(gentiles) and especially fallen-away Jews were to be looked down
upon compared to us who remained Jews, a "chosen people." Now here
was a Rabbi, although Rabbi Baron was a Reform Jew, telling me that a
Jew is a Jew is a Jew and none is inherently better or worse than the
other. True tolerance is the ability to empathize with another's beliefs
without judging the other person, deciding that they are just different
from ourselves. It also became clear to me that generally speaking, the
more "secularized" one's religious beliefs become, the more tolerant
that person is, not only of other religions, but also of non-religious
people. This strongly influenced my thinking of Jewish heroes.

        Rabbi Baron and Mr. Marcus, secular Jews, were two of the
most tolerant people I have ever known. I was lucky to have met them
so early in my life and I am convinced that they were instrumental in
fostering a "live and let live" attitude, promoting within me, a
reluctance to judge others. But since I am not a saint and do make
judgments, I found helpful the saying from the Ethics of Our Fathers:
in judging a person, tilt the scales for grace (or to his/her merit)." (Avot
1, 6) If we had more Rabbi Barons who would encourage young
scholars to study our culture, we would have less of a crisis in
transmitting our rich cultural heritage to the next generation.

        At the University of Wisconsin, I completed my Masters in
Social Work, my Masters thesis, Jewish Youth in Milwaukee, An
Exploratory Study in 1954, and my Ph.D. in Sociology in 1956. My
doctoral dissertation was entitled The Great Defense, A Study of
Jewish Orthodoxy in Milwaukee. I have always believed that research
should be based on theory or a conceptual framework, and, whenever
possible, on the one's direct personal experience. This combination

works best for me and I was fortunate to be able to do my research according to these two criteria.

I believe social scientists, or anyone for that matter, do not approach research without some assumptions about the world, "truth," social interaction, the nature of people, etc. Therefore I was shocked to hear recently a colleague at the Columbia University School of Social Work, say that there is no theory in social work. He maintained that the researcher has a problem, collects data, and publishes the findings. Bingo! The truth! I find that perspective terribly naïve and counter-productive. Researchers always have some prior orientation to research even if they are radical empiricists who, to my mind, delude themselves when they claim that they bring to their studies no values, biases or cognitive beliefs.

A concept is an idea with empirical content. A theory is a set of inter-related concepts that connect phenomena to one another, usually in some cause-effect fashion and often with some predictive value. Our greatest thinkers, Marx, Durkheim, Weber, Freud, etc., generated the most powerful generalizations about people, society, culture and methodologies (epistemology) for studying ourselves. Most of us researchers and scholars work at a more modest level, what Robert K. Merton referred to as "middle-range concepts." Kurt Lewin's theory about the marginality of American Jews discussed above is an example; another example is Zangwill's "melting pot" notion about America in the beginning of the twentieth century with the huge influx of immigrants melding into a "New American" character. Zangwill was mostly wrong and fifty years later, Glazer and Moynihan wrote a book called Beyond the Melting Pot that severely criticizes Zangwell. But that is the way science proceeds with new ideas, erasing or modifying old ones.

When I returned to the States from Israel, I continued my studies at the University of Wisconsin in Madison and Milwaukee. My major mentor was Hans Gerth, a truly Renaissance scholar (someone with wide interests and who is an expert in several areas), who was a theoretical descendent of giants like Marx, Weber and Mannheim. Gerth was an outstanding journalist, a classical pianist, a translator of books and essays by Max Weber, and, as much a sociologist and psychologist as an outstanding historian.

His classes had a constant stream of scholars who came from all over the United States to hear his lectures and to interview him. Phillip Rief, the author of The Mind of a Moralist, an important

critique of Freud, along with his wife, Susan Sontag, who wrote
Against Interpretation often attended his lectures. I was entranced by
his free association of theory and history and inexhaustible treasury of
anecdotes and could listen to him all day. If S.N. Eisenstadt at Hebrew
University persuaded me to become a sociologist, Gerth convinced me
to do so. It is sad to report that today there are few professors that have
Gerth's breadth of knowledge. Gerth was also a great narcissist and I
always thought that he took a special liking to me and made me his
teaching assistant because of the total undivided attention I paid to his
lectures.

Gerth influenced me far more than any other professor in the
theoretical orientation that I used for my studies, especially about
Jewish life. When I was at Wisconsin, he and C. Wright Mills wrote
Character and Social Structure, which Robert K. Merton, in a foreword,
characterized as an "historical oriented psychology of social
institutions." As a student of Max Weber, Gerth mastered the method
and theory of typologies and he was a genius in capturing, through
cross-classifications, master cultural and social trends. Gerth borrowed
from Marx and institutional sociology, primarily represented by Max
Weber, a unique "middle path" between radical and conservative
orientations.

Nowhere is this clearer than in his typology of individual
orientations of minority group members. A minority group, like the
Jews, is a status group based on descent, with members denied status
equality, irrespective of their achievements, with the majority group. It
is important to stress that Weber invented the concept of "ideal type" as
a heuristic device to better understand people's different responses to
cross cultural and institutional pressures. No one person may fall
completely into one category but social patterns may be revealed in
which people with varying orientations emphasize one ideal type. Gerth
developed a typology of Jewish individual reactions to the cross-pulls
of Jewish heritage and identification with American culture.

It is of great importance to understand the difference between
cultural and social structures. A cultural structure, in this typology,
consists of the values, beliefs, philosophy and orientations, which Gerth
defines as "the symbols and styles by which status is sought; social
structure refers to associations, organizations, institutions,
neighborhoods and communities which Gerth defines as "the groups in
which status is sought." An example can make this distinction clear.
Einstein, for instance, considered himself "culturally" Jewish and a

Zionist, but at the same time, divorced himself from Jewish institutions
and Jewish groups that included the synagogue, Jewish community
centers, Jewish landsleute groups, Jewish study circles, celebration of
Jewish holidays with others, and so on and so forth. Einstein refused to
be the first President of Israel. Simply put, the so-called "cultural Jew"
can identify himself / herself as a Jew and not participate in any Jewish
organization; a religious Jew obviously believes in Jewish values and
participates in Jewish organizations; an assimilated Jew neither
identifies as a Jew or belongs to any Jewish social groups; most rare of
all is the cosmopolitan or Zen Jew who has significantly modified his
Jewish beliefs, but nevertheless belongs to a synagogue or a Jewish
brotherhood like Bnai Brith or a Jewish community center.

     The above theoretical distinctions are vital for understanding
the transformation of the Jewish experience in the United States and I
adopted this overall typology for my studies of Jewish life as well as
my personal cultural transformations. I will describe my identity
journey in terms of this typology at the end of this chapter.

     Below is Gerth's Typology of the ethnic group experience in
the United States. (Gerth, 1953, P. 326)

	The Groups in Which Status Is Sought	
The Symbols and Styles by Which Status Is Sought	In His Own Minority Minority	In The Majority Society
Of His Own Minority	I	II
Of the Majority Society	III	IV

     It is important to emphasize again that most Jews probably do
not fall neatly into one or another of the above categories. Nevertheless,
the scheme affords us an opening into understanding how Jews'
reconcile their minority and majority statuses in succeeding generations
as Jews assimilate more fully American norms and values. The
typology also can be used to compare the accommodation of other
minority groups to American society.

     In Box I are Jews who are the most exclusively oriented to the
Jewish culture and institutions, which certainly is represented by
extreme Orthodox religious groups. Reform Jews best represent box II,
more so in the past than today perhaps, who adapted more fully Jewish
customs and rituals, particularly the synagogue service, to fit into and
mimic the gentile's status. The organ in the temple, the celebration of

the Sabbath on Sunday, the reduction of two days of a Jewish holiday to one day and the removal of hats in the synagogue are a few of the examples of melting into American society and de-emphasizing Jewish institutional and cultural differences.

Box III are examples of Jews who have achieved prominence in the majority society and also participate fully in minority institutions. An excellent current example of course is Joseph Lieberman, who ran for Vice-President of the United States while remaining an Orthodox Jew. In Box IV are assimilated Jews who successfully escape any Jewish status by using the styles and symbols of the majority society to seek status among non-Jews. I gave before the examples of Robert K. Merton and Walter Lipton; others include such diverse people such as Barry Goldwater and Benjamin Disraeli. We refer to them as assimilated Jews.

I have used the above typology to understand the accommodation of other religious, racial, and gender minorities to American society. Cultural diversity is a subject that is taught in all Schools of Social Work in the United States, Canada, and other countries. The above scheme can be useful in charting the acculturation of the recent explosion of Hispanic and Asian populations.

The above typology became the theoretical basis for my research of the Jewish community in Milwaukee. I wanted to explore two main areas: (1) The identification of Jewish youth with the Jewish community in terms of their beliefs and institutional membership and religious rituals (my masters thesis in social work). And, (2), the beliefs and religious practices of adult Jews who at least nominally belong to Orthodox synagogues (my doctoral dissertation). My masters thesis states that the acculturation of the native born Jewish youth will be largely determined by the strength and vitality of Jewish institutions; the thesis of my doctoral dissertation about a case study of Jewish Orthodoxy in Milwaukee, was that religious Eastern-European Jews' acculturation to American society consists first in systematically abandoning religious practices and affiliation to Orthodox institutions, primarily the synagogue, and then, diluting their Jewish cultural values and identity.

When I returned to Milwaukee from my two years at the University of Chicago, one year in the army, and one year in Israel, I was astonished by how much the Jewish community had changed over the ten years since my Bar Mitzvah. Milwaukee Jews had greatly improved their economic status, moved from the lower North-side to the much more affluent West Side, and owned their own homes. "Synagogue road" with its huge high domed synagogues and even Rabbi Twersky's modest home-synagogue had all disappeared. The Jewish Center was gone, all the kosher butcher shops and delis had left, the O.K.U.V. Hall where Jews played pinochle nightly was closed down, and the region was rapidly becoming a "Negro ghetto". Some of the growing numbers of successful business and professional native-born Jews had moved to the East Side and joined the Reform temples. My cousin, Phil Rubinstein, who inherited a successful bag business and was the grandson of an Orthodox Rabbi, became eventually president of the oldest Reform Temple, Emmanuel-El, and also president of the Milwaukee United Jewish Appeal.

I was devastated by the loss of my childhood neighborhood and community. I now cherished even more all the Jewish holidays when we would troop back and forth, up and down Synagogue road, and when we teased the girls, played hooky, and would a break by stealing plums, grapes and apples in near-by neighborhoods. Gone were the Wolffs, a hard-working Orthodox family, who made a fortune in the junk business. After playing catch with Joe Wolff for hours, I was always invited for some fantastically delicious home-baked challa and superb sour pickles. Gone are all the Jews from their first and second floor houses on Eleventh Street between North Avenue and Center Street where I rode endlessly my two-wheel bicycle from which I was inseparable.

I am fully aware of the dangers of nostalgia, "…..Praising what is lost / Makes the remembrance dear." (Shakespeare, All's Well That Ends Well (1602-03, 5.3.19) As I sit here working on my computer and listening to my favorite classical music station, WQXR-FM, Sunday morning, the Emmanuel-El Reform Temple suddenly begins broadcasting its semi-operatic service with chorus and organ music. I have to turn off the station. I could cry. The whole-institutionalized service from the stage is totally alien to me. To me it has no soul. I would much more appreciate a gospel service from a Black church. I'm lost. I can't go back and there is nothing for me to go forward to.

Sometimes a richly textured story of one person's odyssey can be very illustrative of change of a large group of similar situated people. But social science is properly wary of generalizing from a sample of one and his / her friends and relatives. I surveyed 160 West

Side middle class male and female high-school teen-agers with parents
from Eastern Europe. I inquired about their beliefs and rituals, and,
their beliefs about their parents' attitudes. My findings can be briefly
summarized.

During High School, boys and girls gain the techniques,
attitudes and perspectives necessary for making money, gaining a good
social position and courting desirable mates who will help them fulfill
certain goals. Going onto college has become necessary for the great
majority of youth. Jewish youth stick together and many live in the
same upper West Side neighborhoods and participate in some Jewish
sponsored activities. Jewish youth make themselves out to be more
liberal than their parents and desire more contact with gentiles than
their parents think is desirable. Large majorities of Jewish youth
assented to obligations such as temple affiliation and continuation of
Jewish education without really wanting to.

I wrote in the summary of my early 1950's research, that after
Milwaukee Jewish families broke out of their initial working class
ghetto, Jewish youth continued to consider themselves Jews and
accepted it, neither being especially proud of it, nor at all being
resentful of their minority group status. Social and economic interests
and obligations far overshadowed further learning of Jewish history and
problems. Jewish leaders in the community had already begun
complaining about the youths' indifference toward their Jewish
heritage. But the youths were "imitating" the primary models they have
---- parents, relatives, neighbors, etc. Jewish youths in Milwaukee
were on a precarious perch between consolidating a positive Jewish
identity and merging further into the general American society,
abandoning or diluting considerably, their Jewish consciousness.

The youths I was studying in the early fifties were only five to
eight years younger than me. It was obvious that they did not have
much of a Jewish education, and were familiar with only the most
superficial highlights of our history, like the Israelites' exodus from
Egypt under Moses. But, this was also true of most of my cohorts of
first generation native-born Jewish youth. The crucial test of the future
of the American-Jewish identity was poised to begin.

I cannot think of one of my high school friends who did not go
on to college. Over 90% of Jewish youth attend college. The great
majority of these youth, and also this is true of Jewish youth today,
attend college away from home and the city where they grew up. In
these crucial years, from eighteen to twenty-five, college and

professional graduates have spent from four to eight years away from home except for visits on holidays. Hillel, the adult sponsored Jewish organization on campus, attracts an extremely small minority of Jewish youth.

Thus for about five to eight years during their early twenties, Jewish youth become totally absorbed in their studies and the mass commercial American culture. In terms of our conceptual framework, Jewish youth have no institutional or communal anchors with which to pursue their cultural heritage. The few Jewish fraternities and sororities for the most part ape their gentile counterparts in the worst kind of anti-academic snobbish social climbing.

But this is only the first chapter in the disintegration of our Jewish cultural heritage. Only about 20% of my Jewish college graduate friends returned to their hometowns. They gravitated to cities where they could successfully practice their professions or advance their business careers.

They found a spouse either in college or in the city to which they have "migrated." They began the two crucial events of their lives, a career and family life, away from their family, relatives, childhood friends, and the familiar synagogue and Jewish center. The continuity with the past is shattered along with their Jewish roots. The pressure of making a livelihood and building a family, the difficulty of a couple moving to a city in which neither grew up, finding new friends both can enjoy, make it very difficult for them to find a new community. And when they avoid membership in a synagogue or a Jewish Center, or become simply temporary nominal members for the sake of their children's bar mitzvah, they pretty much lost further meaningful contact with their Jewish heritage. The lack of social supports during this crucial period for young couples has been cited as the primary cause of their large divorce rates.

The denouement of the above complex of events is graphically illustrated by the journey taken by my younger brother, Morton. He was always a "problem" because he refused to attend Hebrew school and got into trouble in public school. He joined the army to escape the family and went to the University of Wisconsin and becoming a pharmacist. He then went to Los Angeles, became a very successful pharmacist with his own drug store and married Gert, a Jewish College graduate from Calgary, Canada. Gert came from an Orthodox family and spoke Yiddish fluently. They had two daughters, Cheryl and Susan, and had minimum contact with Jewish institutions or the community. They lived in an affluent Jewish suburban neighborhood in Long Island Beach.

My brother died at age forty-nine, the same year my father had died and with the same ailment, heart failure. After his death, Gert finished law school and became an extremely successful divorce attorney. Cheryl, the older "black sheep" in the family married a wonderful Black guy, was disowned by her mother who refused to attend their wedding, had a baby and then was divorced. The younger daughter, Susan, also became a successful lawyer in her mother's firm and married an Irishman. They recently had a child. Gert also married an Irishman and they are a very happy couple.

Is there a moral to the above story and the fifty-percent of Jewish youth that now marry outside of their faith? This stubborn phenomenon for those of us who cherish our heritage but also believe in the maximum right for our children to have the choice to marry whomever they wish, is the dilemma of our generation. We cannot pretend that this is not a dilemma by putting our "ostrich heads" in the sand. One thing that is crystal clear and not debatable is that inter-faith marriage is the royal road to assimilation. <u>The irony of the whole inadvertent process described above is that a cardinal Jewish virtue ---- learning, study, and education ---- has become the vehicle for abandoning the Jewish community.</u> The rich complex of sacred rituals have become an albatross around the necks of young people who rid themselves of it at the earliest opportunity after leaving their families. Young people no longer have anchors for their changing beliefs. We shall take up the manifold complex explanations of the above phenomenon and what to do about it in Chapter Nine, which deals with the vanishing Jewish-American.

My son's generation has further seriously eroded any meaningful identification with Jewish beliefs or institutions. My son's best friend since first grade is Christian and they are still the best of friends. My son was a year in Israel, most of which was spent on Kibbutz Kfar Hanasi in the Upper Galilee near the Syrian border. He loved the experience and contemplated joining the kibbutz, but he left after one year and is now a manager with Sony in San Francisco. He probably dates more non-Jewish than Jewish women and never fails to tell me when he is dating a Jewish woman. I like to think that Josh, my son, has absorbed some of my dilemma, even if it is mostly at an unconscious level, but that could be wishful thinking. He has very little contact with any Jewish institutions or groups, and because there are no relatives in the area, I doubt whether he celebrates any of the Jewish holidays, neither Yom Kippur nor Passover Seders. How long can one live with a dilemma? I am sure Josh agonizes very little, if at all, about his Judaism. I agonize about it all the time.

How did we get to this crisis in our Jewish identity? I think it may be instructive to understand the sources of escalating Jewish disaffection by succeeding generations of young men and women. My doctoral dissertation, The Great Defense, A Study of Jewish Orthodoxy in Milwaukee, sheds light on the disintegration of orthodoxy and the pallid ineffective institutional substitution. One of the oldest, saddest phenomenon in Jewish life is how the strengths of our culture turn into our greatest weaknesses and impediments to change. One factor is that our secular education leads to the abandonment of religion and rituals.

In the early 1950's in Milwaukee, Jews experienced a phenomenal rise from the working and lower middle classes into the middle and upper-middle classes. The obvious sign was the movement of the entire Jewish population from the North side of Milwaukee to the middle and upper class West Side. All the synagogues on Synagogue road were abandoned and sold to 'Negro' churches. All that remained on the North side were small shops like grocery stores, delis, barbershops, shoe repair shops and tailor-cleaning stores. Only Rabbi Twersky, because of the charismatic force of his personality, was able to relocate somewhat intact on the Upper West Side. And his favorite Hasid, my father, bought a house one block away so he would have to walk only one block to pray in the morning and on all of the holidays.

Most of the members drove in cars on the Sabbath and holidays to Rabbi Twersky's shul, and the Rabbi in his diplomatic wisdom was grateful for the "sin," for which the members could pray for forgiveness in their prayers. What I found in my study is that only a minority of Orthodox members carry out the requirements of Jewish law and rituals in their personal lives. Orthodox Jews had become an aging group that was not reproducing itself. I think nostalgia accounts for the fifteen percent of the nine hundred and five Orthodox members who retain dual membership in an Orthodox as well as a Conservative or Reform Temple. The huge flashy Conservative Temple on the West Side had more members than all the Orthodox synagogues put together. A drastic reduction in attendance occurred, with seventy percent attending the synagogue only several times a year and a much smaller ten percent attending daily. The shrewd practicality of Orthodox Jews, most of whom were rapidly becoming nominally so, is illustrated in their responses to Orthodox rituals and beliefs. 82% fast on Yom Kippur, 12% do not handle money on the Sabbath and only 7% wear tsitses (prayer fringes) every day.

The manifest contradictions in rituals is revealed by the 62% that keep separate meat and dairy dishes at home and the high 32% who eat meat in non-kosher restaurants. 96% prefer their children to marry a Jewish person and 99% would have their child circumcised according to Jewish law. But over 60% believe that most Orthodox synagogues in the United States will become Conservative. The demographic trends appear to seal the doom of Orthodoxy as a mass movement in the United States. Deviancy from Orthodox norms increases drastically among native born-Jews and conformity increases proportionately with age. Increase of income was associated with deviancy; a public school education or college attendance, entering the ranks of business or other professions, or gaining an income over $5,000 (equivalent to $50,000 today) were all associated with increased deviancy.

Thus it is clear that the monolithic sacred culture of Orthodoxy gradually disappears in the daily business of making a living and imbibing the cultural values of American society thereby. An increasingly secularized membership faces off with the crystallized dogma of rabbinical authority. And the Orthodox Rabbis can only stand-by helplessly. Moreover, very successful young Jewish entrepreneurs and professionals who move to the upper class East Side have waiting for them three Reform temples and no Orthodox or Conservative temples.

Another revealing aspect of the suicide of Orthodox synagogues is that the increasingly small number of aging conformists supported by their Rabbis, feel more strongly about maintaining the traditional norms than the deviants feel about changing procedures in the synagogue. The deviants have no recourse, but to show their displeasure "with their feet." One-third of the married sons of Orthodox members are not affiliated with any synagogue or temple; another one-third have joined Conservative and Reform temples; only one-third became members of Orthodox synagogues. Of the latter one-third, my estimate is that 90 percent are nominal members out of respect for their parents. I'm a perfect example. I don't even live in Milwaukee, but still maintain my membership in Rabbi Twersky's shul, which is now led by his twin sons.

One of the big "winners" in the demise of Orthodoxy as a mainstream religion in the United States is the recrudescence of the ultra-Orthodox Hasidic movement. They accurately read the handwriting with large letters on the wall. The only way to hold on to young Jews is to lock them in an eighteenth century super religious shtetl and literally throw away the key. By demand allegiance to all the laws and rituals, no exceptions, and by maintaining exclusive control over their education and lives they, "save" young Hasidics from the seductions of the modern, satanic world. And it works. But at what a cost!

A cult is a group of people who are isolated and alienated from society and mainstream religion. Above all, a cult brooks no dissent from its dogma and deviancy from its rituals. In a cult there is no choice about modifying its practices. Choice about any departure from the beliefs and practices is taken away. It's an all or none proposition. Members are preoccupied only with their religious practice and the relief from stress and meaningless it may bring. Charismatic, frequently mystical, people lead cults. The comfort and security of common beliefs and practices from the cradle to the grave are enormously satisfying and self-sealing. The Hasidim have an enormously rich cultural heritage with their own stories, legends, heroes, music, and dance which totally encompasses every person from the youngest to the oldest. Borough Park has become a must sight seeing stop for tourists to New York. Here, the visitor is transported to a 300-year-old way of life, with the language, smells, sights, sounds, clothes and food of the East-European shtetl. Because of the large families Hasidim spawn, enclaves of the cult are spreading out all over, including wealthy suburbs where they have begun to become a "problem" to secular Jews who resent some of the practices they impinge on their lives.

Conservative and Reform Rabbis and synagogues, and Jewish professional fund-raisers, social workers, educators, and the presidents and members of Jewish associations like B'nei Brith, have not learned much from the widespread demise of Orthodoxy as a mass movement. The first and foremost fact that they refuse to acknowledge is that what they are doing now simply does not work, and that young Jewish men and women are leaving Judaism in droves.

The main lesson of my studies is that it simply is not enough to preach and bewail the loss of our rich heritage and accept meaningless paper membership in Jewish groups and institutions. The old-time religious rituals don't work anymore and we have to put our heads together to figure out the functional equivalent of these old-time religious rituals for they are now out of date for us. Beliefs have to be anchored in meaningful social groups, in institutions, in a community, in common collective practices and rituals. The alternative is that our alienated and disaffected young men and women will be picked off one by one and become assimilated. Even widespread anti-Semitism, which the Jewish institutional professionals depended on, will not be able to stem the assimilation tide. Psychology tells us positive beliefs to believe in are much more powerful than negative reasons for staying Jewish to combat anti-Semitism.

My personal history, after receiving my doctorate in social psychology and masters in social work, graphically illustrates the abandonment of my Jewish identity and absorption into my professional career and the general mass American culture. I fled to New York after receiving my doctorate. My father had died and my mother had settled in Florida. I was welcomed to the Big Apple by having my car broken into Sunday evening in the middle of the night and all my clothes in the back seat stolen. Little did I know having just arrived from Milwaukee, where people did not lock their homes and cars, that the norm in New York City is that clothes or anything left in a car anytime is an invitation for burglars to help themselves. This important lesson in cultural diversity taught me the necessity for locking everything, better with at least two locks. Even at Columbia University whenever I left my office to go to the men's room I always locked my door.

Without contacts, I rode into New York on a wave of chutzpah and my impressive scholastic credentials. I got an extra academic push by publishing an article on my Orthodoxy study in a respected edited book by a very respected scholar. (The Jews in America, by Marshall Sklare) Luckily, I learned that a former University of Wisconsin sociology professor was now at the Russell Sage Foundation. The Foundation had a special program for Ph.D's in sociology to receive a stipend of $7500.00 for each of two years to do research in some social service field. The only requirement was to find an agency in which to do the research. I called one of the largest family and child agencies in New York, the Jewish Board of Guardians (now called The Jewish Board of Family and Children's Services) and learned that they ran a 205 bed residential treatment center, the Hawthorne Cedar Knolls

School in Hawthorne, New York, twenty five miles north of New York City.

My dream, to do an in depth study of a group of youngsters, was about to materialize. I went up to Hawthorne and received a cold wary welcome. The assistant director, Renee Schulman, had been at Hawthorne, it seems, forever and was very psychoanalytically oriented, as were the social caseworkers and the clinical director, a psychiatrist. The main reason they accepted me was because they wanted to stay in the good graces of the influential Russell Sage Foundation, and besides, they would not have to pay me.

The Director, Jay Goldsmith, a student of the legendary Herschel Art, a former director and one of the Great Leaders in institutional care, carefully explained to me that he wanted to see before any publication, all my writings about Hawthorne. I naively agreed without realizing at the time that this could be a form of censorship on my research. The best sign of Hawthorne's belittlement of me and my work was that they totally forgot about me and permitted me the freedom to spend my time as I wished and never asked about my research. My goal of studying the culture of the cottage was believed to be quite inconsequential to the psycho-dynamics of each resident and his / her family upbringing.

I have always been extraordinarily fortunate to have an inspiring, supportive and intellectually challenging mentor at critical periods in my career to guide me in my research and professional development. The Director of Russell Sage the Foundation, Dr. Leonard S. Cottrell Jr., took a personal interest in my work. Dr. Cottrell was identified with the University of Chicago School of sociology when it amassed a brilliant record of intensive participation studies of communities, neighborhoods, gangs, occupations and professional careers. Durable classic studies such as Street Corner Society, The Gold Coast and the Slum, The Gang, The Professional Thief, and shortly thereafter, Erving Goffman's Asylums and The Presentation of Self in Everyday Life are all required reading by any serious student in sociology. Cottrell did some groundbreaking work in role theory and empirical studies of occupations.

In manner, Cottrell was a New England patrician, yet he was very relaxed and embracing in his ability to listen and he always permitted me always to take the lead, and discuss whatever was on my mind. He looked a little like Spencer Tracy, and had a wonderful laid back attitude that in time all will come together. He was the soul of courtesy and politeness, and would direct me with 90% sheer positive re-enforcement and 10% negative comments. I greatly looked forward to our monthly meetings and I was always stimulated to go full speed ahead on my project.

Cottrell helped me through two critical periods. Towards the end of my project I came to him with over 1000 pages of notes and observations. It was impudent for me to believe that he would even attempt to plow through all this material, but he did and we sat down together one afternoon for five hours and hammered out an outline that eventually became the chapters of my book. He would not let me get away with some glib generalities or fuzzy formulations and kept on hammering me to get to the main thesis of the book, how each chapter advanced the main thesis, and that the message eventually emerge loud and clear.

In fact, it was too clear! Jay Goldsmith, the director of Hawthorne, his assistant, Renee Shulman and the Director of the Jewish Board, Herschel Alt, were furious at my findings and vowed Cottage Six would never see the light of day. Cottrell patiently and firmly insisted that they present him with a critique, and that all distortions and inaccuracies would be corrected. Of course, they never did, and eventually Russell Sage published the book, which many of my colleagues in the field consider "a classic." It went through many editions and sold over 80,000 copies. I received a two million-dollar grant to create a new program of group treatment at Hawthorne, which was suddenly delighted to have me still on board. In fact, Hawthorne and the Board boasted that they were proud to permit a sociologist to do independent research at Hawthorne!

But actually, they never forgave my chutzpah, and tried hard to become amnesiac about Cottage Six. More of that later. My book quickly propelled me into Columbia University School of Social Work and a quick tenure and full professorship. This success, however, was achieved at a fearful cost. Despite all my solid achievements, my personal and professional selves crossed over each other and produced a truly existential crisis, much of which I was not even aware of at the time, and for the next forty years of my life, and only with the writing of this memoir have I begun to see some light at the end of a very long dark tunnel.

CHAPTER SEVEN
HOW THE CROSSOVERS OF MY PERSONAL AND
PROFESSIONAL LIVES CREATED AN INSUFFERABLE EGOIST

This is an extremely painful chapter to write. Our sages say, "confess and be not ashamed." Easy to say. I think the Catholics are wiser than we Jews are for institutionalizing the Confession. It may very well be that Confession cleanses the soul. But before one confesses, does not one have to know that he / she has something really important to confess? My difficulty in realizing my fatal defect is that it is perfectly syntonic with the competitive and alienated culture that I entered into, and contributed to. We have a lot of metaphors to describe this dilemma, for example how does the fish know that he is in the water? How can one pull oneself up by his own bootstraps?

As I inferred above I had many collaborators on my path to hell, but this in no way excuses my nefarious role in the whole sorry mess. When I came to New York in 1958 I had two goals. My first preoccupation was to advance my professional and academic career, and a far second goal was to meet a woman and eventually be married and have a family. I was 30 years old, the whole wide world awaited me, and the Big Apple especially beckoned because everyone knew that if you could make it here, you could make it anywhere. Instead of going into therapy, I met a woman and after six weeks, we were married. After six months both of us realized that we had little in common intellectually, emotionally, sexually and spiritually --- you name it. Luckily she never became pregnant, and the divorce was amiable because neither of us had any assets worth fighting over. I seem now to speak very glibly about this experience, but in fact I was quite shaken by it and had the good sense to seek psychotherapy.

Psychotherapy for all young intellectuals in New York City was rigor-de-guerre and the newest rage was Albert Ellis, who was anti-Freudian and known to work very fast, with an optimum of six sessions, often less. He had already published a half-dozen books on psychotherapy and was not too expensive. He was known for special problems, especially dealing with sex, guilt and anyone who was particularly critical of himself /herself.

He occupied a book-lined apartment on West 57th Street and I had an appointment one day after I had called.

I entered the apartment, shook hands, sat down facing him and, with his renowned greeting already securely established, he asked, "now Howard, what problems can I solve for you?" Ellis had an extremely broad, friendly smile that showed all his teeth, and was very thin with large glasses, dressed in an open shirt and sandals. Ellis projected a unique attitude that has not changed over the forty years that I have known him. For the first few moments he listens intently to the presenting problem and in an airy very light hearted manner, re-formulates your problem. Quite amazing! It takes him about two minutes to get the gist of it and for the next forty-five minutes, he earnestly and systematically reveals your crooked thinking and self-talk that perpetuates your problems. I don't think anything really surprises him. He's been there and solved the problem before and knows how precisely to solve your problem. You never see, hear or feel a flicker of a doubt from him about what you have to do to be maximally productive and happy. You are compelled with very little argument or resistance to take his prescription immediately and start "popping pills" into your mouth. And you know you will be well very soon because Ellis says so. Ellis recommends reading his books for back up and it is true that he does exactly what he writes about.

I had a retinue of problems that ranged from erectile difficulties to guilt about my marriage, doubts of succeeding at work, anxiety about securing a University position, occasional depression, inferiority with women, and just plain loneliness. All of this for beginners.

Ellis was relentless in pointing out that my problems were the result of crooked thinking. My preoccupation with what others thought about me had led me to perceive defects in myself. My establishment of standards of how I must behave had led to my beating myself up because I did not attain such standards. Ellis is especially demonic about the "mustabutary" attitudes we develop, and how to dismantle them. For example, when a woman rejected me, I automatically assumed that there was something wrong with me. That's a prime example of crooked thinking. Ellis systematically destroyed this distorted process of reason by disputing this "dumb unscientific idea," that has no validity whatsoever with a number of direct assaults. I had created, in my mind, a totally false image of myself by adopting other people's real and imagined opinions of me. And then Ellis gives you homework to "purposely" get rejected and use the experience as information to do better next time. For example on the first date with a woman I asked her to go to bed with me and she immediately stood up and left and I never saw her again.

It took six sessions over six weeks to root out many of the artful self-put-down stratagems that I had developed over thirty years. I was an outstanding Ellis graduate! Once I grasped the principle and began practicing it, I felt invincible. No one could put me down, or make me feel bad, and very soon thereafter, I could not for the life of me put myself down!

I want to take a few moments to emphasize my enormous feeling of liberation, which came with daring to realize I am inviolate. "Nobody can hurt me; only I can hurt myself. I rob everyone of any power over me. I joyously take responsibility for my feelings and actions and I nurture very positive feelings about myself and who I am."

Practically, this has meant that I carefully evaluate others' opinions and attitudes about me and my work with the powerful caveat that there may indeed be some merit in another's assessment of me, but always with a circumspect perspective of questionable reasoning and motivation. I decide what is valid. Period. This self-psychology held me in good stead at Hawthorne where I did my research, because everyone there was extremely Freudian and tended to put down my social psychological orientation.

After my six sessions with Ellis, and his reminder that whenever I needed a booster shot to simply call him, I was walking on air for at least a year. I have always had this tendency to try out immediately any new theory or practice strategy. I tried to convert everyone to Ellis' rational behavior therapy. I read voraciously every article and book that he wrote and I attended innumerable discussions, workshops and demonstrations. Later I invited him to my classes at Columbia, and to colloquia with the faculty. Not everyone of course would agree with him, but he was very charming, gave very clear, excellent examples, and above all, it became clear to me that he really didn't give a damn what the faculty thought of him.

It is no exaggeration to say that at this point in my vulnerable, fragile self, Ellis "saved" my life. Without him I am convinced that I could not have marched with so much confidence into the future to slay the dragons that were lurking everywhere. I was joyously responsible for myself and I never wanted to be anyone else.

I am enormously indebted to Ellis in liberating me from destructive self-talk and attitudes about standards that I must reach in order to feel accomplished. At this point in my life it was exactly what I needed. I completely mastered the theory and practice of rational emotive behavioral therapy as it applied to my personal life.

I learned in graduate school about Robert K. Merton's theory of manifest and latent functions and have always found it useful in realizing that when some things are accomplished by an individual or an institution, covertly or latently, there may be unintended consequences that will also occur that are not so readily seen, understood, or even able to be grasped. For example, on the kibbutz, I realized that despite the camaraderie and common splendid socialist vision, lurking underneath was a deep fissure that had to do with the tension between individual and kibbutz obligations and responsibilities.

It took many years for me to understand the downside and powerful negative side effects of rational behavioral therapy. I accept my responsibility for swallowing whole the theory and discounting any criticism of it. In a sense, I got to be to be too good in the practice of the theory. The feeling it produced in me is that no one in the whole wide world can adversely affect my self-esteem. But such a point of view easily slides into the feeling that I really don't need anyone else. "Like me, respect me, admire me or 'bye-bye.' There is always other fish to fry. Always." An arrogance creeps into one's armor so that anyone who criticizes you is suspect of having a personal problem and the criticism has very little, if any, validity. Positively, Ellis succeeded in arming me with the ultimate weapon to slay all dragons and that is to serenely go forward with any relationship or project without any fear of failure. I largely eliminated "failure" from my dictionary, and in fact, I wrote an article, "The Strategy of Failure," that was published the same year that I worked with Ellis.

So what could go wrong with all these good feelings and my successes? Just everything. I turned into an egotistic monster. This took time for me to understand fully, almost forty years, and I am still trying desperately to repair as much as I can of my humanity. Ellis' "system," at least for me, resulted in a closed fortress that did not let anyone else really in, nor permit me to exist spontaneously outside of the fortress. The fortress of course was mental and therefore escape-proof.

Now I am sure that Ellis would say that he did not imply, in any sense, the arrogant egotism that lies in looking out for number one.

To turn Ellis on Ellis, it's perfectly okay with me for Ellis to deny any culpability to what happened to me. He can think whatever he likes, but the consequences of his theory for me were disastrous. I kept everyone at a distance. I got so good that no one could possibly hurt me. Because of my invincibility, women that went out with me and I continued to see became dependent on me, and then I rejected them for being overly dependent. I doggedly ploughed ahead with my research and fended off three research directors at Hawthorne and at the main Jewish Board office who wanted joint authorship of Cottage Six. All the nasty remarks of the social workers about my alleged voyeurism swept off me like water off a duck's back.

I boldly applied for a professorship at Columbia University and was immediately accepted. I went on to write six other books and over fifty articles that were accepted by peer review journals. I wrote the only humorous article to appear in Social Work, our flag ship journal, in over 50 years. I made a ton of money consulting and training staff in social work agencies and in the business world.

I now also look at all these accomplishments as so much cotton candy that conceals a corrupt self-aggrandizing monster. I could not stop feeding the success machine that I had gotten so good at manipulating. Everything, but everything, was sacrificed for the greater glory of Howard Polsky. It is really sickening when I think seriously about what happened to me. When anyone becomes fixated on what she / he wants, then it is inevitable that all people become means, or "tools," to get what you want. How can anyone rise above a culture that tells us that individual achievement is the way to be happy, wealthy and wise? Ellis' theory is based on the premise that each one of us wants to be wealthy and famous, and in effect he tells us don't let anyone else, or your own crooked thinking, stand in the way of you getting what you want. If the culture dictates what we should want, then therein lies the vaunted choice that indeed I choose what I want.

Erich Fromm differed from Ellis, for he never tired of reminding us that we want what we are supposed to want. And our society tells us "go for it," and don't let anything stand in your way. Ellis not only never challenges this premise, but adopts as a central principle that this "choice" dictates how the client can achieve their goals and be happy. Ellis is merely a mechanic who will help you build a machine that will get you to where you want to go quickly and efficiently. But one can also argue that if a person unconsciously believes and does what his culture prescribes, he may also be building a kind of life that, at the same time, makes him desperately unhappy and lonely too. In other words, Ellis' method also can generate very unhappy unintended consequences. Ellis rarely explores with the client needs that go beyond success, status, and power, and takes at face value the client's stated needs and wants.

In a recent article that updates three decades of rational emotive behavior therapy, Ellis realizes that a person's negative self-talk may be only the surface feelings of self-worthlessness. It may be the "....basic meaning of her core philosophy that largely created her general feelings of worthlessness." ("Early Theories and Practices of Rational Emotive Therapy and How They Have Been Augmented and Revised During the Last Three Decades," Journal Of Rational-Emotive & Cognitive-Behavior Therapy,Volume 17, Number 2, Summer 1999, p.91) It took a lot of guts for Albert Ellis to admit that for thirty years he had been listening only to the overt message .... Which "loses much of the cognitive and philosophic complexity of the 'meanings' we create about ourselves that we use to denigrate our entire being." (Ibid., p. 91) At this point Ellis simply drops this admission and does not refer to it again. What is implied is that Ellis believes that the so-called "core philosophy" is important only in how it contributes to the clients' sense of worthlessness, which is a very restricted way to think about the meaning people give to their lives.

It never occurred to Ellis that an individual's sense of worthlessness might be the basic driving force of our competitive society. For over forty years, Ellis has profited from clients' sense of worthlessness and his diagnosis is that only thinking that you're worthless "makes" you worthless. So, he recommends stop thinking and talking yourself into worthlessness. But, why do so many people feel worthless?

I will suggest a hypothesis that above all comes out of my own life and personal experience. Fundamentally, I think people feel worthless because they are lonely and isolated form other people. The community, for many people, has disappeared. Each person is on his / her own. In this vacuum, the pursuit of success goes hand-in-hand with the pursuit of loneliness. When I first came to New York I was all alone. To be sure, I made friends, but I was not close to any of them. I became what I could succeed at. This is always a precarious basis for self-worth, because then one achievement has to be superceded by the next. Thus, the more I wanted to achieve, the more I cut myself off from meaningful relationships and relied on my achievements. Now I realize that my rupture with Judaism also cut off a powerful source of community, based on the heritage of balancing self-interest with responsibilities and obligations to others. I was left the superficial and anti-humanistic commercialism of Coca-cola, Andrew Carnegie, and Albert Ellis. I fondly remembered my pre-teen years in Rabbi Twersky's shul.

This helps me understand the phenomenal behavior of a renown professor emeritus at my school who I have known for over forty years. It is impossible to say anything to him about one's accomplishments without him immediately responding that he has done it better. If, for example, you tell him that you were a featured speaker recently at a conference, he must tell you immediately that he was the featured speaker at a half-dozen conferences in the last year. If you published an article, he must tell you immediately that he published five, and one book. It is impossible for him not to tell you immediately how he has bested you in whatever you have done. And he never lies! For a long time I have pondered how someone of his stature has persisted in behavior that is so obviously childish – "I can do anything better than you can!" Now I realize that his is an extreme caricature of what many of us have become.

Is my colleague is so disconnected from other people that he compulsively has to broadcast constantly his achievements to be recognized as important? I don't think that he would ever consider therapy, because he feeds himself constantly with his achievements that he must let others know about. In our achievement culture he is a great man; but does he also feel way down deep that he is lonely, worthless and scared? I think so.

Now I understand how much better the emptiness that I felt as I got more and more into the New York scene. I am part of what has been called the Jewish "lost generation," for we abandoned our cultural heritage and could not be integrated into American society. We were caught betwixt and between two cultures. I never applied the notion to me personally and now I think I realize its full meaning. I became totally absorbed in my career and proving myself as a scholar, and teacher, and I considered myself very successful. I was worthwhile just because I was a success in my field. Along the way I also became an insufferable egoist, but that did not stand in the way of feeling worthwhile and important. I was important enough to be able to ignore totally anyone who criticized or who did not like me. That was their problem.

I was "lucky" to end up in a school, ironically the Columbia University Social Work, whose faculty, for the most part, were also insufferable egoists. There was absolutely no community. Everyone was on his / her isolated perch; each office was a self-enclosed cubicle in which each faculty member was obsessed with publishing and becoming famous. We all walked right past each other and the most meaningful conversations took place waiting for an elevator. We were so alienated from each other, especially during the last fifteen years, that we could not sustain a communal coffee break for fifteen or twenty minutes during a break in classes. Nobody showed up. We didn't have time for each other, we did not like each other and besides, every moment was precious to publish, get famous, and be worthwhile. And all our students were educated in a completely alienated community and aped the faculty by having very little to do with each other, or the faculty. Thus, I was successful and worthwhile in a community that prized individual achievement to the point that any sense of community was obliterated. I was normal because I was succeeding at what my society said I should succeed at. I think that this mad drive for individual success can be generalized to much of our society, especially our successful middle and upper class models. A special example of alienation, I believe, are those members of ethnic groups who completely abandon their cultural heritage and institutions and communities. Ellis is an excellent example of a Jew who rarely acknowledges that he is a Jew. That part of him is totally wiped out! How much more true is this of Jews who change their names and hide their Jewish backgrounds or convert to the majority religion?

Even Ellis, with all of his vaunted individual achievements and worthwhileness, needed comfort from some sort of community. So he created the Albert Ellis Institute which is lodged in a three-story brownstone in the heart of Manhattan. In this busy center, teachers and students go about their work, which is modeled completely after Ellis both in theory and practice and is re-enforced by classes, seminars, workshops, videotapes and some fifty books published by Ellis himself. In this self-sealed community, everyone feels enormously worthwhile and is highly motivated to bring worthwhileness to all of their clients.

If Ellis himself admits that he "missed the boat" in not including the issue of "the meaning of life," then it is truly time for all of us to pay attention. Psychology goes through cycles of fashion that psychologists board in order to be au courant. Psychoanalysis, behaviorism, cognitive behavior, motivation theory and rational-emotive-behavioral theory are only a few examples of trendy, then outdated fashions inpsychology. A recent book gave brief descriptions of some thirty different types of therapy. "Meaning-making" is "hot" now and the indispensable psychologist of meaning-therapy, known also as logotherapy, is the brain-child of Viktor Frankl, our latest guru.

I believe that anyone who takes a serious look at this "theory" will find that it is fuzzy, abstract and ephemeral --- now you see it, now you don't. This theory of meaning-making lacks clarity, definition and any analytical "punch." Frankl's assertion that the capacity to make coherent meaning within a social context, enables an individual to better negotiate his / her world, to better predict the actions of others, and more effectively accomplish goals. That's it. Total mystification. What does the ability to make coherent meaning mean? If you can figure that out you are a far more able psychologist than I am. For example, "meaning and reality are created, not discovered." Good luck. Or this: "an identity capable of encompassing the meanings found in a variety of contexts and cultures... leads to a healthy personality." None of the above statements are elaborated or explained.

Viktor Frankl was a holocaust survivor, who put meaning-therapy or logotherapy "on the map." He evolved this theory while in a concentration camp and it enabled him to survive its horrors. I am extremely interested in the concept for very personal reasons because I am at a crossroads at which I am trying to understand who I am and what the meaning of life is to me right now. Any help will be eagerly grasped. Our Jewish leaders, prophets, sages and teachers constantly fought each other about the ultimate meaning of life. Frankl joins this distinguished company.

Frankl's <u>Man's Search for Ultimate Meaning,</u> first published in Germany in 1948 and recently published by Perseus Publishing, (Cambridge, MA, 2000), and <u>The Will to Meaning</u>, first published in 1968 and then published by Meridian in 1970, are my two sources. The books are repetitive and often use the same anecdotes and illustrations. Of his twenty books, Frankl claims that the "Ultimate Meaning" book is his most organized. In the preface to "Man's Search for Ultimate Meaning," (Frankl, 1948) he sets the stage in a mental hospital, where a patient feels locked in a cage, but nevertheless, feels God is there with him. In this same hospital we also find a jailed, financially ruined prisoner who found a Higher Will and began to reconstruct his life. Thus, despair is turned into hope and eventually success is achieved by way of an Ultimate entity. Belief is trust in ultimate meaning. I find all of this circuitous logic refreshingly naïve, because it reminded me of my adolescence. Throughout both books is a glib pop psychology (which I define as a commonplace idea disseminated via the commercial mass media). For example, Frankl (1948, p.19) asserts that a weak faith is weakened by predicaments and catastrophes, whereas a strong faith is strengthened by them. Abstract faith? Thus "ultimate meaning" arms you to turn disasters into successful achievements. There is something ido latrous about Frankl calling on Ultimate Meaning to save you and advance your good fortune. The Jewish concept of practical spirituality (see Chapter Two) I find much more real and helpful: "What's in the hand is the best prayer." Actually Frankl later says the same thing, albeit somewhat more pompously: the meaning of life is in the response-in-action. (p. 29) Okay I'm for that ---- get off your behind and do something ---- and the Jewish proverb adds comfortingly, "let it be worse, but something different." I like that kind of sauciness.

"Love alone enables the loving person to grasp the uniqueness of the loved person." (p. 43) I find this a meaningless reductio ad absurdum not worthy of serious discussion. I think that the most silly and shallow assertion is Frankl quoting Goethe: ".... whenever man wills, this act of will presupposes a grasp of what he ought to do." (p. 64) When I read this ridiculous statement I was ready to bid Frankl good-bye. I think in our society the opposite of this is much more true. Most often I find people will what they are supposed to will and do what every one else is doing and precisely <u>do not</u> think through what they really want to or ought to will. Writing this book is the hardest task I have ever set for myself, precisely because I had "willed " unconsciously what I was supposed to will all my life, and now began seriously to deconstruct all my "willingness", to find out what I am all about and want to be on a deeper level.

I find it incredible that thousands of people can find any meaning in a statement such as (p.84) ..."identity is available only through responsibility, through being responsible for the fulfillment of meaning."

I happen to agree with this statement, but find it as useful as discovering that the sky is blue. Why is it necessary to write twenty books in order to repeat this sensible counsel? Okay, okay "meaning is the search for meaning." (p. 87) I think it is very nice that Frankl does not use another human being, but encounters himself. (p. 92) Very nice. The opposite of meaningful is futile, which is as important as inferiority was for Alfred Adler. Frankl emphasizes over and over again that … "meaning must be found and cannot be given." (p.112) I guess this is repeated so often because many people are seeking someone to tell them what is meaningful. I think what is useful is to describe one's own search for meaning in detail to give others an idea of the difficulty and challenge. That is a good definition of the meaning of this book. I really think it is a bit too much to write twenty books telling people that they should have meaning to their lives. But, who knows? Perhaps another twenty books on the same theme could indeed be helpful to people. Frankl also spends lots of time trying to convince people about what he calls "height psychology," that is our aspirations and the fountainhead of ultimate meaning that is belief in God.

Let us consider what another book, "The Will to Meaning," published twenty years later adds to the above. There are a couple "new" nuggets. For example, on page 35: "'Success'" and happiness must happen, and the less one cares for them, the more they can." Says who? Says Frankl. This reminds one of Coue, who swept America in the early twenties with the slogan, "Every day in every way I am getting better," which if repeated three times a day will happen. Norman Vincent Peale's "power of positive thinking" slogan also was very popular. I think the above slogan by Frankl is irresponsible.

Ultimately, the lesson to learn from his book, Frankl concludes, is that despite all our suffering, catastrophes turn to Habakkuk's triumphant hymn: … "Yet I will rejoice in the Lord, I will joy in the God of my salvation."(p.157)

In summary, I agree with Frankl that the search for meaning is important, but that saying this over and over again is not enlightening, but rather boring. I think a much better strategy is to read books about people's search for meaning. Such diverse books as Catcher in the Rye, Somerset Maugham's The Razor's Edge, Richard Bernstein's recent The Ultimate Journey, Herrigen's The Art of Archery or Crime and Punishment, or War and Peace, Herman Hesse's novels, or Robert Pirsig's Zen and the Art of Motorcycle Maintenance.

Psychology is still catching up with literature …. and life. I believe most of psychology misses the important point of the disconnection between people and any serious community, which results in evermore preoccupation with the self as separate from other people. My disconnection from Judaism at this point of my life contributed importantly to an estrangement from caring for and loving other people.

The two years following my 30th birthday defined my professional career for the next forty years. With a two-year Russell Sage grant, I immersed myself for eight months in <u>Cottage Six</u> at the Hawthorne Cedar Knolls School. I was highly motivated to use my experience for writing a book to gain access to a University position. "Me," as usual, was the center of my universe. I was using the institution to advance my professional career, which was also true of all the professional social workers, administrators, and psychologists. In the "helping professions," I have found that self-interest far outweighs concerns for clients.

Despite living in a kind of commune at the University of Chicago and my six months on a kibbutz, I was totally unprepared for what awaited me. Cottage Six had the most "aggressive" youngsters in the institution and they were proud of their reputation. The youngsters, 15 to 18 years of age, came from broken families and anomic neighborhoods and created a powerful hierarchy of aggressive bullies and con artists that terrorized the younger, more passive, peer "followers." Literally every encounter among the boys and between them and the helpless cottage 'parents' was laden with threats and intimidation. I had to directly intervene when a boy was threatened with his life. I had to intervene when the cottage parents returned from a week-end away and were dead drunk. The peer leaders helped me put them to bed. The cottage parents courted the aggressive leaders and literally begged them not to be too violent with the younger kids.

The boredom was overwhelming. By four or five in the afternoon and every entire week-end the social workers, administrators and teachers disappeared and the boys went nuts. There was no recreation. So the boys played cards, beat each other up and ran over to the girls' cottages for unsupervised recreation. The boys made a lot of derisive fun of the social workers who saw them individually once a week (when they showed up) for psychoanalytic therapy in the clinic building and who had no idea about what was going on under their absent noses. The campus supervisor, a social worker, appeared briefly twice during the eight months I was in the cottage. The social workers, along with the child-care workers, went on strike because of their abysmally low pay. If anybody in the institution could help it at all, this was one of the last places on earth that they would want to be. And, in fact, social workers left as soon as they accumulated enough private clients in the their offices at home.

It took me many years to grasp how all of us professionals used the residential "treatment" center first and foremost to further our own private interests rather than treat the troubled teens. I used it to get tenure and ultimately a full professorship at the most prestigious school of social work in the world at Columbia University. The psychiatrists who showed up one or two days a week got enormous salaries for their "expert" knowledge. Social workers remained in the institution primarily to get paying private referrals from psychiatrists over-loaded with clients in order to make some real money so that they could leave Hawthorne. The Hawthorne director built a beautiful mansion on grounds, curried the ignorant wealthy board for money and worked himself into becoming the director of the entire agency for an obscenely high salary.

Now let us take a closer look at what was going on "back at the ranch." The main job of the large contingent of professional therapists was to pin psychiatric labels on all of the residents, and often the untrained paltry paid cottage workers as well. The all-utility psychiatric label, fashionable at Hawthorne when I was there, was "border-line", which was used interchangeably with "character-disorder." Each kid, in other words, had a faulty super-ego or conscience that made for difficult treatment. In fact, the largely useless therapy was rationalized as ineffective because the kids were too sick and not "ready" for serious expert psychological treatment.

Initially, I fell for all of this psychological claptrap hook, line and sinker. Besides, it handsomely paid off. Here's how I fell into a terrible trap. First Hawthorne tried to suppress my book and were unsuccessful. Then they decided to support me to secure a grant to hire a professional social group worker to work in the cottage. I received two million dollars from the National Institute of Health, with the help of Russell Sage and my mentor Dr. Cottrell, for the purpose of program evaluation.

And it worked. The cottage with the group worker created a much more "therapeutic milieu," relationships were far more trusting and communal, and boys did better afterward compared to the two other conventional senior control cottages. Alas, after money for our project ran out, Hawthorne reverted to its previous state, wherein psychiatric caseworkers and psychiatrists gained full control again, and shortly thereafter, Hawthorne became a cesspool again. A private security organization was hired to protect the kids and workers from each other. The psychiatric labeling of the kids again flourished.

But the "institutional cat" was out of the bag. Institutions by and large flourish because of secrecy about what is really going on in them. The institutional field had become so dysfunctional that it became increasingly difficult to hide all of the violence and manipulation that was occurring. My book, Cottage Six, became a classic in the institutional treatment of delinquent and emotionally disturbed youngsters and went through many editions and sold over 80,000 copies. Something now had to be done.

That "something" was essentially a positive peer culture (PPC) movement that emphasized influencing the peer youth culture with daily meetings guided by adult facilitators. This helped ameliorate some of the hostility and tension between residents and staff but unfortunately, outside of the meetings, institutional life resorted essentially to a bitter them-us war between the residents and staff. One of the major universal problems in raising children is that they do (and perhaps must) become hostile to adults in their drive toward independence. But emotionally disturbed and delinquent youth peers are drastically cut off from adults and their institutions and are then dominated by the most aggressive and manipulative peer leaders. I subsequently was able to conceptualize the interlocking aggressive cycle; staff bullying kids and youth peer leaders simultaneously reacting with hostility toward staff and peer followers. In turn, aggressive staff accelerated their bullying of kids and fellow workers in ways that mirrored the students. Not a pretty picture, but an accurate one of the great majority of residential institutions.

I was only able to develop the above conceptual framework long after Cottage Six. I now realize that I could not possibly have conceptualized the basic issue of alienation in institutions, because of my own total alienation from any community. I abandoned my Jewish community and lived for forty years with total preoccupation with my career. Every community, except my immediate family, were so secondary that eventually I had no community.

My personal alienation mirrored the breakdown of community in all of our institutions (including my School of Social Work at Columbia University), but was more extremely demonstrated between the keepers and the kept in locked facilities. The slogan in institutions is, "each person for himself and against everyone else." What binds everyone to each other is total unremitting distrust and never turning one's back. In these closed, isolated, institutions of alienation, psychologists have a field day endlessly diagnosing the individual disorders of residents and inmates and often their keepers. And the public at large is bullied into believing that only harsher treatment can correct inmates.

A recent editorial in the New York Times (April 22, 2001) cites a new report by Human Rights Watch which documents the rampant sexual abuse behind bars. Prison authorities rarely investigate complaints of rape and prison rapists rarely face criminal charges. Behind the cruel abuse is an expanding prison-industry complex that is furiously building new prisons, and reviving communities plagued with high rates of unemployment. Everyone knows prisons, jails, detention centers don't work and no one knows what to do about this appalling dehumanization of the keepers and the kept.

It takes someone with a gargantuan chutzpah to even dare to suggest an entirely different kind of institutional set up based on some form of a community rather than a debilitating war that dehumanizes everyone. Let me say immediately before I lose you, that I do not propose one whit less concern about the safety of the keepers, the kept and the community. I am saying, however, that we could create an institution that tempers "the stick" with the evolution of a kind of community in which everyone respect each other much, much more and be responsible for one another and their community. Amitai Etzioni, an American-Israeli sociologist, has brilliantly formulated the practical-philosophical basis for the community I have in mind, in one of the most important books of the last one-hundred years, The New Golden Rule.

On the last page of this book is a pictorial representation of Etzioni's new golden rule. It is the lynch-pin of a book, From Custodialism to Residential Community, The Future of Institutional Care, that my wife, Dr. Roni Berger, and I have written. The new golden rule: "an individual upholds and respects the morality of society as society upholds and respects each person."

For "society" one can substitute "community," or virtually any group or organization. I want to emphasize that it is not necessary for each person to "love everyone." That is foolish and unrealistic and probably not moral. "Loving all" is not the goal, but rather as the society evolves, a culture of respect for each person, might develop so that then people would want to protect and advance that culture and society ----- precisely because it respects every person.

I turn now to the thorniest issue in the trade-off of respect for the individual and the latter's support of the community. David Ben-Gurion once said that the test of a democracy is the freedom to criticize and dissent. This can become quite messy, as evident especially in Israel, but clearly no other system can match our cherished democracy. Please believe me when I say that I am quite aware of the many pitfalls and impossible difficulties in evolving a community and culture of democracy in which people can learn to voice differences and listen to each other and go with majority decisions.

My choice for experimentation with an institutional democratic community would be precisely in residential treatment centers for children and youth. I would build on the experiences of some institutions that have tried to install democratic communities so that we can learn from each other and go forward together. It is extremely important for those of us who want to build democratic communities as an alternative to increasing repression, to know about each other and to learn from each other.

The vision comes before its implementation. Before my Bar-Mitzvah, I studied the "Ethics of Our Fathers," a compilation of sayings by Talmudic scholars that emphasized our responsibility not to separate ourselves from the community. Community activity is as important as studying the Torah. A vision must be workable, but first it requires enormous faith and empathy to withstand attackers' arrows and the indifferent reactions of non-believers. A Jewish proverb says a prophet is a half-fool. I have always been moved by a speech by the socialist and one-time third party candidate for President of the United States, Eugene V. Debs: "While there is a lower class, I am in it, while there is a criminal element I am of it; while there is a soul in prison, I am not free." (Speech, Cleveland, Ohio, Sept. 9, 1917)

In my rich Jewish cultural heritage are many models of the prophetic calling to identification and care for the less fortunate in our midst. From Isaiah to the Baal Shem Tov the call has gone out over and over again to make real our essential brotherhood. My favorite story about the Baal Shem Tov is his practice of distributing every day to the poor any money left over in his household. As human beings, and as a society, it would be fatal to forget these calls to our common humanity. This is one reason I am proud to be a Jew.

CHAPTER EIGHT
GOD, RITUAL AND RELIGION

For the first fifteen years of my life I thought about God as my personal savior. I think now that this must have had to do with the narcissism of youth. It never occurred to me that God may have something more important to do than think about Howard Polsky. Surely, He didn't waste His time helping me pass important exams. I wonder if the widespread belief in God is related to the early anthropomorphism of children and youth to attribute a human form to things or spirits not human. I had a very vague picture of God, and it certainly was not the muscular version depicted by Michelangelo on the Sistine Chapel.

When I became a radical communist in my late teens, I aped my new Marxist catechism that religion is the opiate of the masses. It seemed indisputable that religion supported the ruling class, with of course the exception of radical priests who led peasants and the working class against the capitalist hegemony. As Jews around me shed most of the ritualistic routines of Orthodoxy, we were left with increasing minimal obligations like circumcision, the bar-mitzvah and bat-mitzvah, the chupah, the Passover Seder and Yom Kippur.

I don't think elders realize that the perfunctory adherence to rituals and their corruption by conspicuous displays of wealth, instill in young people a sense of their parents' and their Rabbis' hypocrisy. Despite the massive exit of half our young people into intermarriage and indifference to our rich cultural heritage, our institutions, led by our huge synagogue-mausoleums, have displayed a spectacular paralysis to examine their dismal failure to hold onto their flock. Paralysis is a complete or partial loss of sensation and motion of the body; it indicates a loss of the ability to move and increasing powerlessness and incapacity of any action to address their defunct condition. Half the population of Israel no longer bothers to go through the motions of synagogue activities. What is going on here?

The greatest thinker about the role of religion in society is, of course, Max Weber. My professor at the University of Wisconsin, Hans Gerth, translated Weber's main books and essays on religion [Ancient

Judaism, H.H. Gerth and D. Martindale, trs. Glencoe,Illinois: Free Press, 1952; and From Max Weber: Essays in Sociology, H.H. Gerth and C. Wright Mills, trs., and eds., N.Y. Oxford, 1946, Part III.] According to Weber, the biblical prophets were the first "men of conscience," ready to obey God rather than other men. They agitated for true Judaic conduct in daily life, and were unafraid to confront Kings who turned away from God. When the Second Temple was destroyed under the Roman Emperor Hadrian and the Jews went into the Diaspora, the Rabbi took the place of the prophet and the priest and became the unchallenged religious leader.

The decisive break, represented in the development of Christianity, was its renunciation of the ritualistic commandments of Judaism. In place of a complex of self-segregating ritual practices, a much more palpable Son of God emerged and, like the Old Testament prophets, the Christian apostles lived for religion rather than to make their living off of religion. A host of religious leaders ---- saints, founders of monk orders, reformers, plebian prophets and self-made evangelists ---- constantly reactivated Christianity.

Weber's greatest and most controversial thesis is in his book, The Protestant Ethic and the Spirit of Capitalism, [Talcott Parsons, tr., N.Y., Scribner's, 1930]. Weber maintained that modern industrial capitalism could not have emerged without "inner-worldly asceticism" which contributed to the formulation of the personality of the entrepreneurial middle-classes. Inner-worldly asceticism is man setting out to master the world; he stays in the world, yet is not of it, and his work is part of his crusade for entering the kingdom to come. The world of work equips him to fight the devil and all evil. Weber's thesis also includes an abnegation of worldly pleasures. Work became the major ascetic technique and obsession. Specific psychic attitudes that flowed from work as God's work included thrift, diligence, control of "idle words," humility, continuous self-control, purposiveness ---- all splendid attributes fitted to develop and propagate capitalism.

I think Weber vastly overestimates inner worldly asceticism as the original engine of capitalism. Religion is much more fungible and adaptive to the economy than appropriate entrepreneurial attitudes are to succeed. The Hasidic movement, which took off in 1700 and coincided with the remarkable expansion of capitalism in Europe, was actually based on a diametrically opposite psychology from asceticism. A populist revolt against the rich and the arrogant learned Rabbis, returned God to the peasants and workers with the philosophy of His divine sparks abundantly spread out in everything that man possesses and does, including the tying of one's shoelaces. This was one of the great democratization leveling of holiness the world has ever seen. A Jewish "saint," or the nearest equivalent, the Tsadik (the "Righteous" or "Pious One,") could now be a humble peasant. And, in contrast to the Catholics, a cumbersome bureaucratic process for canonization was totally avoided by keeping the Tsadik the best-kept secret in the Jewish community, a feat in itself. In fact, one of the most important reasons this secret was so well kept is that the Tsadik himself (rarely a "she") did not know that he was a Tsadik: "A Tsadic who knows he is a Tsadik is no Tsadic." Clearly Jesus Christ would have had a lot of difficulty establishing his saintly credentials among Hasidic Jews.

How did <u>work</u> figure into the new Hasidic movement? Very simple. The Jews extended the concept of the holy Sabbath to all of internal Jewish life. The home, synagogue, rituals, holidays, prayers, and their closeness were all holy-endowed. The workplace, in contrast, was essentially profane, a necessary burden. A Jew's greatest mitzvah during the work-day is to take time out and pray to God. The Hasid traveled daily and weekly between two worlds, the profane arena of work and the holy space of home, community and synagogue.

The advantage of this may have been that in the workplace the rules were not so constrained as the behavior in the synagogue. In fact, the separation of work and community opened up for Jews, enormous possibilities for using the skills that they had mastered in Jewish studies in the world of commerce. A wealthy Jew could "buy" a lot of prestige with his money in the community, but was also for the most part not to be completely trusted: "Treat me honorably but with suspicion." A widespread saying maintained that "the bigger the merchant the smaller the Jew." Financial success was not a ticket to salvation or any sign of special holiness. However, earning a livelihood was regarded as the best cure for every earthly ailment; financial success was not considered a ticket to salvation or any sign of special holiness.

When I pointed out all of the above to my professor, Hans Gerth, he was genuinely impressed with my conceptualization of the Jewish ethic toward work, but had a ready answer: "Find the rule, exceptions always come later." I repeated this in Yiddish where it is a very well known saying and then we both laughed.

One of the most important contributions of early Hasidism to our heritage is their formulation of the key problems of God, God and evil, and God and the pious. They worried constantly about these problems and came up with solutions that I don't think have been improved upon for the last 300 years.

The essential method for thinking about God is to treat Him as a mystery. It would take a lot of chutzpah for us far limited mortals to even begin to understand the infinite complexity of God. So, the first thing is to remember that you cannot ever comprehend this grand mystery. Even Moses was not allowed to behold Him so we far less mortal beings also have to live with the mystery. But is there "Some Entity" behind the mystery? Of course! That is the whole point! [The following stories and anecdotes are taken from Martin Buber, Tales of the Hasidim, The Early Masters, 1947, and Tales of the Hasidim, The Later Masters, 1948, Shocken Books, N.Y.; and Louis I. Newman, The Hasidic Anthology, Tales and Teaching of the Hasidim, Shocken Books, N.Y., 1963.]

The best way to deal with a Mystery --- like the mystery of God --- is with mysterious stories and anecdotes. Shrouding the mystery with a story, especially by endowed wise people who are unusually pious or learned or both seems to resolve the mystery at a gut or emotional level rather intellectually. When Rabbi Hanokh, the brilliant Rabbi of Alexander was thirteen, he was examined by the great Rabbi, who was known only by the name, Yehudi. Hanokh grieved that he had spent several weeks on a passage in the Talmud and could not understand it. Yehudi comforted the boy by telling him it was quite common for anyone not to understand something and it happened to him often. Then Yehudi added the following story: "Our Father Abraham explored the sun, the moon and the stars and did not find God and in this non-finding, the presence of God was revealed to him." Then Yehudi added: "For three months I mulled over this story until I too reached the truth of non-finding."

I frankly was stumped in "not-finding God." This issue about whether there is truly a God weighed heavily on the Hasidim, if the large number of stories devoted to this subject is any proof. The following story is the most poignant, heart-wrenching story I have ever read about the belief in God:
Silently his wife held the hungry child. It was too weak to cry. Then --- for the first time --- the maggid [preacher-rabbi] sighed. Instantly the answer came. A voice said to him: "You have lost your share in the coming world."

"Well, then," he said, "the reward has been done away with. Now I can begin to serve in good earnest."

I certainly hope that included getting out and getting something to eat.

Not only is God a mystery, but His ways are mysterious. To even hint at challenging His existence and His ways is blasphemous. But even more. Whatever suffering and pain you undergo are evidence of the strength of your faith in Him. By making God inscrutable, His followers lock themselves into a box with Him and His Torah from which there is no escape. God never fails us. We fail God by challenging our faith in Him.

A Hasid does not say, "If I helped a single person, I have saved the world," but rather, "If I knew for sure that I had helped a single one of my Hasidim to serve God, I should have nothing to worry about." (3D) The only way for a man to grasp the greatness of God is to be truly humble. (4A) Self-improvement is an endless process to make oneself worthy to give true service to God. Forget about persuading others to serve God, a Hasid never completes learning how best to serve God.(4B) Self-conquest in the service of God is without bounds. The best shortcut to love of God is to love fellow human beings.(13C)

People try all kinds of tricks to get God on their side and are foiled every time. A rich Jew decided to change Rabbis to increase even further his wealth, but instead he kept getting poorer. He complained to the Rabbi, who told him that when he began to seek more distinguished Rabbis, maybe God did exactly the same thing and sought more distinguished recipients. (14A)

A Jewish wag best summarized any attempt to influence God for self-enrichment: "If prayers could help you get what you want, they would be sold in pharmacies." The only way to God is total spontaneous heart-felt dedication, which is best shown by maintaining your faith in God in times of dire misfortune. Getting to know God is like meeting a stranger, only it takes a lifetime to get a "glimpse" (metaphorically speaking) of Him.(16) Fortunately, since God's divine sparks are everywhere, a Hasid can work his way to God by the most mundane acts of eating, sleeping, walking, washing dishes and sitting by a river. (21B)

The only real problem is to question His existence. The Rabbis invented fool-proof evidence. A student suffered from some doubt about God hiding from him, and to strengthen his faith went to seek counsel from the eminent Rabbi Pinhas. The Rabbi consoled the student: "God ceases hiding, if you know He is hiding." (21C)

To believe God is hiding reveals a deeper faith in His existence. Part of the genius of The Baal Shem Tov, the founder of Hasidism, is to wed faith with creativity, another mysterious activity. He once said: "When I weld my spirit to God, I let my mouth say what it will, for then all my words are bound to their root in heaven." (26B) The point is clear. Faith in God should be unconditional and complete, so get out of the way of faith and let it commune directly with God. I think this idea of getting at some of the mystery of God by losing oneself in heart-felt faith is derived from the Kabbalah, the secret teachings and the kavvanot, mystical concentrations, which are directed toward superhuman effects. But Hasidim, for the most part, eschewed these flights of fantasy. A student once boasted to his teacher, Rabbi Elimelekh, that in the morning he saw the angel who rolls away the darkness and, in the evenings, the angel who rolls away the light before the darkness. Rabbi Elimelekh told him that he saw the angels too when he was young, but "later on you don't see those things anymore." (38C) One appropriate example of the triumph of faith over reality is holding the Torah which an elderly, frail Rabbi stoutly maintained, "once you hold it, it isn't heavy any more." (37E) I believe that.

The danger is ever present that faith can fall into "ecstasy" and the resulting mysticism can make us fall prey to various forms of "miraculous happenings." The Hasidim addressed miracles with a huge chunk of tongue-in-cheek levity. Thus Rabbi Zalman once asked his disciples why the Master Rav went to the pond everyday at dawn. The answer is that "He was learning the song with which the frogs praise God. It takes a very long time to learn that song." (47C)

Another one of my favorites is the story about Heaven (God) revealing to Rabbi Shlomo of Karlin the language of birds, the trees, and the serving angels. But he refused to learn them before finding out the importance of each of these languages for the service of God. (54D) The Hasidic distrust of the miraculous bordered on ridiculing the whole idea. Rabbi Yehiel once said that as a boy, on the night before his Bar Mitzvah, traveled to the upper spheres to choose a soul of his own liking. He selected a great soul, but could not quite reach it, so he remained a little man. (61D)

A main way to reach God is by prayer. If a man can pray to God, he lacks nothing at all in the world. This is the sine qua non of Godly Judaism. I think that one who faithfully prays daily, achieves the detachment from worldly concerns every bit as effectively as Zen and Buddhist meditation. This is the reason that the rich man who depends on his wealth is to be pitied and the poor man who believes in God is to be exalted. Of course Marx ridiculed this belief because it also supported the exploitative status quo of the wealthy against the poor. This passive resignation to the status quo echoes the great Bratslaver's statement that, "the knowledge that whatever occurs to you is for your good, raises you to the heights of living in Paradise." (71G) This kind of passive fatalism supports the fundamental belief that God does not give rewards for your faith, including suffering and deprivation. Faith always trumps reality. Hence the belief is that if a man is poor and meek, it is easy for him to be joyful, inasmuch as he has nothing to guard against losing. I think this kind of faith is a "baba-meinsah," that is a story believed and repeated by elderly brainwashed grandmothers. In reality I don't think that many Hasidim are convinced that "poverty is a great treasure." (84F) This borders on a reverse psychology of the miraculous that the Hasidim ridiculed.

Ritual was used by the Hasidim to weld their souls to the Divine Spirit. A Hasid confronted the Bratslaver Rabbi about his skepticism that reciting psalms and prayer engrossed the faithful with the heart with God. The Bratslaver replied: "The recitation of Psalms and prayers has the virtue of awakening the heart. Make use of your lips and your heart will follow their lead." (82A)

The ideal of Hasidism was man's immersion in God. This of course presented often the possibility of some mystical identification and interpretation of God's mystery through the miraculous manipulation of numbers and other esoteric interpretations. The Hasidim avoided taking that path as a rule, but of course there were always some exceptions.

The most powerful metaphor to describe the essential ideal relationship with God was a special kind of lovers' relationship. The story below best describes the Hasidic ideal relationship between man and God:

Concerning the verse in the Scriptures: "I stood between the Lord and you," Rabbi Mikhal of Zlotchow said: "The 'I' stands between God and us. When a man says 'I' and encroaches upon the word of his Maker, he puts a wall between himself and God. But he who offers his 'I' --- there is nothing between him and his Maker. For it is to him that the words refer: 'I am my beloved's and his desire toward to me.' When my 'I' has become "my beloved's," then it is toward me that his desire turns." (49A)

If the grand metaphor of Christianity is "Father and Son," the Hasidic metaphor is a merger of love between himself and God without the interference of the earthly 'I'. This submergence of the 'I' with God is the closest Hasidic mystical formulation that I am aware of, in the God-man relationship. In a previous chapter, I have discussed at length the "I and I" and the "I and Thou" relationship. Most psychologists today, following Erich Fromm and Andreas Angyal, believe that the ideal human love relationships include a healthy dose of "I and I" in the I-Thou relationship. Apparently for some Hasidim, the 'I" interferes with the ideal union with God.

I have gone on at great length about the Hasidic attitude toward God. The rich cultural heritage forged over 200 years in Eastern Europe by the Hasidim can be understood only by fully realizing the central role of God in the life of the Jewish people. My ancestors, my father's father, was a Rabbi as was my mother's father, and they were God-intoxicated. I grew up in an Eastern-European shtetl in Milwaukee, Wisconsin. To abandon God, as I did, is akin to a kind of cultural suicide. Can our rich cultural heritage continue to survive and be creative without God? Are we doomed to be swallowed up by a mass American culture that is increasingly gross, infantile, ego-centered and mindless?

Before I delve into this issue ---- is God mysteriously hiding or is there no God in hiding ---- it is extremely important to point out that the Hasidic Rabbis' elaborate defense of a God in hiding, although accepted without reservations by Hasidim, was the core but by no means the full story of the great cultural heritage created by the Hasidim. The rich, variegated, vibrant, creative culture created by the Yiddish-speaking Hasidic community was full of a distinctive medley of humor, dance, music, songs, stories, theater, proverbs, sayings, rituals, etc., and an array of institutions ranging from the burial society to the steam bath and the mikvah (the ritual bathing place for women), and the Hebrew schools and yeshivas). A galaxy of characters emerged; the schlemiel, the meshugana, the naar, the tsadik, the smart-Alec, the balabusta, the melamed, etc. made famous by Shalom Aleichem and other Jewish writers (and featured in the Broadway production of "Fiddler on the Roof"). The holidays and communal weddings, funerals, care of the poor and the disabled and the sick, etc., cemented the shtetl, the Yiddish East-European community, as one of the great cultural achievements of the eighteenth and nineteenth centuries.

At the heart of this Yiddish renaissance elaborated by the people of the shtetl in their daily life was the emergence of a practical spirituality, which was a belief in God <u>and</u> the all too human foibles of their friends, lovers and enemies. The Jews of the shtetl honed a healthy skepticism and let loose a barrage of devastatingly clever wit directed against the high and mighty, the arrogant, the greedy, the show-off, the manipulator, the untrustworthy dealer, the hypocrite, the liar, etc. This rich cultural heritage is beautifully and lovingly described in <u>Life Is with People</u>, by Elizabeth Herzog and Mark Zborowski. This folk culture, for those of us who were exposed to it in our early years, still weaves a magic spell over us.

I would like to give you a taste of this folk culture with a small sample of proverbs and sayings that were known by all shtetl people and woven into their daily life. Many of them were the favorites of my mother and father and their friends and our relatives. The sayings were all based on the common sense of their shtetl experiences and many were said with a self-parodying air in which they made fun of themselves with obvious-profound axioms of life. (Some of the following sayings are taken from <u>Words Like Arrows, A Treasury of Yiddish Folk Sayings</u>, compiled by Shirley Kumove, Warner Books, Inc., N.Y. N.Y., 1984.) Let me hasten to add that the sayings in Yiddish are much more salty and barbed. I briefly offer my "interpretations" at my own peril!

"One hand washes the other and both wash the face." Sometimes we have to trade-off our assets and sometimes they work together. I may very well be citing my idiosyncratic reactions and you can have yours. "Just because you're angry at the cantor, you don't say "Amen?" Many proverbs deal with the stupidity of maintaining grudges. "When you climb a ladder, count the rungs." Always figure out your way back wherever you are going.

"Treat me honorably, but with suspicion." Just don't ever completely trust anyone. "So the Messiah will born a day later." I love this and I am always reminded of it whenever I go crazy about making deadlines. "What's in the hand is the best prayer." Again, a warning about others' promises. "The pig grabs the best apple." How true! "If there is no other way, then commit a sin you may." A far cry from "turning the other cheek." "The eggs want to be smarter than the hens," describes the inevitable conflict between the generations. "God protect us from Jewish chutzpah, Jewish mouths and Jewish brains." A warning about our all too human fellow Jews.

My mother's most used saying: "The way you make your bed, that's how you will sleep." How true! "They are both in love --- he with himself, she with herself." Perhaps even more common today with 50% of marriages ending in divorce. On the other hand, "lunacy without love is possible but love without lunacy is impossible."

Jewish curses are renown: "May all his teeth fall out and only one remain for a toothache." I don't think Satan himself could think up a more devilish fate. People in the shtetl never tired of putting rich folk in the right place: "Rich or poor, as long as no one's less or more." Or, "Six feet deep makes everyone equal." "The bigger the merchant the smaller the Jew." Boastful people were especially lampooned: "With the tongue anything is possible." Or, "He can bring walls together." And making the obvious sound profound: "If you go to the steam-bath expect to sweat." Again a warning: "A friend is a friend up to his wallet." A bit of advice for lovers: "It's good luck to look at the beautiful and live with the wise."

Some of the proverbs are very subtly wise: "What is inferred is worse than what is heard." "An example isn't proof." "Find the rule, the exceptions will come later." "The sun will set without your assistance." The work ethic was a very strong value: "Livelihood is a cure for every ailment." "If you don't have enough to do, shitting is also work." "One chops the wood and the other does grunting." Learning was a cardinal virtue: "A bastard who is a wise student is greater than an ignorant high priest."

Yiddish sayings of flights of fancy remind one of the paintings of Marc Chagall. "A cow flew over the roof and laid an egg." I love this one: "When an ass talks like a human being everyone is surprised, when a human being talks like an ass no one is surprised."

Every culture creates a distinctive composition of values that gives a unique meaning to peoples' lives and bonds them together as a community. The shared values depicted in the Yiddish proverbs and sayings above illustrate that the peoples' powerful beliefs in God, were edited by a shrewd practical-spiritual wisdom that stemmed from their close-knit everyday life in the shtetl. Hasidism that flourished during the eighteenth to twentieth centuries was rent by a host of challenges from Reform Jews, secularists, assimilationists, socialists, bundists, Zionists, conversions, a largely secular Israel, and most devastating of all, the Holocaust.

The key question of Jewish life remains: How central to our continuing vibrant and rejuvenated Jewish heritage is God and Torah and all the rituals? A story is recounted about Franz Rosenzweig, the great German-Jewish scholar who was near to converting to Christianity. However, he had an epiphany in a small Hasidic synagogue when he observed and felt the passion of the members' prayers, and realized that as a Jew, he was invested with 5,000 years of a transcendent eternal culture. This rich heritage he could not abandon. Another story about Rosenzweig I find impossible to forget is about a Hasid who once asked him: "If there is no personal God, to whom do I pray?" Arthur Hertzberg recounts the above in his latest book, Jews, The Essence and Character of a People. (with Aron Hirt-Manheimer, Harper, San Francisco, 1998).

I greatly admire Rabbi Arthur Hertzberg. His credentials are substantial: a Conservative Rabbi, professor at Columbia, Dartmouth New York University; former president of the American Jewish Congress and vice president of the World Jewish Congress; author of seven books on a variety of Jewish themes. Most impressive is his desire in Jews to write a no-holds barred personal account of his journey through the Jewish Establishment over the last eighty years. As a progressive, liberal, open-minded Zionist and religious believer, his eyes are wide open about the crisis of Jews like myself and about God and religion.

I believe that most of the 19th and 20th centuries is an end run about the orthodox God. A new faith was required to take the place of God and the network of outmoded rituals to fervently affirm our cultural heritage and avoid the wholesale assimilation of Jews into modern secular societies. First, I want with Hertzberg's help, to review briefly this end run about our Jewish God over the last 300 years and then describe Hertzberg's and my personal "solutions".

Ironically, every Jewish encyclopedia that I have seen includes (with a picture) a brief account of Spinoza's excommunication from the Amsterdam Jewish community in 1656. Spinoza sought to dehumanize God and think of Him as Nature. "God did not create nature, He is Nature." For this pantheistic blasphemy he had to leave Amsterdam, and settle in Hague, where he became an optician grinding lenses for a living. Ben Gurion asked the Amsterdam Jews to lift the excommunication, but they refused.

In the middle of the nineteenth century, German Jewry began tinkering seriously with the traditional Orthodox God. Mendelssohn, the founder of Reform Judaism, distinguished between morality and ritual and decried God as a scorekeeper of ritual observances. Krochmal was one of the first to declare that Jews are not simply a Jewish faith, but are a people with history through which God is progressively revealed. In many different versions this is by far the most common end run around the Orthodox God. Zionists were less polite, and believed that the old God stood in the way of a modern secular society. Ahad Ha'am denied the existence of a personal God, but held on to the idea of the Jews as God's chosen people and then substituted a rich evolving cultural heritage for God. Rabbi Mordecai Kaplan rejected the idea of "choseness," and thought of Judaism as a civilization of which God was only one part. Franz Rosenzweig introduced the idea of the Jewish calendar and all the rituals were a reflection of eternity. The Jews' past was a part of every Jew and distinguished him / her from other peoples.

The Zionists became the most important foes of the Orthodox God, so much so that nearly half of the Israeli population no longer believes in a personal God. Buber's ideal became the kibbutz, not God, and he also believed in the mystery of life, but equivocated about a personal God. In the land of Israel, Jews would live by the highest ideals of the biblical prophets.

Hertzberg declares flat out that the crisis in Jewish identity began when Jews no longer believed in God, and started to feel that anti-Semitism was no longer permanent. I strongly disagree with his assessment of anti-Semitism, but that is beside the point here. After this discursive review of the end run of God, Hertzberg offers his "solution" to this crisis. He believes that Judaism will not be able to hold onto Jews if nothing more than Jewish music, art, or rituals make them feel better. He sardonically comments that Jews who feel that the Kabbalah, or Jewish mysticism, makes them feel better, may wake up one morning in an ashram in India.

But then Hertzberg launches, like from the head of Minerva, into a plea for Jews to return to the Jewish texts. He equates being Jewish with believing in the Jewish God. However, Hertzberg wants to include under his Jewish tent all Jews who may not believe in God, but work to preserve Jewish institutions from the United Jewish Appeal to Jewish Centers and Jewish burial societies. This is a strange dichotomy. He apparently is willing to settle for an increasingly large number of Jews who are substantially ignorant of Jewish texts, as long as their hearts and their actions promote Jewish causes. For many observers of the Jewish-American scene, this is precisely the prescription for the vanishing Jew in America. All our great Jewish institutions, the enormous synagogues, our substantial Jewish health clubs, to our prodigious yearly money-raising efforts, demand less and less conviction and knowledge about what it is to be a Jew and is exchanged for mindless participation in activities orchestrated from above by wealthy Jews, equally ignorant about our tradition.

I am deeply disappointed in Rabbi Hertzberg's conclusions. His willingness to "settle" for Jews participation in "paper organizations" I find quite astounding. Surely he knows that a culture is sustained by active organic participation of people in a Jewish community. The East-European shtetl, the "Lower-East-Sides" of large American cities, Israel, the Essenes, Kibbutzim, one could go on and on, are powerful examples of communities of Jews forging new life into our heritage. To settle for what our Jewish institutions are creating is to settle for more and more substantially large numbers of cultural ignoramuses who will find less and less reasons for remaining in the fold.

Intellectuals often fall prey to the "academic fallacy." This is the belief that if one knows something, he or she will become committed to an appropriate way of life based on that knowledge. While Hertzberg does recognize that "actions speak louder than words," he does not recognize that his solution consists of individual activities isolated from meaningful communities. A vibrant Jewish culture can be sustained only by active community participation, and our present institutions stand in the way to rejuvenating our communities.

In the last chapter I will turn to the chavurah, Hebrew for "fellowship group," in which a small group of Jews band together, usually in the members' houses, to talk about Jewish affairs, pray or meditate, and find innovative ways to celebrate Jewish holidays and rituals.

To return to the main theme of this chapter, the belief in God, I find myself continually moved by Rosenzweig's story about the Jew who asked to whom he would pray to if there was no God. This anecdote haunts me. I make a distinction between belief and faith. Belief is a cognitive assertion that something is so, or happened in a certain way, or tells us how things are connected, or what may happen in the future. But faith is a deeper and more profound assertion, often with considerable passion, that something is about which there is

absolutely no objective evidence. Faith goes beyond belief in that it
refers to a conviction often with blind acceptance and the probability
that its validity will never be proved. For thousands of years Jews have
had faith, not belief, in God. Many still do, but many do not. Behind
and underpinning our Jewish God is 5,000 years of a glorious heritage,
which Rosenzweig dramatically believed stretches into eternity. We
have our heroes and heroines, our great wars, our martyrs and miracles
and of course the Torah, written or dictated by God Himself, thousands
upon thousands of pages of brilliant impeccable logical commentaries.
Our holidays and festivals, our 613 commandments dictate all the
precise rituals from waking moment to restful sleep, and then of course,
to top it all is the Holy Sabbath, which we celebrate weekly since the
time God Himself rested on the seventh day of creation. But this is
only the beginning! God is presented to us by our learned holy men,
and recently, women Rabbis. They speak to us from the Holy Ark in
appropriate holy attire. And they in turn are backed up by great
theological seminaries in which the study of God and the sacred texts
are rigorously supervised. Every major transition from birth to marriage
and death are religiously subscribed. All our institutions are respectful
of our Houses of God, and are its most devoted financial contributors
and supporters.

        So when the Jew asked who he would pray to if there was no
personal God, he was obviously asking a rhetorical question. Clearly,
his faith is majestically backed up by a massive array of institutions and
rituals, and a past, present, and future fully endorsed by our wisest men
and women. In addition the comfort he experiences in his prayer to God
he is now supported by a host of studies since the early fifties that find
belief and faith itself, endorsed by respected legitimate authorities, can
be enormously beneficial emotionally, physically and spiritually. A
direct link between faith and physical and emotional relief is now
indisputable.

        I am speaking of course of the placebo effect that was
discovered in the late fifties. Hundreds and hundreds of studies have
shown that dummy pills with nothing more than a dab of sugar have
been proven to be as effective as therapeutic medicines in relieving
patients' symptoms and curing their diseases. Surely this is one of the
great discoveries of the twentieth century and a powerful affirmation by
extension of the faith in God as a legitimate source of spiritual and
psychological well-being. It gives legitimacy to the idea that behind the

mystery of God. The belief that a God is hiding somewhere is sufficient not only to spiritual well-being, but to salvation after death. The belief in God is infinitely more important than whether there is a God or not. Science and religion have become bona fide partners. God, or the belief in God, not only makes us feel good, but positively gives us an edge in coping with all the setbacks and tragedies in life. This could very well be the reason, in addition, of course, to our shared mortality, that virtually every society has some sort of God or Gods. It is no wonder that, despite all our hardships, we are unwilling to give up this haven of grace and salvation.

It is now estimated that of the over 2,000 drugs used in ancient China virtually all lacked specific-disease relevant effects. The placebo will not work unless it is administered and backed up by an authority. The placebo of course will not be accepted, or believed to be efficacious, unless a reputable authority says so. For most people, when an authority says a placebo will work, it is quite irrelevant whether it works in "reality," but only whether the mind influences the body when one believes that it does work. Our faith and beliefs have enormous consequences for our behavior. In the growing debate whether science or religion merely describes rather than explains anything, it is quite evident that the placebo will effect remarkable cures, which in the past, were often referred to as "miracles." If it "works," it's "right."

For example, late in his life, the renowned Nobel Prize chemist Linus Pauling devoted his career to curing the common cold. He maintained that large doses of Vitamin C can prevent the onset of colds and minimize its symptoms. Whenever anyone has or thinks a cold is on the way, I automatically say, "lots of C's, hot tea, lemon and rest." I have total faith in Pauling and therefore in his belief in vitamin C. However, most scientific research has shown, that vitamin C does not prevent colds. Guess what? Right, I still automatically tell people, "lots of C's, hot tea and lemon and rest." In general, patients who expect to improve are more likely to do so.

My favorite placebo story is about surgeons at the University of Kansas Medical Center, who performed real operations on one group of patients and "placebo operations" on another group. The "placebo group" was told that they were going to have heart surgery, were given a local anesthetic and incisions were made in their chests, but the surgeons simply fiddled around for show. The patient placebos left the hospital with scars and some pain at the incision sites, but were convinced that they had undergone proper surgery, although they had not had any surgery. Result? Seventy percent of the patients who had the real surgery reported improvement, while all the "placebo-group" reported long-term improvement.

We return to our orthodox Jew who prays to a personal God with a better understanding of his great comfort in believing in God. But for many of the rest us, does the above research make any difference in our belief in God when we know that it is not God, but the belief in God that provides comfort? Until we have a better grasp of how beliefs influence our bodies and spirit, the deep connection between mind and matter, and the effects of placebos and God will continue to be regarded as miracles.

Meanwhile, it is important to underscore some of the negative and downright destructive consequences of faith. Nietzsche wrote: "A casual stroll through a lunatic asylum shows that faith does not prove anything." Another irreverent wag, Havelock Ellis, once wrote: "The whole religious complexion of the modern world is due to the absence from Jerusalem of a lunatic asylum." History is replete with demagogues who were extraordinarily successful in manipulating faith in themselves as emissaries of God. In 1665, more than half the world of Jewry believed that Shabbetai Zevi, a Turkish Jew, was the Messiah. Jews from all over the world packed up whatever belongings they had and made the long arduous trip to Palestine to sit at the feet of the Master. The Turkish sultan obviously was not taken in, and threatened Shabbetai to convert to Islam or be tortured to death. Shabbetai wisely and quickly abandoned his Messianic faith, and became a Muslim.

Later, it was revealed that Shabbetai was somewhat unbalanced, for he had a symbolic marriage with the Torah, pronounced the ineffable name of God, and married twice without consummating either marriage. Decades after Shabbatai, a new nut appeared on the Jewish scene, Jacob Frank, who claimed to be a successor to the previous nut. Frank voided all Jewish laws in the imminent arrival of the Messiah, and organized wife-swapping parties. (David Koresh, the Messiah at Waco, also slept with about half the women in his commune.) Apparently there were enough sane Jews around who remembered the Shabbetai fiasco so that Frank disappeared relatively quickly.

The most recent heralding of the Messiah is by a group of followers of the Lubavicher Hasidim, who were about to elevate their Master, Rabbi Shneersohn, to a messianic status when he died.

Apparently this movement died with his death and there are no reports about his resurrection and since he also did not produce a male heir, he had no successor, which was a bitter pill to swallow because of the Hasidic belief in a genetic basis to specially holy men. Rabbi Shneersohn created a global Habad network, sending young Lubavicher families as emissaries all over the world. He created a mobile unit of vans to reach out to disaffected young and old Jews to come back to God. Doesn't this globalization thrust and the use of modern techniques of "conversion," portend the great potential of global God-faith movements in the future? But the sad story is that Messianic movements since Jesus and His Apostles have not had a very successful track record.

The development in Israel of extreme Orthodox movements in which the Rabbis exercise complete autocratic domination and have moved into the political, economic, educational and civil spheres is really scary. The possibility, even remote, is that Israel could become a theocracy, which scares the hell out of me. It is, of course impossible to debate issues with extreme fundamentalist religious groups because they have God on their side. If they have God on their side then ipso facto they must be right and that ends the debate.

Recently an article appeared in the New York Times about Orthodox government officials inspecting the food that patrons in a restaurant were eating to insure that it was kosher. The often tolerant secular Israelis made such a huge outcry that the Orthodox government officials had to get their noses out of people's plates. Ultimately, there will be a show-down about whether Israel's democracy will have a complete separation of "church and state" or will drift into a theocracy.

I think that faith, the belief in something larger than one's individual personal well being and comfort, is of vital importance. This is one of the main purposes of this search into my Jewish identity. Viktor Frankl's belief in some ultimate Meaning in life is too abstract for my taste. I think also a belief in God as the Ultimate Meaning in life is a lazy, uninspiring and basically empty solution for me. Many of the mechanical routines and unchallenged rituals seem just plain silly to me. In my high-rise apartment building, young Orthodox Jews get the doormen to push the button to get the elevator and then press the button for the right floor. In this way, the Orthodox Jew is not violating the law of doing any work on the Sabbath. It is inconceivable to me to believe that God has any concern whatsoever about any one pressing an elevator button on the Sabbath.

I have enormous faith in the prophetic principles of justice, of peace, of help to the poor, the orphan, the widow, the diseased, the disabled and the eventual elimination of war. I am totally opposed to selfish egocentrism in which one looks out for one's individual comfort and salvation and "the devil take the hindmost."

I believe that a person has to work very hard to craft his / her mission in life. Without that effort I believe a person will easily slide into what his culture tells him / her is important and what to have faith in. That, to me, is deadly and precisely what I have been doing unthinkingly for the last forty years. Our American culture fosters narcissism. That has become very clear to me. I love my Jewish heritage and want to see it evolve further and flourish.

Throughout this book thus far I have stressed over and over again that a people's culture or heritage consists of a set values or beliefs <u>and</u> a network of institutions and shared activities in which our values are anchored. Both are necessary if a culture is to continue to flourish. Rabbi Hertzberg believes that even if a Jew is culturally an ignoramus, as long as he or she "acts Jewishly ," that is to say gives money to the United Jewish Appeal or gives his children a bar or bat mitzvah or shows up in a synagogue once a year on Yom Kippur then he / she is a Jew. Or, if a Jew continues to read Jewish books (in English of course) then he / she definitely is a Jew and will remain a Jew.

I think if that is what we Jewish Americans end up doing than we will gradually, but substantially, lose our Jewish identity or soul. My mission as a Jewish American becomes clear: I want to dedicate myself to joining a group of other Jews to study, discuss and create collective actions that will be based on our values. My guess is that this will probably propel me to join a chavurah of kindred Jewish-American and Israeli souls.

In our past, God was wrapped up with our sense of community. Did the break-up of our community turn us to agnosticism too; or, did the abandonment of God lead us also to the breakup of our vital community? Take your choice. But it is clear to me as I travel through my life in this book that I have a deep, deep need to belong to a community, probably without God.

CHAPTER NINE
ME AND ISRAEL

My wife is Israeli. Since we have been living together for over fourteen years, I am certainly qualified to have some thoughts about Israeli Ashkenazi Jews of Eastern European origin. Dr. Roni Berger was born in Tel Aviv, educated in the best high school in Israel, was a captain in the Israeli army, received a doctorate in Social Work from Hebrew University and taught at Tel Aviv and Hebrew Universities. She was married once before, adopted a boy and then was divorced ---- in that order.

I met Roni on my Sabbatical year in Israel and a year later Roni, her son Dan, and I were living together near Columbia University. In rapid order Roni became an American citizen, passed a New York State licensing exam to do therapy, taught at Columbia University School of Social Work and then at Adelphi School of Social Work, published a book in English, <u>Stepfamilies, A Multi-dimensional Perspective,</u> based on her doctoral dissertation, secured tenure and associate-professorship, and last year, single-handedly published 45% of Adelphi's School of Social Work publications. She is now consultant to major social service agencies in New York City. I will not delve into her activities, such as daily aerobic exercise, mountain hiking, guitar-playing and a passionate obsession for travel to everywhere in the world she is allowed into.

The only other point I want to make for now is her passion for taking care of her son. Wherever she worked, she was always home in time to greet her son when he returned from school. She could not imagine sending him away to summer camp, but she finally relented when he was fifteen years old so that he could be with his friends.

Roni was born in 1945, three years before the birth of the State of Israel. I know she will be angry with me when she reads about my description of all her accomplishments. But I risked taking my life into my hands for the purpose of making an extremely important point in a personal way about the Israelis. A great controversy prevails among academics about the extent it is possible to generalize to a large group of people from an in-depth analysis of one of its members. Many autobiographies by anthropologists and others certainly attest to the belief that this indeed is very possible.

Except for her first three years, Roni, the daughter of a Romanian father and Polish mother, grew up in the State of Israel. Her father was an orderly in a hospital. Life was hard and food was scarce, but there was never a doubt that they would manage on their own and that things would get better. Her "rags to riches" story mirrors my upbringing. She achieved considerable recognition in her field as quickly as I did in mine. Clearly, Roni is much more talented than I am. She has a fine grasp of Western literature and is more familiar with the Bible and other Jewish and Hebrew writings and history than most Rabbis.

Although Roni is fully acquainted with all the holidays and rituals, she is an atheist. Thus she is a deeply knowledgeable and committed Jew with the absence of our Jewish God and ritual observances. So much for the argument that God and religious rituals are the only salvation for Jewish survival.

Roni buys two weekend Hebrew newspapers and a Hebrew magazine every weekend. She is a member of a powerful Israeli "mafia" that knows and transmits to each other the very latest news in Israel. She reads all the current best-selling Hebrew novels and maintains an extremely active network of colleagues and friends both in the States and Israel. When we were living in a high-rise apartment building in Riverdale that had many Israeli families, monthly events took place for celebrating holidays. A Hebrew accordionist would lead the groups in Hebrew songs that went back to the childhoods of the Israelis present. Israelis use other Israelis for travel tickets, moving, buying real estate, repairs, etc., and they frequent Israeli restaurants, Israeli movie festivals and concerts and shows of a variety of Israeli artists and musicians. Many of their children attend private elementary and Junior high schools in which they are bilingual and study in both Hebrew and English.

Roni frequently visits Israel and teaches an intensive summer course at Beer Sheva's Ben Gurion University every year. A steady stream of Israelis stay over at our apartment when they come to the States. In short, Roni is very much a bi-national that is similar to bi-coastal Americans who live in Los Angeles and New York City. Many Israelis intend eventually to return to Israel to live. They never surrender their Israeli citizenship. If Israel would need them, as in case of another war, they would be on the next plane to Israel. No doubt about that.

The large influx of Israelis to the States reinvigorates Jewish Americans' commitment to Jewish values and identity as Jews. For example, I have become vastly more knowledgeable about Israel and our cultural heritage because of our Israeli friends here. My knowledge of Hebrew has greatly increased and made more dimensional my interest in our rich cultural heritage. I have visited every ancient site in Israel and explored every nook and cranny of the old city in Jerusalem. My wife and I have become heavily invested in Elem, an American foundation that raises money for distressed children and youth in Israel and sponsors numerous exchange missions with Israelis around new programs both in the States and Israel. Faculties in departments, like in Social Work, across all the Universities in Israel all know each other and are in frequent contact with one another. My study of the peer youth culture in a residential treatment setting, <u>Cottage Six</u>, has been translated into Hebrew and is well known in Israeli Universities and social service agencies.

In the future, especially after peace comes to this war torn land, I envisage a vast increase in exchanges between Israeli and American Jews. My vision also includes the proposition of a vast increase of "inter-marriages" between Americans and Israelis that will result in a new and exciting commitment of American Jews to our cultural heritage. Jews through the centuries have been wanderers and both American Jews and Israelis will increasingly seek exotic adventures with each other.

Why not? It is unfathomable to me that young Jews feel they have to go to ashrams with loin-cloth gurus in Tibet when they can experience a lifetime of mysticism by going up to the magic city of Safed and its art colony in the mountains of the Upper Galilee and bathe in the glorious sunshine and cool delicious air of Israeli pastures and hillsides ---- "....kissing with golden face the meadows green, / Gilding pale streams with heavenly alchemy." In the 15th century two of our greatest Cabalists, Rabbis Isaac Lure and Joseph Karo settled in this breath-taking panoramic city, said to touch God. Here you can meditate on <u>En-Soph</u> (the transcendent God who remains forever beyond the grasp of the human mind and can be comprehended only through the <u>shirt</u>, the ten Divine potencies (wisdom, intelligence, lovingkindness, power, beauty, eternity, majesty, etc.) Here through mystical piety you can experience a unique adherence to God called "<u>devout</u>." You can become familiar with <u>Tzimtzum,</u> the God who originally is "all in all," contracting Himself into Himself," leaving a vacuum in which creation can take place by an emanation of a spiritual beam flowing from the En Sop. Here you can experience Tikkun ----- releasing the holy Divine sparks from defilement and through mystic meditation, help bring about redemption and the advent of the Messiah. How can you possibly compare all of this Divine mysticism to learning "ahm" meditation on some Himalayan mountain?

Israel is replete with miraculous sites that will beckon you to return to them again and again. If you know anything at all about our rich past you may want to get down on your knees and kiss the holy ground as I do when I get off an El-Al plane or listen to the pounding of your heart when you go up to Jerusalem, the spiritual capital of the world.

I am convinced that if we could create a stimulating year abroad exchange program of American and Israeli students while in college, we could have a new commitment to Judaism that goes far beyond the conspicuous consumption and display of our disgraceful bar mitzvahs and bat mitzvahs. What if all the vast sums of money which go into our fossilized synagogues could be used to create a new flowering and renaissance of Jewish identity among our young folk and adults both here and in Israel? Israel is not just there across the ocean, it is in our hearts, but now must become an integral part of our minds and souls.

If mysticism is not your cup of tea, a year on a kibbutz will flood your mind and senses with a completely different kind of social order than we have than in the United States. This can give you an alternative to your narcissistic preoccupation with yourself and becoming rich and famous. Despite all of its current problems the kibbutz remains one of mankind's finest experiments of a society built on democracy and socialism. To be able to participate in such a cooperative society before you embark on your "pursuit of loneliness" is a privilege that you can experience only in Israel.

To return to the deconstruction of the European-Israeli character that I rudely interrupted with my paean to Israel, I want to extract a cluster of traits that I find typical of Israelis. My list includes the following:

Independent, ambitious, high self-esteem, intense loyalty to family and State, disciplined, strong belief in democracy and separation of "church and State", individualistic, intellectual, assertive, social welfare oriented, "second to none", even highly consumer oriented, invincible mentality.

All of the above character traits are brilliantly portrayed in the opening scene of <u>Kippur,</u> an Israeli film by Amos Gitai about the Yom Kippur war. The war started on October 6, 1973, the holiest day in the Jewish calendar. Egypt and Syria simultaneously invaded the territories Israel conquered in the 1967 Six-Day War. Egypt attacked in the Suez, and Syria in the Golan Heights. The size of their attacking armies equaled the combined forces of NATO in Europe.

Within a week, Israel had driven Egyptian and Syrian forces back to where they had been before the war. The price was very heavy, by the time the war ended 2,700 Israeli soldiers were dead, four times as many as had died in the Six-Day war. Let us return to the <u>Kippur</u> movie.

The opening scene is eerie ---- it is very very early in the quiet morning of Yom Kippur, the high holiday of penitence, and the streets are empty and forlorn. The scene shifts to a soldier in a battered compact car who is picking up another soldier to take to their army units. The soldiers are nonchalant, very relaxed and calm, almost as if they were gong to the office, or perhaps on an outing to the countryside. The sneak attack and looming war is never referred to.

In the car, the picked up soldier kids the driver about his beat-up car and refusal to get a decent car. The driver then launches into a discussion about the evils of consumerism and then quotes from Herbert Marcuse's <u>One-Dimensional Man,</u> which is a very powerful, deep, complex Marxist critique of how people are brainwashed under capitalism to insatiably crave always newer and better things until they turn themselves into one dimensional people or things.

I was absolutely flabbergasted. I don't think there are many professors at Columbia University who have ever heard of Marcuse, much less of course ever having read this brilliant critique of Western civilization. Harry Goldin, the writer and journalist, wrote a book called <u>Only in America.</u> Well, only in Israel, I believe, could you have two soldiers talking about Marcuse's critique of capitalism, especially at a moment when they are about to go into battle and possibly lose their lives. Only in Israel!

Sometimes an incident, real or imagined, can speak volumes about a people, their relationships, and their culture. That opening scene of <u>Kippur</u> will forever be etched in my mind as the epitome of the Israeli character. The Arabs continuous dream about throwing all the Israelis into the sea is the triumph of wishful thinking over reality.

For me this incident has deep significance. Two reserve soldiers go off to war with complete confidence that they can cope with the sneak attack and soundly defeat the attacking Arabs. Echoes of Pearl Harbor. But, the difference is that for two thousand years, Jews were on the defensive. They had mastered, to a large extent, the skills of a persecuted minority, passively sucking up to the <u>goyim</u> so that they could survive rather than be subjected to overwhelming extinction forces when they rebelled. And what a terribly bloody cost; the crushing of the Maccabean revolt against the Romans; Masada; he Spanish Inquisition; the innumerable pogroms and forced ghettozation in Russia and Poland. Then, of course, the beastly and unspeakably barbaric Nazi genocide and the complete destruction of ghettos such as the Warsaw Ghetto. And how about all our martyrs and scapegoats ----- Bar Kokhba and his followers, Rabbi Akiba, Juda ben Bava, Hananiah ben Teradion, Mendel Beilis, Dreyfus, Leo Frank, Anne Frank, Hannah Senesch, Walter Benjamin and on and on and on? Millions of helpless martyrs. And what about all of the defamation, vilification, taunts, insults, ridicule, derision and ever present threat of annihilation for two thousand years?

And now, two Israeli soldiers and the Israeli armed forces move the entire world experience of Jews for 2000 years from a passive helpless defensive stance, to a self-assured, aggressive, offensive attacking position. It is only many years later that I began to fully realize the enormous impact of Israeli's military victories on me personally. I "marched with the Israelis" spiritually; when the 1967 war broke out. I joined the same day millions of Jews all over America flocked to the synagogues with wide-open pocketbooks and purses to support the Israelis. Their fight was our fight and I was prepared to go to Israel myself to do what I could to help the war effort (it was one of the great disappointments of my life that before I could ship out for Israel the war was over!)

Two soldiers, calmly and totally self-assured, completely transformed Jews all over the world from passive accommodation to the status quo to taking their destiny in their own hands. No Rambos, Clint Eastwoods, Pattons, Gary Coopers at "High Noon, no way, none of that bull-shit, two soldiers welded to a people who would not only "never forget or never forgive," but will force the current enemy never to forget. The days of a cowered Jewry, passively insinuating itself to a prejudiced authority and the anti-Semites, is over for good. I feel more proud of and aggressive about my Jewishness because of the emergence of the State of Israeland - its stunning victories, bolder than ever before.

The phrase now used in Jewish academic circles to describe Jewry before the State of Israel is the "ideology of affliction." For two thousand years Jews debated about martyrdom or conversion, Orthodoxy or assimilation and everything in-between, but because of the creation of the State of Israel, these choices can no longer be imposed by Gentiles. How much we want to hold on to our tradition is entirely our choice as Jews. Israel liberated us forever and presents us with new challenges.

The main issue now pervading American Jewry is the extent of its shift in orientation to Israel from "mobilization" to "personal meaning." Mobilization refers to the primacy for years of American Jewry mobilizing its economic, political and spiritual resources to support the Israeli State, especially its war effort and the immigration of millions of destitute Jews from Arab countries and the former Soviet Union. It is clear that in recent years, the urgency of Israeli support has definitely waned, particularly among younger Jews. Many believe Israel is out of mortal danger. Its survival, stability and growth are assured. Now what?

Many writers and thinkers would like very much to believe that a shift in relating to Israel would now move to considerations of the meaning of Israel in their personal lives, very much like my effort in this chapter. The question of course immediately emerges ---- personal meaning about what? Here I think Liebman and Cohen and Sklare and Greenblum have developed an important theory about the specific significant paradigmatic shift in values by non-Orthodox Jews both in Israel and the States. [Charles S. Liebman and Steven M. Cohen. 1990. Two Worlds of Judaism: The Israeli and American Experiences (New Haven: Yale University Press) and Marshal Sklare and Joseph Greenblum. 1979. Jewish Identity on the Suburban Frontier (Chicago: University of Chicago Press.)

According to Liebman and Cohen, American Judaism is characterized by four distinctive features: universalism, moralism,

individualism, and voluntarism. I have tinkered with these terms and I
have my own spin which I think makes them more clear. I think it is
also useful to contrast each of the above traits with its opposite with the
proviso that this is only a typology that contrasts the two orientations
on the following page in terms of emphasis and they have a lot of
overlapping. I also highlight the trait contrasts by giving to each group
a title that integrates them into a gestalt.

HUMANISTIC	GOD-CENTERED
UNIVERSALISM	PARTICULARISM
MORALISM	RITUALISM
INDIVIDUALISM	UNIVERSALISM
CHOICE	COERCION

PARTICULARISM VS. UNIVERSALISM. Particularism
refers to an emphasis of the special features of Judaism and its religion.
The idea of a "chosen people" via religion sets the Jews off as different
from other people. This orientation focuses on the distinctive rituals,
symbols, prayers, etc., of the Jewish religion. Universalism, by
contrast, stresses the common humanity of all peoples. Jews are no
more "chosen" than any other people. All people are to be treated
equally without regard to race, religion, national origin, sex, sexual
preferences, etc. In Alcoholic-Anonymous (AA) meetings, reference is
made to a "Higher Power," which includes all the various Gods,
including simply a Transcendent Spirit.

RITUALISM VS. MORALISM. In ritualism the focus is upon
the scrupulous observance of a set of routines to fulfill religious
obligations. Moralism, in contrast, concentrates on ethical behavior,
what is right and just in human relationships. Moralism is much more
philosophically oriented, whereas ritualism is preoccupied with
following rites that have not much changed over generations.

INSTITUTIONALISM VS. PERSONALISM. An
institutionalism orientation follows, without questions or exception, the
prescribed traditional way of carrying out rules, regulations, and
routines. Any institutional modification has to go through a
complicated and sustained system of prescribed institutionalized
methods for change. Personalism focuses much more on the personal
meaning of any act, routine or belief. The authority shifts from God, or
the institution, or the ritual authority to the individual. In the parlance

of psychology the locus of control is inner-directed rather than outwardly directed.

COERCION VS. CHOICE. Coercion consists of control, vested in some external source, and is the way for one to identify with an ethnic group, a religion, a particular synagogue, etc. Choice gives individuals the freedom to decide how "Jewish" they want to be without any social sanctions. Like in personalism, choice turns over to the individual, the autonomy to express his identity or religion or affiliations.

Over forty years ago, in my study of Jewish Orthodoxy in Milwaukee (described in Chapter Six), I showed how Jews gradually and systematically abandoned rituals that significantly interfered with their work and newfound leisure activities. The inexorable march toward more and more self-fulfillment and personal choice over institutional coercive rituals has continued unabated as more and more American Jews become non-observant. A recent report (The Jewishness of Israelis: Responses to the Gutman Report) from the Gutman Center, a prestigious Israeli survey organization, states that the "totally non-observant" Israelis represent twenty per cent of the population. The "catch" is that this group is disproportionately Ashkenazi, the best educated sector of the population, and exercises great influence in the elite media and higher education.

So what is going on in the States and in Israel? For a significant proportion of Jews in the States and Israel, individuals are free to decide whether to be "Jewish," how much so, and at what intensity, with very little concern of the sanctions from institutionalized Judaism. And like what I am doing right now, the search for a meaningful Jewish identity can occur at any time. The really sad caveat, however, is that Jewish institutions have done such a terrible job in educating us in our rich cultural heritage, that the choice of how and what Jewish elements to integrate into our life style is based on a terrifying ignorance of our own culture.

We are a steadily fragmenting people. Many of us do not get what we want, or what we think we want from our present Jewish institutions. Why should we support them? Israel is becoming more distant as it exercises less and less impact personally on our Jewishness. It is fairly clear that younger Jews especially, are continuing systematic abandonment of not only Orthodoxy, but also the ersatz opportunistic creations of the Conservative and Reform Establishments. If the latter believe that their huge paper organization of indifferent adherents is going to last much very much longer, I think that they are in store for a big big surprise.

The movement toward a humanistic philosophy outlined in the previous pages does give a direction for those of us who are seeking a progressive Jewish-American identity. We want a more universal connection with progressives of all faiths. We want an ethical rather than a ritual foundation of our beliefs. We want a faith that has an impact on our daily thinking and activities and above all, we want the right to choose to include, in our philosophy, what makes sense to us. But there is a big catch here. How do we integrate the above perspective with specific elements from our rich cultural heritage?

Progressive American and Israeli Jews share a deep fissure in our tradition. In the States, young people are assimilating in droves, and in Israel, a large number of Jews are unable to find meaning in the power of Jewish traditions and in our heritage. The challenge in Israel and the States is to fashion a meaningful Jewish consciousness in progressives' current life-styles. It is not too late. We liberal-democratic Jews for the most part feel that we are a part of the Jewish people and want to preserve some of our Jewish traditions. But we are selective.

Within the next 25 years, the core of Jewish life will revolve primarily around the two remaining major Jewish "civilizations" in the United States and Israel. In both societies, an increasing number of Jews will become disaffected by Jewish religious institutions. Jews have become, and will continue to be, significant in the world at large. The three greatest creative figures of the nineteenth and twentieth centuries, Marx, Freud and Einstein, were Jews. Marx converted. Freud and Einstein did not, but all three shared a deeply humanitarian philosophy that is now characterized by a credo that emphasizes a common progressive destiny and ethical rather than ritualistic behavior. Personal meaning of traditions rather than institutional preservation and the right, rather the mandate, for people to choose for themselves what makes sense is the direction we must continue on.

The beginning of wisdom is to admit and to welcome the recognition that you may be lost. Many of us are adrift. We have lost our moorings. I don't think the way back to Judaism is for each of us individually to find the key that will re-open the door to our rich heritage. I think we progressives have to band together to work together to evolve creatively, a viable Jewish communal ethos. We need new forms of how to commune with each other which will be addressed in the next last two chapters. When I go to Israel for extended periods, which included two sabbaticals, a very subtle and profound psychic change occurs, which I just recently recognized. In Israel, I shed my Jewish defensive armor and stop recording my automatic categorization of people as Jewish or non-Jewish. My sensitive smell of anti-Semitism atrophies and my self-consciousness as a Jew evaporates. In Israel I am a member of the majority group in contrast to the minority group status that I have in the States.

But another insidious attitude infects me. I am not going to get embroiled in the unproductive assertion that Israelis are racist visa-vie the Arabs, and, the Ashkenazi visa-vie the Sephardic Jews from Arab countries. I don't believe that American Jews are any less racist than Israeli Jews. So far as I know I don't think there is a society in the world in which the dominant group is not prejudicial toward minority groups in their midst. In all these societies, prejudice and discrimination are masks for privilege, status and power; they are used as weapons against insecurity and threats to their domination.

Since racism is endemic everywhere, the more useful discussion is how to confront it. Since the gross overt discrimination against Jews in the United States is far less prevalent than in the past, prejudice is now much more subtle, but often it takes only a few words to illuminate its covert, deep and widespread existence.

Just today, May 25, 01, a strange concept appeared in an article in The New York Times on page twelve that I had never heard of before. Reverend John D. Castellani, president of the drug treatment program Teen Challenge International U.S.A., had spoken in testimony before a House subcommittee regarding President Bush's proposal to channel government money to religious social service programs. Most Jews adamantly oppose this legislation as violating the church-state separation principle and that there is no way to separate the efforts to proselytize from the efforts to treat people.

Reverend Castellani testified that while some of the Jewish clients who had gone through his evangelical Christian program returned to their Jewish faith, others had become "completed Jews." In a follow up interview, he maintained that although converting was their choice, the program "naturally encourages embracing Christian teaching." This is a bombshell that will probably help kill the proposed legislation.

Now I learned that the term "completed Jews" is used by some evangelical Christians and Jewish converts to describe Jews who have accepted Jesus as their Savior. Thus a Jew who has not accepted Jesus is not "complete." I can think of only two explanations for this weird testimony. One is the idea that Jews are an inferior people, note the term "completed Jew," who have not accepted the true religion of Jesus is so embedded in some Christian teaching and churches that it could possibly not be disputed. It's the gospel truth. Thus the good reverend could not even imagine that some people, especially most Jews, would consider this term as gross insulting prejudice. Why else would he publicly announce this outlandish remark before an open Congressional committee? The only other reason that I can think of is that he is just plain stupid for revealing to the world the revelation of inferior uncompleted Jews.

It is precisely these kinds of stupid blunders that help us Jews understand how endemic anti-Semitism can be in a Christian society. The Anti-Defamation League will make sure that everyone will learn about this strange new concept and increase the opposition to the government giving money to religious organizations. The general point I want to make is that in recent years, American Jews have become so sensitive to prejudice that when it is revealed, it is immediately publicly attacked and "never forgotten." Years ago Jesse Jackson, who is mostly friendly to Jews, called New York "Hymietown" and we Jews will never let him and others forget it.

The way to curb prejudice is to resolutely attack it, even the most casual remark, whenever and wherever it raises its ugly head. Jews in the States and Israel are increasingly confronting other Jews and gentiles who express prejudicial attitudes. The major problem is to expose the more subtle forms of prejudice. For example, some American Jews (notice I did not say, "American Jews") believe that Israelis are aggressive, brash, rude, arrogant, aggressive, etc. Prejudice essentially consists of creating a category of negative traits and identifying particular individuals as belonging in this negative category. The "logic" is impeccable: Israelis are aggressive. Yossi is an Israeli. Therefore Yossi is aggressive.

In Israel I have often heard repeated that Arabs cannot be trusted. The same process occurs as above: Arabs cannot be trusted. Ahmed is an Arab. Therefore Ahmed is not to be trusted.

This prejudice is backed up often by statements such as, "you don't live in the Middle East," "you have never dealt with Arabs. Arabs say one thing and mean just the opposite," and so on and so forth. The most frequent story that I have heard in Israel is about the frog and the scorpion that made a deal for the frog to carry the scorpion on his back across a pond. Midway the scorpion bites the frog and they both drown. Then the story-teller usually adds, "that's the Middle East." I suppose in the Arab version the Israeli is the scorpion. It is very difficult to change this stereotype that many Israelis have of Arabs.

Some Israelis often have extremely negative attitudes toward Sephardim, dark-skinned Jews from Arab countries. This prejudice accounted in part for the ouster of Labor as the dominant political party in Israel. Recently, I attended a joint mission meeting of Israelis and Americans who were concerned about the high dropout rate of Sephardim from school. The group of highly educated professionals included social workers, psychologists, educators, counselors, child-care workers and top government officials from the ministries of education and social welfare. At one point, one person said that not only were Sephardic youth dropping out of schools in high numbers, but that those who did go to school were getting an inferior education. She used the specific phrase that the "teachers were babysitters." No one reacted to this blatant discrimination and the conversation continued.

I was furious. I seethed. I had to use all my self-control not to shout: "Racism! How would you feel if your child went to a school in which the teachers were baby-sitters?" Then another Israeli had the gall to say, "what's wrong with baby-sitting, at least that's something." Both American and Israeli members of the commission seemed to think that there was nothing wrong with this attitude. I think that if teachers and administrators in the States publicly expressed this kind of wholesale prejudice they could very easily be fired from their jobs. A protest group of minority group parents would appear the next day in front of the school.

Both Israeli and American Jews have a lot of work ahead of them to root out prejudice and discrimination, both toward outsiders and within the Jewish community of one group toward another. I love Israel. I am better, a "complete Jew," for its existence. Israel is my homeland even though I am not an Israeli citizen. I like to consider myself an honorary Israeli citizen. Like most Israelis in the States who believe that they will eventually return to Israel, I too can see myself retiring in Israel. Meanwhile at the end of the Passover Seder I say the immortal words ---- "next year in Jerusalem."

CHAPTER TEN
HOW THE JEWISH JOKE BINDS US TOGETHER

The Jewish joke binds together all the Jews of the world. The Jewish joke is a major defensive response; part of the "ideology of affliction" that we have evolved over 2000 years of oppression, anti-Semitism and expulsions. 2000 years of persecution are packed into the "innocuous" joke.

The Jewish joke consolidates our identity by contrasting our "superior" values and beliefs with Gentiles, or Goyim. It is our way of overcoming minority status in an overwhelmingly Christian world with "them," non-Jews.

Lenny Bruce, the irrepressible stand-up comic who performed in Greenwich Village and was mercilessly persecuted for his explicit sexual references, had a popular routine that contrasted "Jewish and Goyish:"

Dig: I'm Jewish. Count Basie's Jewish. Ray Charles is Jewish. Eddie Cantor's Goyish. B'nai B'rith is Goyish; Hadassah, Jewish.
If you live in New York or any other big city, you are Jewish. It doesn't matter even if you're Catholic; if you live in New York, you're Jewish. If you live in Butte, Montana, you're going to be Goyish even if you're Jewish. Kool-Aid is Goyish. Evaporated milk is Goyish even if the Jews invented it. Chocolate is Jewish and fudge is Goyish. Fruit salad is Jewish. Lime jello is Goyish. Lime soda is *very* Goyish. All Drake's Cakes are Goyish. Pumpernickel is Jewish and, as you know, white bread is very Goyish. Instant potatoes, Goyish. Black cherry soda's very Jewish; macaroons are *very* Jewish. Negroes are all Jews. Italians are all Jews. Irishmen who have rejected their religion are Jews. Mouths are very Jewish. And bosoms. Baton-twirling is very Goyish. Underwear is definitely Goyish. Balls are Goyish. Titties are Jewish. Celebrate is a Goyish word. Observe is a Jewish word. Mr. *and* Mrs. Walsh are *celebrating* Christmas with Major Thomas Moreland, USAF, (ret.), while Mr. and Mrs. Bromber *observed* Hanukkah with Goldie and Arthur Schindler from Kiamesha, New York.

Many second and third generation American-born Jews would not "get" Lenny Bruce's humor. Many of them have been so acculturated that they have lost some of the subtle, precious distinctions delineated by Bruce. I, on the other hand, not only love this routine, but could easily add my own observations:

Pastrami is Jewish, roast beef is Goyish; a Chevrolet is Jewish, a Jaguar is Goyish; lox is Jewish, kippers are Goyish (English-Goyish); whiskey is Jewish, gin-and-tonic is Goyish; chicken soup is definitely Jewish, clam chowder is Goyish; Saturday is Jewish, Sunday is Goyish; the Catskills are Jewish, Bermuda is Goyish; El-Al is Jewish, TWA is Goyish; kishkas are Jewish, steak is Goyish; heartburn is Jewish, liver problems are Goyish; near-sighted is Jewish, far-sighted is Goyish; God is Jewish, Jesus is Goyish; masochism is Jewish, sadism is Goyish; a psychiatrist is Jewish, a physician is Goyish; Miami Beach is Jewish, Paradise Island is Goyish; a doctor and lawyer are Jewish, an engineer and an architect are Goyish; Jerry Seinfeld is Jewish, Humphrey Bogart is Goyish; Einstein is Jewish, Newton is Goyish; Bill Clinton is Jewish, George W. Bush is Goyish; a baked potato is Jewish, French fries are Goyish, Martin Luther King is Jewish, Norman Vincent Peale is Goyish.

In most of the above contrasts, Jewish is portrayed as simpler, cheaper, less ostentatious, more direct, and more "real," as opposed to the sophisticated, snooty, superficial, and conspicuous "Goyish." The disappearance of these differences, still most pronounced among immigrant Jews, points to the evisceration of specifically Jewish mores, customs, and habits among second and third generation native-born Jewish Americans.

Jackie Mason contrasts Gentiles and Jews after seeing a play. The Gentiles say:

"Drink?"

"Yep."

"Good idea."

Jews say:

"Let's eat," or:

"Does anyone know a good Chinese restaurant in the neighborhood?"

A Jewish and Gentile boy were arguing about the existence of Santa Claus in Santa's presence. "Santa Claus is real," the Gentile boy was arguing. "It's just a story," the Jewish boy replied, "make believe." Santa leaned over and whispered in Yiddish: *"Naar, darfs ihm sagen?"* Translation: "Foolish boy, why do you have to tell him?"

Significantly, the Jew is dressed up like Santa to make some money. (Wearing disguises to survive is a well-known Jewish experience!) He enlists another Jew in his "conspiracy" to fool the "enemy." He does this in part by using a language, Yiddish, that the Gentile could not understand. The subtext is that clever deception is one of the main guns in the Jewish armory, and the Jewish boy needs to be taught this.

A teacher asks the students in her class to each consider who their favorite hero is. A French student says "Napoleon." An English student says: "Churchill." Then, a Jewish student says: "Jesus."

"Moishe, I thought you were a Jew," the teacher says, confused. "Listen," Moishe answered, "business is business."

A priest and a Rabbi were having a friendly chat. The priest said, "In Judaism, there is no central theological figure. In Catholicism, we have St. John the Baptist, Mary, Mother of God, and of course, the King of Kings, Jesus..."

The Rabbi replied "Father, you must understand that we think of Jesus as a nice Jewish boy who went into his father's line of work."

An anti-Semitic minister asked all the Jews to leave his church. He then went on to ask the families of those Jews to leave the church, and then, said their Jewish ancestors would not be honored or welcomed either. At this point, the Virgin Mary whispered to the babe in her arms "Nu zindele, mir darf ahem gehen." ("Now, darling Son, we have to go home.")

A Rabbi and a priest go to Miami Beach to compare their ability to perform miracles. The Rabbi begins to walk on the water, but the priest keeps falling. The Rabbi yells at him "Walk on the rocks, walk on the rocks!"

A few Jewish jokes relate the plight of the Jews to other oppressed minorities.

A Jew boards a train and finds himself seated next to a Black man who is reading a Yiddish newspaper. "Excuse me," he inquires, "are you Jewish?" The Black man looks intensely at the Jew and says (in Yiddish): "Noch dos fallt mir;" translation: "That's all I need."

We see that to be Black or Jewish is tough enough so that one does not need to be both. And even if I am Jewish too, you don't have to broadcast it to the world. Thus the expression "noch dos fallt mir," is used whenever one adds or thinks about adding unnecessarily more burdens to himself.

The Holocaust cemented the distrust most Jews feel toward Gentiles to the point that it sometimes reaches paranoid dimensions. After all, the world did stand by as the Nazis slaughtered the Jews. The less the Jew is acculturated in the host culture, the more suspicious the Jew is of the Goyim, and sometimes, distrust is an almost instinctive expectation of the worst, so that a Jew may never lower his/her guard.

A teacher points to pictures of Hitler and Goering side by side on the wall. She asks a little boy: "Who goes in between?" Little Hans answers "Jesus, of course."

In Nazi Germany there was a blackout in Berlin. In the darkness, a robber holds up a Jew, demanding his wallet.

"Thank God," the Jew tells the robber, "I thought you were the Gestapo."

Storm troopers confront an elderly Jew. "Who is responsible for all of Germany's troubles?"

The Jew replies: The bicycle riders and the Jews.

Storm troopers: Why the bicycle riders?

Jew: Why the Jews?

During the late 1930's, the Grossmans lived in a German neighborhood. A gang taught little Sammy the Nazi salute. The Grossmans tried everything to stop Sammy's outstretched arm from rising like a Fascist, but could not change it. So, they went to a doctor, who was also unsuccessful in getting little Sammy to alter his behavior. Mrs. Grossman finally asked sadly: "Doctor, do you think we'll have to amputate?"

An elderly Jewish woman goes up the aisle of a train and asks each passenger if they are Jewish. The first, second, third and fourth each say "no." Finally, a fifth passenger says, "Yes, I'm Jewish."

"Excuse me," the elderly Jewish woman asks her, "Do you know what time it is?"

We see that complete distrust is the basis for what would be considered exaggerated paranoia in Gentiles.

A Jew arrives at the station as the train is pulling out. He raises his fist and yells, "anti-Semite!"

A Nazi passed by a Jew and hissed: "Schwein!" The Jew doffed his hat and introduced himself: "Steinberg."

The German ambassador was boasting about Nazi Germany. "We have great treasures above and below the soil: below the soil, we have great stores of coal, potash, iron and many other minerals; above ground we have Hitler, Goebbels and Goering." A reporter inquired: "Are you sure those treasures are not distributed in reverse?"

One Jew asks another: "When will Hitler die?"

Answer: "On a Jewish holiday."

Hitler was lowered and raised a dozen times in his grave, and each time he got a bigger ovation.

Under Fascism, the Jews were exterminated, but under Communism, they did not fare so well either.

The commissar insisted that with the Communists in power, everyone would eat strawberries and cream in the winter. Schoenburg objected that he did not like strawberries and cream. The commissar insisted: "In winter, you will eat strawberries and cream!"

Jews are preoccupied (for obvious reasons) with figuring out who is or is not Jewish. An American tourist in China visits a small synagogue in Beijing, and surprises the congregation by praying there. Finally, one of the Chinese asks him: "Are you Jewish?" The tourist replies: "Yes, I am Jewish." "That's funny," the Chinese says, "you don't look Jewish."

Years ago, when anti-Semitism was much more open than it is now, a real estate broker refused to rent a house to a Jew, who told the agent: "This is the reason Jesus was born in a manger."

The Pines, an anti-Semitic resort, did not allow Jews. When Katzenberg tried to register, the clerk demanded to know if he were Jewish. Katzenberg replied: "I'm a Quaker." Then, the clerk demanded that Katzenberg say something in the language of the Quakers. "Geh in drerd," Katzenberg told him in Yiddish to "Go to Hell."

Mikey runs into the house yelling that Babe Ruth has hit another home run. His grandfather asks "Iz das gut far di Yidden?" ("Is this good for Jews?") The exaggerated preoccupation of the Jew for his own and for safety marks Jews off from the Gentiles and warns them never to put their arms down.

Of course, special mistrust is set aside for the presumed motives of Jewish converts and other "assimilationists."

Four converts to Christianity were explaining their conversions. The first speaks about a Gentile girl whom he loves. The second reports that he had an opportunity to become president of a company. The third wanted to advance at his university and the fourth claimed that he had come to believe in the Holy Trinity, but was rudely interrupted by the others "That you can tell to your Gentile friends!"

On his deathbed, Levy declared that he wanted to convert. His family was shocked. Levy explained: "Better one of them than us."

Lewisohn became so successful financially that he changed his name to "Hamilton." His partner Levin did the same thing, so that when someone called to speak to Hamilton, the secretary would ask: "Lewisohn or Levin?" (In a sequel to this story, Hamilton becomes so successful that he changes his name back to Lewisohn.)

The Reform Temple is often criticized for adopting Gentile practices, and watering down traditional Jewish customs.

One Jew asks another, "How can you tell a Reform Temple?"

"It is closed on Yom Kippur because of a Holiday."

Distrust of Gentiles easily spreads to Jews' distrust of each other:

Two business partners are discussing robbery precautions for their mutual business. "For now, we don't have to worry," one says to the other, "we are both here."

A Jew orders a turkey sandwich in a restaurant. "No turkey," says the waiter. "Okay," says the diner, "I'll have a chicken sandwich." The waiter says, "Listen, if we had chicken you would have gotten your turkey sandwich."

A defendant tells the judge his name is "Abraham Solomon Ginsberg O'Rourke." The judge asks: "What's the 'O'Rourke' for?"

Defendant: "For protection."

Jews are so accustomed to having enemies and living with their own opposition to them that they create "enemies" among themselves, and even oneself may become the enemy.

A Jew is marooned alone on an island and after ten years is finally visited by outsiders. He proudly leads them to a clearing and shows them two magnificent synagogues that he has built. "But why two?" asks one of the visitors. The Jew replied: "This one I like; that one is terrible."

Two Jewish salesmen meet in the Minsk railway station. One asks the other where he is going and he says he is going to Pinsk.

"Aha," thinks the other Jew, "he is telling me he is going to Pinsk, but actually he wants me to believe that he is staying here in Minsk, but I really know that in actuality he is going to Pinsk." So, he says out loud: "Liar!"

Mike bought a length of fabric from Italy and asked various tailors to make a suit, but each tailor refused, saying he hadn't gotten enough fabric. Finally, he found an elderly tailor who agreed to make him a suit. Several weeks later, Mike came to pick it up and noticed that the tailor's son was wearing a suit made of the same cloth.

"How did you have enough fabric to make me a suit when the other tailors said they didn't?" Mike asked.

"Maybe the sons of the other tailors were bigger," came the reply.

Jake and Sam had been partners in a successful clothing store for years and they knew each other as you would know the fingers on your hand. Sam finally took his first vacation in Florida in years, but could not resist calling Jake to see how things were. "Oy, Sam, can you imagine? We had a burglary last night and they took all the money." Sam responded in a friendly, but firm manner: "Jake, put it back."

Jewish parents insist that their children become doctors and lawyers.

Two grandmothers are pushing their daughter's babies in strollers. One asks the other how the babies are. The other replies:

"Fine. The baby boy is a lawyer. The baby girl is the wife of a doctor."

A psychiatrist meets another psychiatrist and suggests that they go to his office to talk because his rates are cheaper.

Greenberg goes to a psychiatrist and for the first three sessions, not a word passes between them. At the beginning of the fourth session Greenberg asks the psychiatrist: "Maybe you can use a partner?'

Long before the "Second Opinion" became institutionalized, the Jew had a healthy skepticism about doctors' efficacy. A Jewish man goes to the doctor to find out what to do about a swelling bump on his head. The doctor tells him to put cold compresses on it. "That's funny," says the patient, "my babi [grandmother] says to use hot compresses."

"My babi says cold compresses," the doctor says firmly.

A Jewish girl returns pregnant from college.
Dad: "Who's the father?"
Daughter: "I don't know."
Dad: "Already two years in college and you don't have sense to ask: 'With whom am I having this pleasure?'"

A single Reform Rabbi is given a paid vacation in Las Vegas. He registers in a hotel and is surprised to see the door to his room open and a scantily dressed gorgeous woman warmly welcoming him in. The Rabbi is shocked, and immediately calls the manager to complain. But in the corner of his eye, he sees the young woman getting dressed.
    "Where are you going?" the Rabbi asks her.
    "Well, I just heard you on the telephone," she answers.
    Rabbi: "Oh, I'm angry with the management, not with you!"

A young couple went to a Reform Rabbi because the wife was sexually dissatisfied with her husband. The Rabbi said "I suggest I show him how it is done and he watch me." When the Rabbi was finished, he asked the husband if now, he knew what to do. His wife interrupted his reply: "Rabbi, do it again; he is such a dummy!"

Two stubborn men could not settle an argument so they went to a Rabbi. The Rabbi was out, so his wife, the Rebetzen, agreed to help them. They both admitted that they were the most stubborn people in the world, and the Rebetzen interrupted them. "No way. My husband and I are the most stubborn people in the world. After we were married, we went to a hotel with twin beds. Each one of us refused to go to the other's bed and we went home, where we also have twin beds.""But you have six children," cried one of the men. Rebetzen: "You're right, but the shamus [janitor] is not a stubborn man."

A Jewish woman goes to a psychiatrist. He tells her that they have special tools for finding out what is really on people's minds. He raises a pencil and asks her what she thinks it is, and she says, "that's a pencil." He raises a knife and she says, "knife." He points a finger toward the ceiling and she says, "finger." All the time the doctor is grimacing at her answers, so the woman tells him in some exasperation: "Look, you may think all those things are phallic symbols, but to me, they are a pencil, a knife and a finger."

A man told his psychiatrist that now that he was getting older, he had trouble chasing women. The psychiatrist suggested that he try chasing women downhill.

Irving visits his Mamala in Miami Beach, but tries going in the water without being able to swim. As he's screaming for help, she runs onto the Boardwalk, shrieking "My son Irving the Doctor is drowning! My son Irving the Doctor is drowning!"

Sammy Goldberg is in a marching band. As the procession goes by, his mother announces to the other spectators "Everyone is out of step with my son."

Telling Jewish jokes is an integral part of Jewish daily life. We cannot wait to tell the latest joke that we have heard to a dozen others. My wife and son, my brother, my lawyer, my Israeli travel agent, my Israeli friends, their wives, and my professional colleagues all must hear the latest joke I have heard. And, it is astonishing to witness the speed with which a Jewish joke travels all over the world. Within three days, everyone has heard it.

Some jokes, only Jewish people "get." One Jewish joke tells about a newcomer to a group who hears someone simply call out a number, and everyone laughs. One person is not even smiling, and the newcomer asks why this is so. The response is that he does not find that joke funny. There are some punch lines that are universally known by Jews. For example, when a Jew is accused of not listening, the response, accompanied with outreached hands, is: "Who listens?" Most Jews know that this response refers to the joke (which is one of many versions) about the new psychiatrist who asks the veteran how he can spend the whole day, day after day, listening to patients. The veteran psychiatrist stretches out his arms and says: "Who listens?"

A Jew asks another Jew why Jews always answer a question with a question. "Why not?" the other asks.

Jews love to put each other on the spot and test each other's skills for getting out of dilemmas. Levine meets Cohen on the street and they have been talking for awhile when Levine says to Cohen: "Here we are talking for about an half hour and you don't have the courtesy to ask: 'How's business?'".   "Okay,'   says   Cohen, "How's business?" "Don't ask," replies Levine.

"Don't ask" has come to stand for the bind of asking about touchy subjects to be courteous and then being rebuffed for not minding one's own business.

On the morning of September 11th, 2001, Yasir Arafat called President George W. Bush. He said: "Listen, I'm very sorry about what happened." Bush asks "What are you talking about?" Arafat asks "Wait a minute, what time is it in Washington?" Bush answers: "Eight-thirty a.m." Arafat says: "Call ya in an hour."

More than Jewish music, dance, storytelling, and rituals, Jewish humor lends spice to the daily conversation among Jews, and also between Jews and Gentiles. The Jew has been the quintessential outsider, having had a unique perspective from the underbelly of American culture, and has created a major undercurrent. The Jewish joke shows the underdog undermining the "top dog's" legitimacy, and mocks conventional social norms. Most Americans have heard of Jack Benny, Fanny Bryce, Molly Goldberg, Milton Berle, Burns and Allen, the Marx Brothers, the Three Stooges, Joey Fay, Syd Caesar, Carl Reiner, Mel Brooks, Sam Levinson, Tom Lehrer, Al Franken, Mort Sahl, Adam Sandler, Buddy Hackett, Joey Adams, Jerry Seinfeld, Woody Allen, Jackie Mason, and, above all, Lenny Bruce.

The Jewish joke underscores the Jew's legendary automatic opposition to power and privilege. This is one reason why Jews generally are more liberal and progressive and more desirous of change on behalf of the powerless against the powerful. That is why, for instance, in general, I support the workers and their unions against the bosses. I am against big corporations like Nike, who pay starvation wages to their factory workers in South America and exploit children as laborers.

I fully support the New York Times editorial of June 16th, 2001 regarding patients' rights: "He [President Bush, the second] ought to reconsider his opposition to empowering people to seek meaningful redress from their health care plans when they are wrongly denied medical coverage." Also, I totally support the Reverend Al Sharpton in his and Puerto Rican's opposition to the United States Navy's bombardment of the Puerto Rican island of Vieques, which further impoverishes and endangers the health of its 9,000 already economically depressed inhabitants. Wherever people are struggling against oppression, I am with them.

And that is the reason I support the Peace Now movement in Israel. Admittedly, the mad terrorist attacks by Arab kids who are brainwashed and bullied by their fanatical leaders has shaken my trust in the more progressive, but silent Arabs—why aren't they outraged by this barbarism? Nevertheless, I still empathize with the Arabs' contention that they are occupied by a colonial power, and support their struggle for an Arab state that is not eviscerated.

The greatest lesson of the 20th century is that blind obedience to authority can lead to the destruction of all of us. That lesson was paid for with the lives of six million Jews, while Nazi judges, lawyers, professionals, philosophers, academics, doctors and millions of workers silently stood by. The Jew has been a force in the world, challenging blind obedience, and often with a "crazy" defiance! Did we not create "chutzpah," and brazen impudence to challenge authority everywhere? The Jewish joke embodies that chutzpah, and chutzpah can always undermine corrupt and cruel dictatorial authorities.

I do not believe in balancing the right and wrong sides of the powerful and the privileged "objectively" with the right and wrong of the powerless. I am prejudiced to support the underdog and I am proud of my bias. My bias against what "is," is a very special contribution I feel Jews have made to the progressive intellectual revolutionary history of humankind. I am as proud of Spinoza and Marx as I am of Moses and Isaiah.

CHAPTER ELEVEN
AM I A VANISHNG AMERICAN-JEW?

This question, like all good questions, raises more questions than it answers. The provocative title of Alan M. Dershowitz's recent book, THE VANISHING AMERICAN JEW, In Search of Jewish Identity for the Next Century, [Little, Brown and Company, 1997. New York] states the issue as a "fact," rather than as a question. Of course an immediate question that arises is which American Jew? Certainly Orthodox Jews are not vanishing. And as Dershowitz himself points out, Jews who intermarry may not vanish, and even their children may not all vanish. It is also clear that not all secular Jews world-wide, especially in Israel, are about to disappear.

Our losses in Europe were devastating and resulted in a remarkable shift in the distribution of world Jewry. The Nazi genocide reduced the number of Jews in Europe from over nine million to less than four million. But the latter figure, estimated in 1948, does not take into account the millions of Jews who have since then left Europe for Israel, the United States and other countries. The estimated world figure of thirteen million breaks down roughly into nine million in the Diaspora and four million in Israel. It is estimated that Israeli Jewry will soon constitute more than one-third of world Jewry.

According to Dershowitz, there is good news and bad news about our "vanishing." The bad news is that as a people, we are in danger of disappearing through assimilation, intermarriage and low birthrates. The good news is that we are less dependent on our enemies, especially anti-Semites, for our survival and that it rests on the untapped strengths of our heritage. Institutional anti-Semitism is on its last legs as governments, churches, universities and businesses embrace Jews. We have to change the nature of Jewish life to adapt to new internal necessities. And this, in turn, can be achieved only by a new Jewish state of mind. That's the thesis of the book in a nutshell.

Another bit of good news is that Jews do not convert to Christianity, but "convert" to mainstream Americanism. It is difficult for me to believe that as a our mass culture dumbs down with more infantile, boring, derivative, repetitive, mindless, superficial content, that educated Jews will continue to enjoy it or stick to it. Our rapidly deteriorating mass culture affords no challenge to our rich cultural heritage. The problem here is that we are so immersed in all this nonsense from such an early age that we no longer have any perspective to realize what is happening to us. Truly a "fish in the water" phenomenon in which the fish is not aware of what he is swimming in.

So are we our own worst enemy? Only a new Jewish state of mind can ensure a Jewish future for us and mankind. According to Dershowitz, the biggest obstacle is that 53-58% of Jews are marrying non-Jews. The disappearance of Jewish neighborhoods, the dispersal of Jewish youth in colleges, the lack of parental pressure and the dilution of religious commitment will continue and even increase and thereby result in more inter-marriage.

No more than ten percent of the offspring of mixed marriages marry Jews. Apparently the conversion of Jewish religion into a more vague Jewish faith has very little holding power to keep young Jews into our fold. Jewishness is no longer central to their identity. Thus young Jews do not see any positive reasons for remaining Jews. Young Jews are shifting en masse to humanistic moralism without the burden of rituals. Indeed, the essence of Judaism ---- justice, charity, learning, creativity ---- is also true of other religions and faith.

Dershowitz makes a big point of the marginality of anti-Semitism, particularly institutional anti-Semitism. I believe that he vastly underestimates the scope, depth and significance of social, informal, or subcultural anti-Semitism. I know personally of many instances in which assimilated Jews, who often are not recognized as Jews, were confronted with both subtle and outspoken anti-Semitism. As I pointed out in the first chapter, I experienced first-hand this "social" anti-Semitism exist in wealthy, educated and professional classes and statuses. Thus assimilated Jews have become our new marginal American citizens. Many middle and upper class Blacks are in the same situation.

Young Jewish people feel overwhelmingly that being Jewish does not make any difference in his or her future opportunities in the United States. Among many Gentiles, anti-Semitism is not acceptable. Dershowitz believes that we are no longer second class citizens. But the extreme right, including a spectrum of anti-Semites from the militia movement to Christian evangelicals, maintains the drumbeat of anti-Semitism, but they are relatively marginal to mainstream American society. If conditions worsen significantly they may become relatively more important.

More than half of Dershowitz's book addresses solutions to the catastrophic assimilation of our young Jewish men and women. Three approaches are found wanting: (1) a return to religious adherence which becomes the central unifying essence of Jewish life; (2) "make aliyah," go to Israel and live in a Jewish environment; (3) "be a mensch!", live a Jewish life based on our ethical principles.

I think the reader could probably figure out the reason each of these solutions is unsatisfactory. I think Dershowitz dwells on their deficiencies so that he can then present the solution.

THE RELIGIOUS SOLUTION - American Jews are not going to lock themselves up in a totally Orthodox culture. That's over. The Reform, Conservative, Reconstruction, etc., alternatives have amply proven that most of their members are not moved, enlightened or delighted by what they offer and are members of their synagogues in name only and all of their religious personnel have no idea what to do about all this disaffection.

The "Judaism as a Civilization" idea has enormous difficulty in showing how this could benefit the daily life of Jewish-Americans. More and more Jews are becoming more and more secular and our Jewish religious institutions are at a complete loss of how to address this growing phenomenon. The main problem is the illusion that religious institutions can do anything about this powerful trend. Religious institutions' obstinate repetition of doing what is ineffective and irrelevant, and their lack of self-examination are important contributions to the assimilation of young people in alarming numbers.

ALIYAH: THE ISRAELI SOLUTION - The problem with this solution is that more Israelis are coming here than American-Jews who are going to Israel. Are Israelis telling us with their feet that the United States is the real "promised land?" Of course, most Israelis intend to return to Israel and most of them will, but they are still telling us that the States is more than only a great place to visit. On the other hand, Israel is a great place for American Jews to visit.

Clearly, non-Orthodox Jews would much prefer the state-church separation here than any encroachments on their freedom to do what they want to do when they want to do it. It is easier and more fruitful for secular Jews to pursue a non-theological ethical, culturally diverse and self-selective way of life here than in Israel. The major advantage of Israel is the restricted choice of Jewish marital partners which concerns parents much more than our young men and women. The fact is that Jews' penetration in the U.S of business, politics, professions, academia and the arts opens wide the doors for promising opportunities for young Jews that previously were much more restricted. The materialism and narcissism of the me generation are much better served here than in Israel.

Our Jewish institutions have failed miserably with our young people as far as their identification with our rich cultural heritage is concerned; assimilation is the outstanding symptom of this failure. Now young people increasingly have no choice about how Jewish they want to be because they have no foundation to make this decision.

THE MENSCH TACK: THE "BE AN ETHICL JEW SOLUTION - The "solution" that the Jew should be a mensch is a complete capitulation to assimilation. This "solution" doesn't make any sense at all, except for chauvinistic Jews who believe that the ethical Jew is different or superior than the ethical goy. That, of course, is nonsense of the worst kind because of the hidden sense of superiority of our ethics over the ethics of non-Jews.

Dershowitz's pursuit of a Jewish ethic leads him to identify a number of Jewish "essences" - justice, "repairing the world," (my guess this means helping the poor and needy), charity, learning and study, and dissent and disputation. I think this approach is an extremely counter-productive way of establishing "essence" differences between us and non-Jews. It smacks of a kind of angelic superiority over the ethics of other peoples. I think it would have been a lot more accurate to distinguish us from other people because of our love of pastrami, chicken soup, gefilte fish and Chinese food!

DERSHOWITZ' SOLUTION: LEARNING AND THE "BOOK" - Jewish professionals, from Rabbis to Hebrew school teachers are boring, boring, boring. Dershowitz wonders how we can have such brilliant academics, lawyers, doctors, business executives and mediocre Jewish professionals. Most studies are conducted in a religious mediocre context. Hebrew classes simply cannot compete with "soccer practice, drum lessons and hanging out at the mall." The time has come to give more resources, read "money," to Jewish education so that it can become competitive. This is a classic common American response to problems ---- throw money at them.

Dershowitz develops a fascinating functional approach for persuading young Jewish folk to study Jewish texts. It will not only provide all students with a competitive advantage in their business, professional and personal lives, but will also make them better lawyers, doctors, corporate executives, teachers, literary critics, husbands, wives, mothers, fathers and citizens.

When I read this I became nauseous. Yes, it actually made me sick to believe that one of our great Jewish intellectuals has so succumbed to the success and money idols that he is willing to reduce our great heritage to the function of giving our Jewish youth a material, monetary competitive advantage. Dershowitz has joined the chorus of Bible-hype saviors that can make you rich, happy and, yes, good! I could puke!

Fortunately, later Dershowitz descends from the heights of self-improvement and asserts that Jewish learning is an end in itself. Thank God! He maintains that he thinks Jewishly about virtually every secular issue that is part of his diverse life. Now, I understand why he joined the dream team defense of O.J. Simpson. The Bible and commentators told him that it is perfectly fine to take this course of action. He also believes that it is important to integrate all the great Western thinkers' philosophies and thought with our Jewish texts.

I think it will be news to most American Jews that Marx, Freud and Einstein could have had more of a competitive advantage and been even more brilliant if they had studied the Talmud. Of course that could not be proved now either way. I do strongly believe with Dershowitz that to become a mystic, a Jew does not have to become a Buddhist. We've got lots of diverse mystics in our portfolio to choose from. I was delighted to learn that care for the environment and feminism are also major Jewish concerns.

In conclusion, Dershowitz's prescription for a revitalized Judaism includes: less tribalism and more universality; being open and welcoming to the increasing number of intermarriages. Jews can be Jews if they are secular and do not believe in the "supernatural." There is a need for more Jewish schools on the Quaker and Brandeis models so that non-Jews, if they like, can also learn about Judaism; and, above all educate ourselves in the most open and eclectic manner to have a more open, positive Jewish state of mind.

At the end of his book, Dershowitz does issue a call for action. It is quite interesting to me how Dershowitz resorts to typical American solutions to serious issues. But they are also "Jewish." One-hundred years ago a worldwide conference on Zionism convened in Basel Switzerland to debate the Jewish future. An outsider in a sense, the thoroughly secular Theodor Herzl, convened the conference.

Dershowitz has decided that the time is ripe for another worldwide Jewish congress to consider the Jewish future.

It should be telecast live by satellite so that Jews throughout the world could participate. One proposal that Dershowitz suggests is the creation of a worldwide twenty-four-hour-a-day Jewish television network that would transmit a diverse array of Jewish courses, news, and religious programming. And finally Dershowitz bids us good-bye by saying "shalom" and is looking forward to seeing us on the information electronic highway.

Dershowitz certainly thinks big and has a magnificent vision. One main problem is that it is elitist and top-down oriented by assembling all the Jewish Establishment elite to "solve" the problem of assimilation. But the main problem is the pathetic Jewish institutions that do not know how to attract our young people to our rich cultural heritage. They are the problem. It's like the blind leading the blind. A better analogy is that it is like assembling a world conference of foxes to find better ways for protecting chicken coops.

In the opening chapter Dershowitz shares with the reader his anguish about his son's inter-marriage with a Catholic woman. Dershowitz makes clear that the purpose of his book is to explain his deep seated mission to preserve the survival of Jews. His son Jamin was raised in a very Jewish home but love triumphed over his commitment to Judaism. Dershowitz and his wife accepted and indeed welcomed Jamin's wife and her parents and kin into their family. Maybe it is too painful for Dershowitz to explore in any depth the profound dilemma of writing a whole book on the survival of American Jewry and his total heart-felt acceptance of his son's "inter-faithless" marriage.

Many of my relatives were also confronted with their children's inter-marriages and I live too with the strong possibility that my son will marry a non-Jewish girl. And we all know that what was once the exception is becoming more and more the rule. It is now "normative," fully accepted culturally among most of us to support inter-faith marriages. Writing this book has helped me understand the powerful counter-culture our youth are now adopting while abandoning Jewish survival as one of our most important missions as Jewish-Americans.

I believe that inter-marriages and our "acceptance" of them is the resolution of the conflict between the traditional theocratic tribal culture of our ancestors and the liberal humanistic, democratic ethos of

American society. A culture of an individual, a group, and person is a set of values. And a "value," in turn, is a preferred idea of the desirable that powerfully introduces behavior. Values are the precipitates of experience that emerge from the culture we are born into and a host of other experiences from a variety of influences in our daily lives.

Kurt Lewin invented the idea of "force field analysis." We are constantly confronted with conflicting values and have to make choices among them including the possibility of integrating differences some time. In the previous chapters, I have outlined a force field analysis comprising the contrast and the conflict between a tribal God and a universal God or Spirit; an ethical versus a ritualistic emphasis; the favoring of personal meaning over institutional allegiance; and, choice over coercion. These values form two contrasting gestalts - a traditional / theocentric belief system versus a humanitarian / democratic orientation.

With these two contrasting belief systems, Jamin's and my son's orientation has definitely tilted toward a humanitarian orientation while Dershowitz and my orientation remains transfixed between the traditional and free choice orientations. We are stuck. And what is personal here is writ large in the growing conflict between the generations and the "stuckness" of our Jewish institutions. Reluctantly, and with great anguish, Jewish institutions have had to face the abandonment of our young people. The more they accommodate to liberal values, the more our young people leave the Jewish fold and the more they leave, the more Jewish institutions have to accommodate to our young people's changing beliefs.

In a sense, Jewish youth want the institutions to change more and more to accommodate to them, while Jewish institutions want the youth to come back to the fold. Dershowitz and I deeply love our children and will continue to love them despite their inter-marriage. And our youth know this; they know that their liberal, democratic parents will continue to love and support them 100%.

The over 50% of intermarriages among Jewish youth has made Jewish and non-Jewish marriage normative. That means that young people feel increasing comfortable and conflict-free about intermarriage. The momentum is with them, while Dershowitz, myself, and our Jewish institutions have become paralyzed about influencing this trend. So in ever increasing numbers we will go along with the wishes of our young people.

It is not quite accurate to say that all our professional sages and thinkers are simply standing by. Quite the contrary, the moaning of the "loss of our youth" has become our past-time and lots of half-baked reformist ideas are floating around that do not seem to grab many people. It is also true that many of our finest thinkers believe that nothing can be done to stem this inter-marriage tide so we might as well accommodate, like many Reform temples do, by intensive conversion programs directed at the non-Jewish partner.

I think three simplistic approaches are emerging that I believe will prove to be ineffective. A number of "modern" Orthodox leaders believe that the way to hold on to our youth is to incorporate them into our God-centered ritual traditions as a kind of barricade against the secular trends of our society. To be sure, a small number of young people will buy this "package" and thus they will be saved from inter-marriage. I think its appeal to the great mass of young people is nil.

Rabbi Hertzberg has "settled" for young people continuing to do something Jewish. It could be fasting on Yom Kippur, a bar mitzvah, circumcision, kadish, lighting candles Friday night, attending a Klezmer concert, a trip to Israel, going to a Chinese restaurant with other Jews. It would be great if they would read a book about some Jewish topic. Do something Jewish!

Dershowitz wants young people to adopt a Jewish state of mind. To this end he has a fabulous list of 500 Jewish books that can change anyone's state of mind. This in turn is reinforced by an electronic super highway filled with all kinds of chat rooms where Jewish youth can ponder the dilemmas of their Jewish identity and "vote" against inter-marriage. Where and how young Jews will get the motivation to do these wonderful things is not clear.

In general, our great Jewish sages have an alarming ignorance of what a culture consists of in the first place. At minimum a culture comprises a set of values and a body of activities and routines, knowledge about its way of life, and the belief or the faith that by participating in the culture they will be happy, successful, wealthy, healthy, wise, etc. The traditional orthodox culture beautifully illustrates these principles: a belief in God and His Torah, 613 commandments to carry out God's will, the intensive study of the holy texts and the unshakeable faith that by following all the above routines, they can live well, live long and have a share in the world to come.

The fragmentary approaches of Hertzberg and Dershowitz will not work because culture is a gestalt of behavior, knowledge, and values and when any one of these three legs is missing the "cultural" stool easily topples. The orthodox orientation beautifully exemplifies all three legs to such an extreme that they have been exceptionally successful in holding on to their youth. Orthodox youth simply do not intermarry. Non-Orthodox youth absolutely refuse to pay such a heavy price of exclusivity.

Social psychologists postulate three major ways of influencing change in values, conduct, and knowledge.

(1) Coercion-Compliance. This model consists of a fixed set of rules and total obedience to the enforcement of these rules. This is most successful with very young children, but outside the Orthodox community, becomes increasingly difficult as the children grow older. Youth in every culture rebel to some extent with their adult authorities, otherwise there would never be any changes in the way we live.

(2) Role-model-Identification. Another source of influence that can induce change occurs when the child or youth desires to be like another person --- parent, teacher, coach, older peer, relative, a hero, a movie star or any fictional figure, etc. In the youngster's desire to be like a person he/she admires, he/she also takes over the values and beliefs of the role model through identification with that person. In this book I have given many examples of teachers, Rabbis, Biblical prophets that I have greatly admired and certainly adopted thereby the values for which they stood.

(3) Acculturation-Internalization. The two types of influence outlined above, coercion-compliance and role-model-identification, stem from "outside" the youngster's culture and therefore the locus of control is by and large external to the youngsters' socialization. Acculturation-internalization is more of an in-depth and comprehensive absorption of the values of the culture in which the youngster grew up, and therefore, become part of his personality in largely subconscious ways. Ahad Ha'am got it absolutely right when he wrote: "What is the true national education? That which makes children absorb the national spirit unconsciously." This observation epitomizes the brilliance of Ahad Ha'am. He deeply understood that the creation of an Israeli state was the sine qua non of our survival. Here is where children and youth are socialized in our language with our national holidays and memorials, with all the symbols that identify the culture of a people from the flag and the national anthem to the mezuzahs on most door posts. From the moment a child is born he / she breathes the Jewish culture every second of life and afterwards rests in peace in a grave on

our land. It is impossible for an Israeli to have an identity crisis about his Jewishness.

The reverse of the above is true in the States. Here the Jewish child is drowned in a "foreign" country with a non-Jewish set of symbols, rituals, obligations and expectations. Jewish identity begins to take more and more of a "back-seat." Here in the United States who we are as Americans has its unique dynamic development in which we Jews as Americans are integrally related. Our most perspicacious thinkers and writers from Mark Twain to J.D. Salinger (a Jew) and Phillip Roth (a Jew) have written about the dark, greedy, uncaring, anti-humanistic subculture underlying our magnificent values in our Constitution, the Bill of Rights and Declaration of Independence.

This "me generation" prevails today in all our generations and infects Jews as much as anyone else. This powerful informal but pervasive culture of individualism runs riot; greed, materialism, selfishness, and indifference to and disregard of millions of people who go to bed hungry every night is what our children and youth are immersed in. To survive and to flourish today in the United States the national prescription is unambiguous: "look out for number one!"

We Jews have taught our children how to succeed in this culture, not how to be Jews. And we are really good at this. Our children and youth are primarily and overwhelmingly interested in "making it". As Dershowitz pointed out, we know how to give our children a competitive edge. In this functional subculture for promoting number one, why on earth should our young people saddle themselves with "useless" outmoded rituals and values?

In addition, as I have pointed out previously, an impressive rhetorical positive humanistic philosophy has emerged to displace the tribalism of our ancestors. Our superior educated youth value a "universal" God rather than a unique Jewish God, an ethical rather than a "ritual" life, a philosophy that makes personal sense rather than mindless allegiance to institutions, and above all the total absolute right to make choices about how they want to live as an American and a Jew including the right to decide for themselves about intermarriage.

If the above cultural diagnosis makes any sense, then a two-step strategy suggests itself to reclaim culturally our Jewish youth. We have to infuse our youth from a very early age in very specific ways how to implement Hillel's famous admonition: "If I am not for myself, who will be for me, but if I am for myself alone, who am I?" When this balance is destroyed, as what is happening to many of us now, we in danger of creating a jungle of each for himself and against everyone else.

I want to share an anecdote related to the above which occurred about two years ago. I was sitting on a bench in Riverside Park down the street from the Columbia University School of Work where I teach. Suddenly I heard a commotion behind my back and when I turned, I saw a young man and woman harassing a Japanese nanny who was holding on to a stroller with a baby in it. The two kept yelling at her and reaching for the watch on her wrist and her purse. She was utterly disoriented and started crying and kept on resisting her attackers. I immediately rose and approached them and yelled as loud as I could to leave her alone. Out of the corner of my eye I saw some men and women watching from across the wide, two-lane street. As I approached the young attackers, a man and a woman, the man took out a knife and started waving at it me and warning me to stay back. I kept walking toward him, yelling "police, police, police" as loud as I could.

As I got closer the young man kept yelling at me to stay away. Then he said: "get back, this is none of your business, this is none of your business. I'll get you, this is none of your business." I go crazy in this kind of situation and I really did not care what would happen to me and I kept approaching them and yelling at them. Finally, they began withdrawing while continuing to threaten to me and proceeded down Riverside Park. I immediately went over to the nanny who was crying and trembling and overcome by fear and confusion, and tried to calm her and then accompanied her to her apartment building. She did not speak any English. When I crossed the street one of the onlookers came over to me and said something to the effect that I did a great job. I wanted to ask him where he was while all this was happening, but I didn't.

Continually ringing in my ears is the attacker's refrain, "this is none of your business, this is none of your business." I find amazing that this young man had internalized a cardinal American value of everyone minding his / her business and was using it to justify his "defense" that it was "none of my business" and he should not be interfered with in his "business" of robbing this defenseless elderly nanny.

I believe that this is the ultimate logic of our me-generation: "look out for yourself and stay out of trouble." This portrait is purposely exaggerated. I realize that we still have many pockets in our society of people who care about others and about themselves in balanced ways that Hillel intended. "Teach America" college graduates are willing to work at least for two years after graduation in the worst schools in the worst ghettos.

The best antidote to the "me first, second and third " syndrome is the concept of the Tsadik, that the great 18th century Hassidic rabbis evolved in Eastern Europe. The ideal person gives and gives to others because he /she enjoys to give to others and this is done to help the giver as much as the given. In colloquial Yiddish this is referred to as a gute neshama (good soul), someone who looks out for others for the sake of looking out for others. In our cynical society, many of our "me-firsters" would consider them suckers. I want to remind the reader that an ideal need not be fulfilled one-hundred per cent. An ideal is a guideline of behavior that we can aspire to and work toward without achieving it completely. Jews are not "saints."

The first step then, toward a revitalized Judaism, is to dig deep into our heritage and come up with an idealistic alternative to "me-ism," which youth who have not been completely corrupted can be attracted to. If we really subscribe to the idea of tikkun olam (repair of the world) we certainly can find many many people with specific concrete needs that we can help. This is what our great Jewish institutions should be fostering among our young men and women.

A second vital overall step is for our institutions to demonstrate our famous flexibility for enlarging our "tent" to include Jews who are attracted to an ethical humanistic philosophy. If we don't significantly alter our "tribal" ways to include our disaffected youth then I think intermarriage and assimilation will continue to expand.

We must continue to explore in much more depth the alienation of young people from our institutions. We are doing something wrong, not our youth. We have to fashion a new cultural gestalt of values, practices, and knowledge that can appeal to our young people.

But us disaffected adults also have to re-examine our commitment to Judaism and I want to suggest in the next last chapter a course of action we can take to this end.

CHAPTER TWELVE
I CONVENE A CHAVURAH

The inimitable Yogi Berra once said, "When you come to a fork in the road go forward." I never subscribed to Robert Frost's famous decision to "take the road least traveled by." 1 like the philosophy of Rabbi Hirsch Rimanover (79A) who spoke about some Hasidim that took the main highway, others took the side road, but the best is the road of one's own choosing. Where do I go from here? I want to deepen my knowledge of Judaism, I want to be a more committed Jew, I want to integrate my Judaism much more into my daily life and I want to contribute to our Jewish community.

An obvious option is the chavurah, a fellowship of Jews who gather regularly together mostly in small groups to share, in personal ways, common concerns about their Judaism. The underlying impulse for most chaavuroth (plural for chavurah) is to synthesize traditional studies and practices with a liberal, autonomous, decentralized, self-propelled personalized group. Many members are turned off by the "one-stop" synagogue services for bar-mitzvahs, memorials, high holidays and watching the Rabbi dance on Simchat Torah.

The synagogue now is a collection of isolated individuals, who sit together during a service and often do not know each other's names. The traditional Conservative and Reform service is boring, bureaucratic, unresponsive to individual needs, filled with entirely non-enchanting mechanical rote prayers that project an outmoded God that has become increasingly irrelevant to many peoples' daily lives.

Most exasperating of all is the total oblivion that Rabbis and other Jewish professionals inhabit about the bankruptcy of their institutions. This is what is truly remarkable about the Jewish Establishment today - its incapacity for self-examination. If Socrates is correct that the unexamined life is not worth living, how much more devastating is the lack of self-examination of our Jewish institutions? Surely they are aware that young people are abandoning them in frightening droves.

Enter the chavurah as an antidote to Jewish institutional decay. Several historical accounts of the chavurah trace its roots to the "social utopia" of the Pharisees around the time of Jesus who formed small groups of worshippers to study the Torah, carry out traditional rites, and pray. The Essenes, on the other hand (made famous by the finding of the Dead Sea ed scrolls in the Qumran caves) were a "revolutionary utopia" of celibate men who meticulously carried out all of the rituals of daily living in a monastic environment. And Jesus, of course, assembled a brilliant chavurah of apostles who dramatically appeared together at The Last Supper (which obviously is our Passover celebration).

After the fall of Jerusalem in 70 A.D., Ben Zakkai gathered together a small community of sages and organized a school in Yavneh, an Old Palestinian city on the Mediterranean coast between Jaffa and old Ashdod. Yavneh remained the seat of scholarship and culture until the Bar Kochba revolt against the Romans in 132-135 A.D. In 1979 a religious kibbutz was established near the abandoned site of Yavneh. If there was ever a community that came full circle, certainly the reestablishment of a school of learning in Yavneh some 2000 years after its original founding, is a spectacular example of continuity.

One of the most important developments of the chavurah occurred in Eastern Europe between 1500 and the Holocaust. Jews lived in shtetles, small towns and villages that were organized around the shtieble, the town shul ("synagogue") where everyone knew each other and which became the "second home" of the Hasidim. What a wonderful, powerful, creative flourishing of a people's folk culture. Stories, dance, music, art and the philosophy of the Tsadic emerged. (See Chapter Two) Remnants of this culture continue to influence Jews and non-Jews all over the world.

The shtieble, the center of the shtetl, was embedded in what Dr. Leo Baeck called milieufrommigkeit, "the piety of the environment." For hundreds of years, the Hasidim lived in villages in which the whole environment was a religious extension of the shul. Villagers lived close enough to the shtieble so that they would not have to drive on the Sabbath and holidays and thus be able to carry out the complex of 613 commandments that prescribed rituals for every day of the week. Extreme Orthodox groups want to turn all of Israel into shtetles with shtiebles and reincarnate the ghettos of Eastern Europe into one huge Israeli ghetto. Fat chance!

The kibbutz movement created a unique form of chavurah. Originally, relatively small numbers of pioneers invented an autonomous, decentralized socialist-democratic, secular way of life that integrated its purpose and its method. It played an important role in the creation of Israel and its unique culture and pioneered a utopian way of life that moralists and philosophers dreamed about for thousands of years. The "noble experiment" has undergone drastic changes since its founding some one-hundred years ago. No matter. It is one of the great social experiments of our time and will be forever a significant contribution to the culture of mankind.

The small group has been the engine of social change since as well as before the dawn of the Christian era and Jesus and his apostles to Lenin and the Communist cells in Russia to Osuma Bin Laden and his world wide "sleeping cells." The small group is also a powerful socializing force for changing individual beliefs and behavior. As I have described before I have been a member of one or another chavurah, fellowship group, since my pre-teens. We called them "social groups," sometimes "clubs,' which is far less colorful and evocative than the term "chavurah." The latter term connotes more solidarity and mutuality and friendship, partly because it is related to the root "chaver," which means in Hebrew "comrade" or "friend." I played hooky with several close friends from school; I was on numerous sport teams, including the high school basketball team. I was in a Zionist youth group. I studied with several close friends in a yeshiva for a year. I was a bona fide member of a youth communist league "cell." I was in a platoon unit in the army. I joined Hillel in college.

In my twenties, I was a close-knit member of a research team at the Jewish Board of Guardians. For my anthropological study, Cottage Six, The Social System of Delinquent Boys in Residential Treatment, I lived with eighteen delinquent boys and workers in a cottage on the campus grounds for eight months. For the last forty years at the Columbia University School of Social Work, I was a member of the social science department. For many years I was a member of two different consultant groups that trained staff and workers in business organizations and social service agencies. For many years I spent a month at Crystal Lake Lodge, a leftist progressive resort in upper state New York, where I developed strong friendships that have lasted for over forty years.

In the 1960's, I became a sensitivity trainer with the National Training Institute. We facilitated many small groups in all kinds of social settings to explore the psychology and art of giving and receiving feedback. This was an attempt to democratize a kind of "therapy" for thousands of people. These "training groups" eschewed psycho-analysis and encouraged group members to be more aware of their own

limitations and strengths and to give feedback sensitively based on
ongoing group interaction. Intensive marathon groups over three days
solidified members' affiliation to each other. These encounter groups
metamorphosed into an amazing array of self-help groups, which are
formed by groups of individuals who share a common problem or
issue. Over 200 different self-help groups currently range from a group
whose members suffer from diabetes to family members of prisoners
and Checks Anonymous for people in debt. Alcoholics Anonymous,
still strong since its founding over forty years ago, is the granddaddy of
the movement.

     The self-help groups have a lot in common with the Jewish
chavurah, which is commonly associated with a synagogue. Common
features include a voluntary small group structure formed by peers who
have come together for mutual assistance in satisfying a common need
and bringing about social and personal changes. Face to face social
interaction is emphasized as well as personal responsibility. The group
promulgates a common philosophy or set of values that enhance social
responsibility, independence, and personal Jewish-American identity.

     When I was on my Sabbatical for a year in Israel, I attended a
unique "chavurah" that met in a different home Friday evening or
Saturday late morning and afternoon. This informal social group was
made up of secular academics and professionals from a variety of fields
and included their spouses. There was no set agenda, although current
events usually were discussed. A lot of joking and kidding around
predominated and the latest jokes were shared. Sometimes someone
would bring up a very serious issue and the group spent a lot of time on
the problem. I looked forward to this "hanging out" every week and
was greatly pleased to be accepted as a bona fide member of the group.
I have called this kind of regular gathering without a specific goal other
than giving its members an opportunity to "sound off" a social, sociable
or "shmooze" group

     This tradition continues with Israelis in the States. We lived
for ten years with many Israeli families in a high-rise apartment
building in Riverdale in New York. The secular Israelis met frequently
in one or another apartment for all kinds of socials with each family
bringing their own favorite Middle-East dish. Israeli Independence
Day, Purim, Chanukah, return of a family to Israel - were all occasions
for Israelis getting together. Invariably, the evening would end with a
sing-along with an Israeli accordionist and slides with cartoons and the
verses of favorite traditional favorites from early childhood to

contemporary songs. These regular get-togethers were excellent example of a secular chavurah.

For the last fifteen years I have been a member of Elem-America, a foundation that raises funds for distressed youth in Israel. Elem, however, is based on principles far more important than merely raising money. Elem is also a research group that studies innovative programs for helping distressed youth in the States and conducts frequent American-Israeli conferences that exchange information about the latest developments in the field of rehabilitation. I have gone frequently to Israel to study first hand their programs as well as conduct training sessions for their staff.

For three years I was a member of a writer's group that met once a month in different members' houses to critique each other's writings. These were in-depth reviews that had a significant impact on all the members and finally broke up when a number of the participants left the city. My undergraduate studies at the University of Chicago were under the spell of the Great Books curriculum, in which we read the great books of the Western canon. After I graduated, I joined a Great Books club that met every two weeks and thoroughly enjoyed debating the philosophies of Plato and Aristotle and fell in love with Montaigne's essays. For one year I attended a yoga class that combined hatha yoga and meditation.

For twenty years I was a member of an early-bird tennis club that would meet Thursday mornings after tennis matches to shmooze over coffee and bialys and cheese. We always told the latest jokes and many of them were, of course, Jewish jokes. I developed close friendships with several members and one of them, Alan, has been my very best friend for over thirty years.

Every ten years I attend a high school reunion in Milwaukee, Wisconsin. I am always astonished how quickly high-school cliques re-familiarize each other without very much contact for years in-between the reunions. Every five years I return to Milwaukee to get together for a week-end with a special clique of Jewish friends who invariably have brunch in our favorite deli as part of our tradition. I also have gone to bar-mitzvahs and bat-mitzvahs of their kids and to their marriages and even to grandchildren brises (circumcision of the male child on the eighth day after birth).

For many years I taught about small groups, especially self-help groups at the Columbia University School of Social Work. Based on personal experience and widespread reading in the literature, I evolved a typology of the small group or what I like to call now the chavurah, or fellowship group. My typology includes four types of small groups that are distinguished by the main function or purpose of the group. Some groups incorporate features of other types, but I think they can be distinguished by its primary purpose:

I. Mission Groups have primarily an external goal to achieve; examples include socialist and other revolutionary groups, a task force that has to come up with recommendations for a course of action, all committees in organizations.

II. Self-help (or feedback) Groups are primarily oriented to helping peers who share a common problem or issue; examples include A-A and support groups for families who are suffering from the trauma of a lost child.

III. Theme-Centered Groups are organized around the study and discussion of a particular theme or issue; Great Books Club, a writer's group, meditation group, nutrition study group, weight-watchers.

IV. Schmooze (or social) Group is built on members' comfort and enjoyment of each other's company.

I want to emphasize again that each group type often includes features of the other groups and may combine several of the purposes of the above types. What members of all the groups share is the belief that present institutions cannot fulfill their needs and that they have to find alternative small group structures to fulfill themselves.

I realize that I have considerably expanded the idea of chavurah or fellowship group. But I think the wider scope enables us to locate the special features of the Jewish chavurah, which has evolved over the last forty years or so. I believe that the heady 1960's released powerful currents of energy that liberated people to take the initiative to create independent self-help structures. I greatly admire people who decide to create their own institutions, traditions and groups when Establishment institutions fail them. One of the fascinating features of modern life is the extraordinary inertia of smart assertive educated people who continue to go along with institutions that for them are "dead in the water." The synagogue is an outstanding example of this passive obedient tendency.

Of course there are important "extra" reasons for continuing membership in a synagogue like a lawyer courting clients among his / her fellow worshippers. Also it is important for the "kids," especially bar mizvas and bat mizvas that are blown way out of proportion to their importance in Judaism. The incredible authority we give to Rabbis, many of whom are extraordinary mediocre, has always astounded me. The Conservative Rabbi of a synagogue in Madison, Wisconsin where I was the principal of the Hebrew School while I attended the University, was a "dandy," who was always quite fashionably attired and totally lacked any vision of a meaningful service for worshippers. The Yiddish proverb, "little on the outside, nothing on the inside," perfectly describes him.

The greatest impediment blocking people from taking their lives into their own hands outside of Establishment institutions is what sociologists call "pluralistic ignorance." This refers to people who have common needs and issues, but are not aware that many other people are in the same boat. The feminist revolution is an excellent example, for when Betty Friedan's The Feminine Mystic exploded in 1963, the floodgates opened for a feminist reconstruction of our society in history, economics, politics, the family, religion, the male dominated business hierarchy, universities and so on and so forth. Women's consciousness raising groups, a feminist chavurah, sprung up all over the country in which women supported each other against a male dominated, authoritarian society.

The chavura was an independent grass roots movement initially, that was invented to fill an important need that Establishment institutions miserably failed to address, the true equality with men. Of the dozen or so books about the Jewish chavurah, I was able to find the following two that were the most useful: Bernard Reisman, The Chavurah, A Contemporary Jewish Experience, (1977) Union of American Hebrew Congregations, N.Y; and, Jacob Neusner, editor, Contemporary Judaic Fellowship in Theory and In Practice, (1972) Ktav Publishing House, Inc., N.Y. Both books emphasize a spiritual rather than God-centered approach, drastic reduction of rote rituals and the key importance of communality.

Of the four types of chavurah described above, the Jewish chavurah has feature characteristics of all them, but it also has a distinctive primary thrust despite the manifold needs it fulfills for its members. I believe that the main impulse of the Jewish chavurah is the feeling of its members that the synagogue is totally ineffective in creating an environment in which a community can flourish. For many the synagogue has become a congregation of isolated individuals who mouth all the prayers and carry out all the religious rituals without any significant meaning or impact upon the worshippers' lives.

Chavurah members want an independent, smaller size group and to simplify modify the traditional rituals so that they fit the needs of its members rather than the members sharply curtailing their needs and desires to out the traditional rites. They found themselves less and less committed to Judaism and more and more alienated from the synagogue, which was also true of their children. The chavurah was regarded as half-way between the temple and family worship at home. They want to transfer responsibility for their religious lives from the top to the base, from the distant authoritarian structure to a consensus-democratic governance.

The Halacha, a term applied to Jewish law as interpreted by Talmudic and medieval authorities, no longer made sense to be followed blindly and actually stood in the way of finding a more meaningful service and fresh normative Jewish way of life to which they indeed could become committed, and which would make a difference in their lives. The Reform movement, of course, made significant alterations in the medieval code, but the chavurah wanted to go much further in modifying this code. The basic idea was to wed selected features of our tradition within an independent egalitarian democratic community. Ties to a synagogue would evolve as needed. Rabbi participation was optional, a radical departure from tradition.

The role of tradition within the community would evolve. The chavurah would become a Jewish community. Activities such as weekly discussions around a theme or book would evolve. The commune wanted to work at creating its unique synthesis of traditional and modern values. The struggle against social dislocation and alienation and for forging a meaningful Jewish identity went hand in hand. Clearly, the massive, expensive, impersonal, synagogue institution was part of the problem rather than a meaningful solution to fulfill the members' needs for a sense of community.

Chavurah members' needs and desires did not automatically mesh, and had to be created through democratic discussions and consensus building. The attempts at chavurah building highlight the strengths and weaknesses of the Establishment synagogue. Instead of responding to the manifest needs of its members, the synagogue is a ringer that compresses out all these different needs and simply puts all people, whatever their needs, through the same outmoded traditional mill. The ancient code takes over and all the worshippers, despite quite different needs and concerns, continue to focus on the same outmoded traditions and rituals that have been used for a thousand years. When contemporary life becomes so different from the past, people are stirred out of their apathy and inertia and finally are moved to the realization: "Hey all this stuff really does not help me and puts me to sleep." But all the "good boys and girls from Jerusalem" (a phrase used for boys or girls who completely conform to adult commands and standards) have been lulled into a dependent sloth from which is very difficult to take spiritual reins into their own hands.

Especially in religion, the rabbis, priests, ministers, Pope, etc., are backed up by God and have a special pipeline to Him / Her, so that shaking up and even revolting against these authorities' legitimacy is considered a major spiritual insurgency. Just like the realization today that all medical doctors are not equally proficient, so is the awareness that all Rabbis are not equally wise and pious, which leads parishioners acting more cautiously when considering in whose hands they place their spiritual destiny. For example, in Israel, Oved Joseph, the chief Rabbi of the Sephardim, Jews from Arab countries, recently publicly announced that he had a dream that the holocaust occurred because the Jews in Eastern Europe had stopped eating kosher food. This is not only a supremely ignorant statement, but cruel and heartless and a terrible insult to the six million Jews who died in the genocide. We must always challenge authorities' legitimacy.

Stupid religious leaders abound in all the religions. Pope Paul consorted with Hitler and the Nazis. Mohammedan Sheiks call for Arab kids to become martyrs by blowing themselves and innocent civilians into smithereens. And remember the minister cited in a previous chapter who said Jews that did not adopt Jesus were "incomplete Jews?" More than ever, we realize that men of God can be as stupid, lazy, hypocritical, opportunistic and corrupt as any one of us non-certified religious mandarins. The bloom is off and the realizations that religious leaders "wear emperors' clothes" is readily apparent to any reasonably educated independent person of average intelligence. Nor should we forget that some of the greatest bloodbaths in history were engineered by "men of the holy cloth." The Spanish Inquisition, the Crusades, the Colonial-Conquistador-Christian decimation of the natives of America, and despicable little atrocities like the excommunication of Spinoza by the high and mighty religious elders of Holland were all initiated my such authorities. Rabbis are like you and me and have no special spiritual certification to be more honest, holy and virtuous than any of us non-professional religious mavens.

Tradition is the handing down of practices and beliefs from one generation to another. But tradition can also be "the dead hand" of the past. In Jewish seminaries, students regurgitate ancient texts to become certified to foist much of the same nonsense on synagogue members who are much too docile, "generous," and ignorant of the sacred texts to openly revolt. The charade is fortified by members simply staying away. It would be farcical if it were not so sad to see our synagogue mausoleums 95% empty for most of the year. A real Jewish institutional mitzvah would be to turn the synagogues into shelters for the homeless, serve delicious Jewish soul meals for which we are justly famous and have our theological seminaries train our students as social workers to help our benighted neighbors get back on their feet. This would be a powerful extended Judaism of our Prophetic heritage.

In the United States today, we need to discuss Judaism as a serious intellectual inquiry; it is too important to leave to the Rabbis to decide our agenda for us. Moreover, the temple is rarely an experience in community which lies at the heart of those of us who sincerely want to bring our Jewish heritage into our daily life and sustain it.

The big problem with the independent chavurah is that people come to it with widely different needs. These needs vary, from Jews alienated from any meaningful community, to people looking for social-psychological support, and to Jews like myself who want to probe more deeply into our values as guidelines of how to live today and how to become more of an activist with other progressive groups to build a more compassionate and caring society for all people. I am not as interested as are more religious Jews than myself, who want to find a better way to commit their souls to one another and to God.

The chavurah in recent years has begun to be co-opted by the religious Establishment, particularly the Reform movement. I think this spells the doom of the chavurah as a vigorous independent movement outside of religious institutions. The Reform movement recognizes a good thing for themselves when they see it, so Reform Rabbis, and some Conservative Rabbis, are now becoming more active in guiding and "facilitating" the development of the chavurah. Now, all sorts of guidelines are offered by Rabbis about how to organize and sustain a chavurah, possible themes for discussions, how to enact various tailor-made rituals and how to tie the chavurah in more closely to the temple. Very sad. Almost all observers of the chavurah are extremely

pessimistic about its future and believe that the movement will
eventually die.

Nevertheless, however chavurah independence is
compromised, it is not inevitable that it must be. As the above cursory
review has shown the chavurah throughout our life span can be and
always will be adapted anew by groups that feel it can serve a useful
purpose in their lives that Establishment institutions do not fulfill. I
decided to convene a chavurah of friends to discuss how our Jewish
heritage influences our daily life as Jewish-Americans. I purposely left
wide-open how this and allied themes could be tackled by the chavurah
so that its members could articulate by consensus how to proceed.

I've come full circle. I began my journey by digging into my
past and present to explore how Judaism affects me as an American.
Before this exploration, Judaism was a residual category in my life that
vied with other interests and was not prominent in my concerns.
Writing this journal has transformed my life so that I am now deeply
concerned about what is happening to us Jews all over world,
particularly, of course, now in Israel, and with every new finding and
exploration of the holocaust.

I have always believed that we can find solutions to problems
that we create. I guess this is why I am fundamentally an optimist. I
don't believe in leaving to others to devise solutions in which I do not
participate. In Yiddish there is this wonderful expression, "far yenem,"
which refers to coming up with great plans and schemes for other
people to implement. Now I want to spread my wings. I have a great
need to join with other Jews to explore ways of integrating our
magnificent Jewish heritage in which I was raised into my current life.
A chavurah, a small independent group of Jews interested in the same
subject, seemed to me, the best vehicle for sharing my ideas with
others, learning how they deal with their Judaism in everyday life and
gaining support for my new confronting attitude of making sure that
other people are clear that indeed I am a Jew and proud of it. In general
I wanted to know how others with similar backgrounds were engaging
their Jewish identity as Americans.

I convened several chavuroth in my apartment around an
ample Jewish Sunday brunch that included selections of the following:
lox, smoke fish, marinated herring and onions, chopped liver, falafel,
whitefish salad, gefilte fish and horse radish, stuffed derma, hard
kosher salami, kigel (hot Jewish pasta pie), bagels, bialys, Levy's
Jewish rye, matzo brae (toasted matzo with eggs), pierogen (potato

dumpling), lochshen and cottage cheese (spaghetti and cheese), vegetables including tomatoes, cucumbers and onions, cole-slaw, sauerkraut, half-sour pickles, hard-boiled eggs, potato latkes (pancakes) with apple sauce, sour cream or honey, humus, tubule, pita, a variety of cheeses, freshly squeezed orange juice, fruits (including watermelon), <u>compote</u> (stewed mixed fruit), baked apple, ruggelach, hamentaschen, strudel, Israeli glazed candies, mixed nuts, mints, dried apricots, raisons, Israeli jams and jellies, Israeli chocolate, strawberries in sweet cream, linzer tart, coffee, tea, apple cider, buttermilk, Dr. Brown cream soda and celery, Kedem kosher red wine, Maccabee Israeli beer, halvah (plain and chocolate-covered), strawberry, cherry and plain cheese cake and the specialty of our house, a classic New York City egg cream. A typical brunch for a get-together of Jewish friends. Clearly the brunch was a success because the group did not move for the next three and one-half hours from the groaning food laden large dining-room table with a skyline view of Manhattan to the living room. Basically, I wanted to know how others with similar backgrounds were engaging their Jewish identities as Americans.

Participants ranged from 50 to 80 years of age and were mostly professionals that included doctors, social workers, psychologists, University professors and school teachers, writers and artists. Religious orientations ranged from atheists and agnostics to traditionalists who celebrated the main Jewish holidays. Very few were members of a synagogue. Most were American-born and several were Israelis and also non-Jews who were married or were companions to Jews.

I will give a composite picture of the sessions that were in most respects very similar. Before my brief introduction, the group initiated a lively discussion about each other's names, especially among members who had the same last name and how people's names were changed at Ellis Island where the immigrants from East-Europe landed when they came to America. I then said that I brought this group together because I had become much more conscious about my Jewish identity recently and was curious about how others of my generations were relating to their Jewish identities. Then I let the discussion flow.

This theme-centered chavurah has three dimensions: (1) the members' personalities and histories; (2) their interaction; and (3) the development of the theme. I chose my favorite people so I knew that generally our backgrounds were in many respects very similar.

Everyone participated and seemed quite comfortable doing so. As is typical in this kind of small group, as the session proceeded, some members were much more personal and disclosing than others ---- a good indication of growing trust. The size of the group ranged from seven to ten members. I steered the group from going "all over the map," to going all over the "Jewish map." I tried to get the members to stick to one issue at a time until it appeared exhausted and then to move on to other themes. I also encouraged, when necessary, the group members to speak from their personal experiences rather than letting the discussion become too abstract and impersonal, although that did happen from time to time and also proved to be fruitful.

Here I will summarize the highlights of the group discussions. One of the very first themes that came up was anti-Semitism. Everyone, without exception, was able to recount anti-Semitic incidents in the course of their lives, which they vividly remember and were eager to share with others. One anti-Semitic incident was recounted by an elderly physician. It occurred fifty years ago, which he remembered as happening yesterday. I call it a "transforming incident," because it reveals in stark profile the depths of anti-Semitism that are too frequently massively covered up, and which is impossible to forget once it is heard. The doctor was called up in the reserves during the Korean war, but was sent to Germany. He went with his wife and two small children and they were lucky to get a superb kind, caring, and pleasant, middle-age German nanny to watch over them. After about six months, the doctor was assigned to a different German city. At the railway station, while they were saying good-bye to the nanny, she remarked that "after all, Hitler did one good thing by getting rid of all of the Jews."

Our very sophisticated group was thunderstruck. Everyone had to express his / her dismay in one way or another. I said that this revelation slipped through the carefully constructed sieve of a massive cover-up in post-war Germany and tells us the true depths of anti-Semitism, particularly in Germany, but all over the world. It reveals that among many many Gentiles, anti-Semitism is totally accepted, and in fact, flourishing and that anti-Semites are extraordinarily successful in keeping in tact their deep, dark, infamous Jew-destruction prejudice.

A social worker in a bad ghetto school in the Bronx, remarked that she did not reveal to her mostly Latino pre-teens that she was Jewish, which was easy to do because she did not look Jewish at all.

This raised a minor tempest in which various positions were taken about when, where, and how to disclose one's Jewish identity. Readers of this book know about the extreme position that I take in letting "the world" know as soon as possible that I am Jewish and proud of it. After a lengthy discussion, I think most chavurah members were convinced that revealing our ethnic identity is important and also I believe that the group was an important source of support for members to become more open, and proud of putting their Jewish identity "on the table" immediately in all our relationships. A member recounted that she saw Mel Brooks interviewed by Mike Wallace on 60 Minutes and one segment showed Brooks amidst a large cast of people who were briefly identifying themselves. When Brooks' turn came, he identified himself as "Jew Exraordinaire," which of course got a big laugh. Another member recalled that at the Emmy Awards where Brooks' musical, The Producers, ran away with all the major awards, Brooks brought on stage about a dozen or so backers and introduced them as his "Jewish backers." I adore this kind of chutzpah.

We tackled the question of Jewish-American versus American-Jew. We went round and round on the linguistic meaning of the two identities. I still maintain my position, which is true also of most of the members, that I am foremost a Jew and being an American is an important secondary component of that identity, which is why I prefer "Jewish-American" in an analogous way to the way that Blacks refer to themselves as African-Americans. "American-Jew," on the other hand, connotes an emphasis on being an American first and foremost; this way my Jewish identity is a component of my identity as an American. A large segment of the chavurah clearly did not go along with that interpretation. I am sure that the subject will be taken up in future meetings.

Israel figured prominently in all the chavuroth. One chavurah exploded over an Israeli issue and it became doubtful if it would be able to continue with its current composition of members. This particular chavurah had some very powerful, articulate representatives of the extreme Left and Right of the Israeli conflict with the Arabs, and internally, with some domestic issues as well.

Israel has always had a small, largely University-based, leftist kibbutznik and professions-based small minority of Ashkenazi-Israelis (mainly from Eastern-Europe). Rather than naming names I will group the three main political sub-groups in the chavurah into roughly Left,

Center and Right, even though there are differences among members within each of the three categories.

Over the last twenty years or so, the extreme Left has launched a powerful critique of Israeli politics and policies, the essence of which, is that Israel has been an integral part of Western, particularly American, imperialism, and is a colonialist country that has occupied the West Bank and Gaza and exploited and subjected Palestine to an economic third rate colony. Israeli colonialism is the primary cause of the unrest and ongoing conflict with the Palestinians. This colonialism also consists of a vicious ideology that attacks Arabs as inferior, completely untrustworthy and scheming and stresses that the Arabs' real goal is to "throw all the Israelis into the sea," and occupy all of Palestine, including Israel, for themselves. On the domestic front, the Left, despite important differences among them, views Israel as becoming more and more "Americanized," or abandoning its democratic-socialist ideals, and as vulnerable to the religious block, which may destroy the vital, democratic principle of the separation of "church and State." The settlements in the West Bank are viewed as provocations that complicate and stand significantly in the way of a peace with the Arabs.

The Right is the complete obverse of the Left, and adopts the view that the aim of Arabs is precisely "to throw all the Israelis into the sea." Arabs are not to be trusted and will never change their scheming ways. Above all, the total lack of any democracy in Arab countries, and their domination by tyrannical feudal despots, is dangerous for Israel's survival. Here too, important differences exist among Right-wing factions, but in general, many oppose the creation of an independent Palestinian state, and adopt a religious "mystical" Biblical identification with all of the holy land, and are not willing to cede an inch of it to the Arabs. Many are ready to go to war with the Arabs for the next one-hundred years.

The Center adopts parts of the Left and Right in a variety of amalgamated positions, but in general, believes that peace between Arabs and Israelis can eventually be achieved, and is unsure about how much to cede to the Arabs. All the main differences on refugees, Jerusalem, water, boundaries, the Israeli settlements, etc., will take a long time to resolve, but eventually can be resolved. This is some of the background to the explosion that erupted in one of the chavuroth.

The issue was an evaluation of the Camp David meetings of Clinton, Rabin and Arafat, where the peace process is now and where it is going. The Left understands quite well that the Arab countries surrounding Israel are primarily feudal, undemocratic fiefdoms, and that many Arabs are intransigent about expelling the Jews from the Middle East. Nevertheless, the extreme Left attacked the "propaganda" that Barak was doing all the compromising and that Arafat was again "taking another opportunity to miss an opportunity."

In the ensuing "discussion" Left and Right talked at each other and past each other. The history of Palestine since the Roman era was used by each side to justify its position. Both sides were adamant about their quite different assumptions about history, the Arabs, prediction of the future, etc., so that at the end of this discussion, each side was more convinced about its position.

The Center was completely incapable of forging any kind of "meeting of the minds" between Left and Right, so that in the end, we all agreed to disagree. Whatever good will and empathy that we had developed for each other evaporated. It seemed to me that members of the Left and the Right and the Center too, said good-bye to each other with their heads shaking in disbelief about how naïve and inflexible the other positions were.

I want to emphasize that the very hard positions taken by the extreme Left and Right represent a very small minority of both Israeli and American Jews. The rest of us Jews got a lot of talking to do with each other! I had one powerful insight that I got out of all of this turmoil. I am more impressed than I have ever been in my whole life that democracy is the one great hopes of Israel, Palestine, and indeed the world. Democracy is the only force, in my opinion, that can hold back the authoritarian collectivist ideology of the far Left and a global corporate take-over and the religious fanaticism on the Right.

These thoughts made me feel immensely proud to be an American. Democracy is our greatest heritage and our most magnificent contribution to humankind. Tyrannies beware! Democracy will mow you down! And I am also proud of the democracy in Israel!

A number of other important issues were taken up in the chavurah, which I don't want to take the time to discuss now. My overall assessment is that most of the chavurah members were very stimulated by the discussion and definitely wanted to continue meeting. We did not take up what actions we might take as a group, but the members wanted very much to discuss this in future meetings.

Completing a book is like a graduation and commencement. I firmly believe that a good book challenges, in a major way the beliefs, values, feelings and behavior of the reader, and even more so the writer. It is not enough for me to have good intentions about my new pride in my Jewish identity; I want my new awareness to have an impact on my conduct and for me this means joining in a sustained way with other Jews to clarify my beliefs, get support, and take some significant actions. I strongly believe that the chavurah is an excellent vehicle for exploring in depth our rich Jewish heritage and how it can influence our daily values, beliefs, and behavior.

Who knows? My next book might very well be the evolution of our chavurah. The journey continues and never can end.

EPILOGUE
I'M NOT MARCHING THIS TIME AROUND

September 11th, 2001 changed out world. The bloody and senseless dehumanization of our species has never made the precariousness of our existence clearer. Our religious differences have taken precedence over our common humanity. The holocaust proved that one nation could nearly obliterate another, and, the terrorist attack on the Twin Towers proved that a fanatical gang of zealots could wipe out thousands of us in a murderous act of self-destruction.

My personal odyssey received a shock that created enormous doubts about certain life-long held convictions of mine. Since my exposure to Marxism as a teenager, only one other experience completely shook up my political perspective as much as this; it was the revelation that the communist Soviet Union was a despotic dictatorship via Nikita Kruschev's 1956 "Secret Speech" to the Central Committee of the USSR.

For about ten years prior to that leaked confession, I knew every reason for defending the Soviet Union's concentration camps and its repression of democratic freedoms (which I became aware of belatedly); they could be justified as a defense against attacks by colonialist, imperialistic, capitalist countries. We young Marxists believed that lack of freedom of expression in socialist countries was largely capitalist propaganda, or, alternately, we asserted that repression was a temporary necessity.

Kruschev's exposé of Stalin's demagoguery in 1956 slowly seeped into our consciousness until our whole outlook fundamentally changed with the realization that socialism was plagued with corrupt tyrants who believed more in maintaining their autocratic power than building socialism.

Then, it finally dawned on us that despite the incontrovertible fact that *even though* Western capitalist democracies were exploiting the vastly underpaid workers in their societies, and viciously exploiting men, women and children in developing countries, basic democratic rights in our homeland still held up fairly well for the most part. This change occurred even though we remained painfully aware that formal democratic principles and processes were undermined daily by wealthy individuals and corporations, and that our class-stratified society was dominated by self-interested ideologies.

So what was the big lesson that we learned? It was simply this: we had thrown the baby out with the bath water. Our attention was so riveted upon building socialism that we carelessly condemned, in total, all democratic-capitalist societies.

Today, those of us who were ardent Leftists when we were young are much more careful about condemning capitalist-colonial exploitation, *and* more careful about excusing the excuses of the anti-democratic, totalitarian, dictatorial regimes for their repression of the "oppressed" and "exploited," whom they are supposed to represent. Many of my socialist friends eventually condemned both systems, and became politically apathetic. But does so doing give us a foundation, or chart a course for the future?

Despite the class inequities in capitalist, democratic societies, are unparalleled in achievements. In such countries, freedom of expression and assembly are guaranteed, as are free elections, the right to due process, the separation of church and state, and all the other familiar pillars of the democratic process as embedded in the Bill of Rights and over 200 years of judicial decisions and legislation. Therefore, democracy, rather than socialism, has converted me and become my preferred political philosophy.

All this meditation now informs my position on the present conflict with Arab dictatorships. Extreme Left-wing radical Jews, both in the United States and Israel, in the wake of the terrorist attacks on the Twin Towers in New York City and the Pentagon, want us progressives to focus *primarily* on America's exploitation of Arab countries and America's propping up of anti-democratic monarchs and dictators. They maintain that the "root cause" of Arab terrorism is a reaction to our economic terrorism of the Arab people via the exploitation of our mighty global corporations.

But is there not a powerful parallel between the attacks of 50 years ago on the United States for its subversion of socialist countries with present condemnation of the United States for its subversion of Arab countries? Fifty years ago, radicals were in denial of the fact that socialist countries ruled in a manner which was both undemocratic and vicious, and their rulers were uncritically defended. Are not Arab countries and their undemocratic dictators defended and excused in like manner by Leftist intellectuals, including Jewish ones, today?

On balance, anti-democratic Arab dictatorships are all much more dangerous to the future of our world than capitalist democracies, therefore I exempt myself this time from siding with them just because they're the enemies of the United States.

An imperfect world compels all of us to make imperfect choices. Why attack U.S. imperialism as a root cause of Arab terrorism without, or instead of, condemning Arab dictatorships that impoverish their countries and completely repress democratic freedoms? Should the rejection of governments like Syria's and Iraq's really be considered Western chauvinism?

Furthermore, the undemocratic, exploitative, corrupt Arab dictatorships, to divert attention from their cruel domination of their own people, use Israel as a scapegoat. Evidence of this exists in their use of pro-Palestinian rhetoric to inflame nationalistic sentiments while doing little to help them.

Therefore, the anti-Israeli and anti-American protests against the present invasion of Afghanistan should be opposed, as both the U.S. and Israel, despite their exploitative, colonialist legacies, have an indisputable right to protect themselves and their democracies against vicious dictators.

Is not the preservation of democratic freedoms more important than the fight against imperialism, at least in a world in which so few countries have them? An Arab "win" could destroy us all.

On the other hand, an Israeli and American "win" enables us to continue the struggle, within and outside the United States and our allies, for economic justice. Since when, as promised, did "the dictatorship of the proletariat" ever flow into democracy, as the Communist Manifesto promised? Besides, the proletariat never got the chance to "dictate," only Lenin, Krushchev, Mao Zedong, Castro, and the rest of their leaders. The fight against economic injustice is equally compelling inside of countries which profess to run a "worker's state" as everywhere else; the failure of socialist countries to deliver the revolutionary promise of economic security to the working classes only lessens their legitimacy compared to our American model of unions, strikes, and the democracy which permits them.

Choosing democracy not only lends the world's working classes a greater chance to have a voice, basic rights and a better life, but perhaps even more important, provides our endangered world with a chance of negotiating nuclear disarmament. There is no evidence that Saddam Hussein, the Taliban, Osama bin Laden or other militantly anti-Western, undemocratic despots would show restraint if they possessed nuclear weapons. Therefore, it is the survival of humanity, not our callousness towards the economically depressed masses of the world, including the disenfranchised Arabs, which compels those of us who historically have opposed capitalism and imperialism to side with the United States in our present military intervention.

Etzioni's New Golden Rule
Respect and uphold society's moral order
as you would have society respect and uphold your autonomy.

Individual Autonomy

Respect/Support

Respect/Support

Community